Odd Birds

HARDING

Odd Birds

ST. MARTIN'S PRESS ❧ NEW YORK

www.stmartins.com

Designed by Anna Gorovoy

Title-page illustrations by Jim Tierney

Library of Congress Cataloging-in-Publication Data

Names: Harding, Ian, 1986– author.
Title: Odd birds / Ian Harding.
Description: First edition. | New York : St. Martin's Press, 2017.
Identifiers: LCCN 2017001939 | ISBN 9781250117076 (hardcover) |
    ISBN 9781250156488 (signed edition) | ISBN 9781250117083 (ebook)
Subjects: LCSH: Harding, Ian, 1986– | Actors—United States—
    Biography. | Birds watching—Anecdotes. | BISAC: BIOGRAPHY &
    AUTOBIOGRAPHY / Entertainment & Performing Arts. | NATURE /
    Animals / Birds. | BIOGRAPHY & AUTOBIOGRAPHY / Rich &
    Famous.
Classification: LCC PN2287.H225 A3 2017 | DDC 791.4502/8092 [B]—dc23
LC record available at https://lccn.loc.gov/2017001939

Our books may be purchased in bulk for promotional, educational,
or business use. Please contact your local bookseller or the Macmillan
Corporate and Premium Sales Department at 1-800-221-7945, extension 5442,
or by e-mail at MacmillanSpecialMarkets@macmillan.com.

First Edition: May 2017

10 9 8 7 6 5 4 3 2 1

For Bubs.
Always.

Contents

Large and isolated in the gleaming whiteness of the page, the hawk stares back at you, bold, statuesque, brightly coloured. But when you have shut the book, you will never see that bird again. Compared with the close and static image, the reality will seem dull and disappointing. The living bird will never be so large, so shiny-bright. It will be deep in landscape, and always sinking farther back, always at the point of being lost. Pictures are waxworks beside the passionate mobility of the living bird.

—J. A. Baker, *The Peregrine*

Odd Birds

Introduction

BRIDGE

TO NOWHERE

The day had been sweltering. I'd spent the last few hours trying to avoid the heat, but as I stood in the river, the icy cold water rushing around my ankles, I began to shiver.

I looked up and down the river. I couldn't find the bird.

A blur tracked across my peripheral vision. I turned to see where it went.

Large boulders interrupted the river in places, and looking out over the water, I couldn't see where the bird had landed. It had been only a shadow of a motion—a flash of gray.

Where the hell had it gone?

Maybe it had landed just out of sight, I figured, so I began to slog through the river, periodically glancing upstream to see if it had landed on any of the boulders sticking out of the water. Bird-less, every last one of them.

Maybe the bird had flown farther upstream than I had realized, and here I was, standing in a river, my teeth chattering, just a bit overeager to find it.

I looked out at the river again and tried to take it all in. White riffles coursed around the large boulders. The water was fast-moving and clear where it had room to flow. A trout rose to the surface of a pool below one of the rocks.

There it was again. The flash of gray.

As I turned to look, the movement congealed into the form of a small bird, its tail bobbing rhythmically as it perched out on a boulder in the middle of the water. It turned back and forth, looking upstream and down, as if trying to make up its mind where to go.

The bird hop-flew to the next rock downstream, toward me, and continued to bob its tail. It blinked—I saw it blink—its white eyelids popping against its slate-gray body.

An American dipper. This was a good bird.

I had gotten a late start that morning. It was a Saturday in August, and I was driving out of Los Angeles—the city I call home. I was going up to the mountains to go hiking and birding by myself, then I had plans to meet up with friends to camp for the night.

I turned the AC up to full blast as I drove: it was a stupefyingly hot day in the Southland.

I've been in LA for just under a decade now, and I love it here. An ocean to the west, mountains to the north. The city stretches east and south, and the mass of humanity here seems more or less continuous all the way down to San Diego. There's a lot to do close by—you can surf in the morning in Santa

Monica and then drive two hours to spend the afternoon skiing at Big Bear.

Los Angeles County is huge—substantially larger than the city itself. It stretches far north over the Angeles National Forest and the San Gabriel Mountains, encompassing Antelope Valley—which blooms orange with California poppies in the spring—the eastern corner of the Los Padres National Forest, and the western corner of the Mojave Desert. Despite the urban sprawl across large parts of the county, which is home to more than ten million people, even larger swathes are covered in oak woodland, pine and fir forest, and desert—and there's seventy miles of coastline.

Because of the diversity of habitat, you can see more species of birds in Los Angeles County than almost anywhere else in the United States.

A little more than an hour on the road, I exited the 210 at Azusa. I was on my way to the Angeles National Forest, which includes the mountain range to the northeast of the city. A few turns put me on the 39, heading north into the park.

As the highway switchbacked up off the valley floor, I started to think about my plan for the weekend. Today I was looking forward to getting outdoors, roughing it for a night. In the morning I would wake up early to drive back to Los Angeles. A stylist was coming over to my house in the midafternoon to make me look presentable, because tomorrow night I was attending the Teen Choice Awards.

For the past seven years I've played a high school English teacher named Ezra Fitz on a TV show called *Pretty Little Liars*. It was a gig I was fortunate enough to land right out of college. Right now, I'm finishing up filming on the last season of *PLL*—its seventh.

As I drove, I thought back to an idea I'd had for a while—three seasons back, my character on the show wrote a book, and I've been thinking about writing one myself ever since. What you're reading now is the result of that crazy idea.

This book isn't a chronological memoir. I'm too young to write something like that anyway. Instead, it's a collection of stories and thoughts I've had about my life in Hollywood and my life outdoors—and a few things I've only recently been able to put words to.

I want to look back on my experiences so far and talk about a few of them: about my childhood, about my life as an actor, and about some of the things I find meaningful. And, yes, birds. A lot about birds. Because they mean a lot to me, and they keep cropping up in my life.

As I continued up into the park, I had to concentrate fully on the winding road. All around loomed mountains covered in chaparral, a tangle of thorns and brush, brown and faded gray-green, vegetation the color of desert camouflage.

A cyclist was pushing himself up and up and up the steep road, and I followed behind him for a ways, watching his legs turn pedals turn gears turn wheels, waiting for a sight line long enough to safely pass.

And then, farther along, the road twisted back on itself, and I got a view back down the valley—where I had been fifteen minutes earlier—and I saw the haze of the heat rising off the endless city, and the thin layer of smog hugging the land below the clear air of the mountains.

I wasn't close to my destination yet, but somehow it felt like I had arrived.

I pulled off the road at a ranger station to see if I could get a recommendation for a hike. The ranger at the station was more goat than man. He had a scraggly white patch of fur under his chin and was wearing a pair of indoor-outdoor glasses—the kind that are always tinted purplish gray, even indoors.

"Hi there," I said, approaching the counter. "I'm looking for a short day hike. Something a few miles long."

"You got enough water?" the ranger asked, not looking up from the newspaper he was reading. "Need a couple of liters today. The sun's brutal."

I know park rangers have to deal with people with death wishes on a near-daily basis, but I know the rules: Take nothing but selfies, leave nothing but footprints. And always carry plenty of water.

"Yup, I've got a couple of bottles," I said. The ranger glanced up from his paper, looked me over, and rolled his eyes.

He pulled out a map of the park, pointing out where we were. Farther up the road, past the spot where my friends and I were planning to camp that night, he pointed to a parking lot on the map.

"This is Coyote Flat. Park here—if the lot is full, park along the road. There's a five-miler here that'll take you to the Bridge to Nowhere."

Perfect. While the name "Bridge to Nowhere" wasn't particularly auspicious, a five-mile hike was just what the doctor ordered.*

---

* I later realized that, to this particular park ranger, "five-miler" meant "five miles each way," which was not quite what the doctor ordered. But at the time I was unaware of this fact.

I glanced at my phone before getting back into the car. I knew I was about to lose the little bit of reception I still had, but I wasn't concerned. John and Walter, the two friends I was meeting up with later that night, knew where we were supposed to meet. I was actually looking forward to being unreachable for a few hours.

Twenty minutes later, I parked in a large lot—it was mostly empty—and started off down a dirt path at the far end. The sun was at its apex, and the temperature must have been in the high nineties.

It was a dry, mind-scrambling heat, like the physical embodiment of white noise—and there was no breeze or even rustle of wind. I slathered sunblock all over my face, and would've dunked my head into a vat of it if they sold containers large enough.

I started up the trail, which follows the east fork of the San Gabriel River.

Walking along, the crunch of gravel underfoot seemed especially loud. You pay closer attention to your surroundings when you hike alone, and even the sound of a twig snapping can make you jump—at least until you get used to being back in the food chain.

The trail dropped steadily from the parking lot for half a mile to a campground set among a small stand of pine trees. There were a few tents scattered about. Some were just tarps draped over cords, others seemed built for more permanent residence, and had strings of laundry hanging out to dry.

Passing through that brief bit of shade under the trees was a welcome reprieve. But then the trail left the trees and the road behind to parallel the course of the river, crossing over it from time to time.

A few hundred yards past the campsite, I realized I hadn't heard any birds. No canyon wrens, no scrub jays—nothing. Too hot for them to be singing, apparently. I was starting to feel a little light-headed myself, and I wondered if it was such a good idea to be outside for so long. I had two liters of water on me, which I figured was more than enough. I took a swig from one of my wide-mouthed Nalgenes.

I could feel my face beginning to burn. I opened up my pack and pulled out a balaclava, which I originally bought for skiing because it covers my entire face—except a thin slit for my eyes. It's also great for sun protection while out hiking, as long as you don't mind looking like a yuppie jihadist. The occasional odd looks are worth the protection from skin cancer.

I took the Nalgene I was drinking from and poured it over my head to cool off, and then reached for the other I'd brought along. To my utter horror, it was empty. I'd forgotten to fill it up. At the next water crossing, I jumped into the river in my clothes to cool off, which was nice, for a moment. Above the crossing, a trio of unkempt redneck "entrepreneurs" in their early thirties was shoveling soil into a sluice box—it looked to be a small-time gold-panning operation.

The water around me was filthy—full of the runoff from their work. I hadn't been planning on it, but now I definitely wasn't going to drink from the stream.

"Finding anything?" I called over to them, trying to be friendly.

They stared at me for a moment. One coughed. They went back to their work.

Sometimes it's hard to make good conversation in the woods. People mostly come here to be left alone.

I realized then that I still had the balaclava on, and must've been a weird sight, sitting there in the river, lightly panting. The men continued to ignore me, and I took my cue to keep walking, a little soggier now, my shoes squishing with each step and the bottoms slowly caking with sandy soil.

I slogged onward, my eyes focused on the ground. I tried not to think about how thirsty I was. The river floodplain widened out, and yucca plants festooned the flats like Koosh balls. I found myself slowly following a path up the eastern side of the valley.

Where the hell was this bridge? Around every turn in the trail, more trail . . . and I was completely out of water.

The sun continued to torment. I kept putting one foot in front of the other, willing them to move more out of spite than muscle memory.

I passed a pair of hikers on their way back down: a mother and her teenage daughter.

"You're almost there!" the mom said encouragingly.

I guess my balaclava didn't frighten everyone after all. I nodded a quick thanks and picked up the pace. I was getting somewhere after all.

I'd gone another fifteen steps or so when I heard a voice call out from behind me—"Ian?"

I stopped and turned around. The teenage girl and her mom were standing in the middle of the path looking back at me. The girl's hands were shaking.

"Ian?" the girl said again. I stared at her, dumbfounded. How on earth could she have recognized me? My face was almost completely covered—all she could see were my eyes.

I couldn't recognize my own mother by only her eyes.

"Uh . . . yes?" I managed to stammer.

Her face lit up. "I knew it!" she cried. Before I knew what was happening, she was hugging me. My clothes were damp from sweat and river water.

"Nice to see you, too," I said.

"This is so exciting!" she chirped. "I'm a huge fan of your show."

I looked down and saw that the girl was carrying a canteen.

"Can I have some of your water?" I blurted out.

They both seemed taken aback.

"Um . . . okay," the girl said, reaching for her canteen and handing it to me. I thanked her and took a few desperate gulps.

"Would it be possible to take a picture with you?" she asked.

"Sure, of course," I said, handing her back her canteen.

The mom took out her iPhone. I put my arm around the girl's shoulder and smiled. The mom held the screen up to her face, framing the picture, then hesitated and put it down. "Everything okay?" I asked.

"Would you mind taking off your face mask?"

I had forgotten all about it again.

After we took the photo, I thanked the mother and daughter for the water and hiked on, hoping that I'd soon reach my destination. I was beginning to worry that the Bridge to Nowhere might not actually exist.

But then, not fifteen minutes later, around a corner, there it was.

Turns out it wasn't some big metaphor, after all. It was real.

The bridge was beautiful—a Depression-era concrete arch that spanned a deep gorge—and far below, a clear mountain stream carried snowmelt down to the valley below.

When the bridge was originally constructed, in 1936, it was intended to connect the north side of Angeles National Forest with the south. Partway through construction, the road leading up to the bridge was washed out by a massive flood. Rebuilding the road was subsequently deemed not worth it, leaving the bridge orphaned in the middle of the wilderness.

There was a hand-pump spigot on the bridge, and I doused my head under it. After thoroughly soaking my hair, I filled my water bottles and collapsed in a sweaty heap under a canvas sunshade that was stretched out over the bridge.

My head was still burning up, that feverish buzzing of dehydration. I closed my eyes for a second and must have dozed off.

When I snapped back to reality, there were three or four other hikers loafing around nearby. Two of them sat, backs against the concrete wall of the bridge, eating cans of Vienna sausage. In a cooler at their feet, I noticed a stack of empty sausage tins.

Off in the distance, a pair of ravens cruised by, their wedge-shaped tails pronounced in stark outline against the summer sun.

I stood up and stretched my legs. I considered walking back down, but I found myself looking to the far side of the bridge. I didn't feel like going back down just yet, so I got up and wandered across.

On the other side of the Bridge to Nowhere, there was a trail, a path to the river below. Picking my steps carefully, I made my way down to the water.

As I stood looking up and down the river, taking it all in, the colors and textures, I thought back to the girl and her mother I'd met on the trail. I replayed the interaction in my head, still amazed that she'd been able to recognize me with that balaclava on.

Had I been rude? I hoped not. I'd definitely come across as disoriented. A little weird, probably. At worst, they walked away thinking I was on drugs—and I could live with that.

A blur tracked across my peripheral vision—I turned to see what it was. It was a motion, a flash of gray. I couldn't find it.

You know what happens next.

I stumbled downstream, planting a foot squarely into the river in my frantic search to find the bird. And there it was again: the American dipper.

There's no wrong way to look at birds.

You can go to the coast and set up a scope and pan across the ocean's edge, looking for shorebirds. You can walk through the woods and listen—identifying them by their songs. You can watch them on feeders in your backyard from your living room, taking in the beauty of their myriad forms.

You can take a reference book out to the woods and compare the pictures to the birds that you see in the wild. You can learn about their field marks—the shape of their tails or the way they bob up and down.

Often though, the birds don't stay put long enough for you to observe them as much as you'd want. Instead, what you see is a motion. Birds aren't static objects, and birding makes you good at identifying blurs.

Sometimes I let my eyes not focus on anything in particular—let them almost glaze over, fall out of focus, and take it all in—and then the motion will register, like a water bug skating across a glassy surface. Out in the forest, or even just walking around my neighborhood, I'll see the motion before I actually see the bird.

But, when my eyes do pick up on that motion, I'm able to trace the bird as it moves through the trees or arcs across the sky.

You learn very quickly to key in on forms. Size alone can be deceiving—depth perception doesn't work as well when a bird is set against an endless expanse of blue sky. You look for the little details, like the shape of the crest—and whether it is rounded or squared off. Or even how it flies. Three undulating wing-flaps, then a wide, gliding dip? Good chance that's a woodpecker.

As a birder, you develop a rough sense of the birds you could see in any given area, so you can know almost immediately when something's unusual because it doesn't fit the forms you're expecting to find.

I sat down on a rock, my shoes dripping, and watched the dipper hop around the stream, disappearing beneath the water's surface from time to time to walk across the bottom of the riverbed, searching for food.

Then the air changed and a cool gust of wind came down the river, ruffling the bird's feathers.

I looked up. The sun had started to set behind the mountains to the west. Shade stretched across the gorge, and there was a sudden chill in the air. I looked at my watch and realized it was getting late. It would be dark soon. Before long, my friends would arrive at the campsite down below.

We would spend the night talking around the campfire, looking at the stars and wondering what the different constellations meant. Later, we would climb into our tents and fall fast asleep, enveloped by the chirping and howls of the mountains around us.

In the morning I would drive back to Los Angeles for the awards ceremony. In the evening I would be on the red carpet, posing and laughing with my costars.

But now? Now I would hike down, into the darkening night, to be with my friends, and fall asleep beneath the stars.

FAMILY

CARDINALS

When I was a kid, my mom told me to keep an eye out for cardinals whenever I went out to play in the woods behind our house.

"They look out for us," she told me. "So we need to look out for them, too."

Cardinals hold a very special place in my family, and much of our family folklore centers around them. I'm reminded of this whenever I go back to Maryland to visit my mom—you can't find cardinals in Los Angeles, they don't make it this far west.

My mom keeps porcelain statuettes of them on shelves and tabletops around the house. She has cardinal coffee mugs, picture frames decorated with cardinals, even cardinal-themed oven mitts. At Christmas, cardinal ornaments overwhelm the tree.

They brighten up her house in much the same way the real birds can appear as a bloom of crimson on a snowy winter's day.

My mom inherited her name, Mary, from her mother, and her love of cardinals from her father, John Collins.

Grandpa John served in the army during World War II. He received a Purple Heart and Silver Star for storming a fortified hillside to hurl a grenade into a Nazi pillbox. After the war, he returned to Virginia, where he met his wife, Mary, and started a family.

John and Mary were Irish Catholic, and they brought their children up in the Church. The family always had a particular fondness for saints and guardian angels. They were always looking for symbols of their faith in their lives—signs of divine presence in the world around them.

Grandpa John was also an amateur naturalist and a history buff, and he loved the cardinal because it was the state bird of Virginia—never mind the fact that it's also the state bird of five other states. He would always point the birds out to his kids when they appeared in the yard. At some point, my mom and her siblings came to believe that cardinals were the guardian angels of the Collins family.

I never met my grandmother Mary. She died of pancreatic cancer when my mom was eleven years old.

According to my mom, the week after her mother's funeral, a female cardinal flew up and perched right outside the dining room while the family was eating breakfast. The bird seemed to be peering in through the window, watching over my mom and her siblings as they ate. My grandfather noticed, and as he pointed the bird out to his kids, it began to sing—its syrupy call inserting itself into the conversation like my grandmother used to do.

Eventually, my grandfather remarried. His new wife, Alice, was squat in appearance and cranky in demeanor. She took on the job of parenting my mother and her siblings as best she could.

So now there was Grandpa John and Grandma Alice in the house—and a cardinal that acted suspiciously like Grandma Mary living in the backyard.

Fast-forward a few decades. I was in elementary school. Grandpa John got sick. Mom, being a nurse, could tell that he wasn't going to get better.

A few days after Grandpa John died, a pair of cardinals showed up at the feeder we had hanging in our backyard.

We'd often hear them calling before they appeared. They'd come in from the forest to the bushes at the edge of the lawn and survey the house. Then, in stuttered flight, they'd swoop across the yard. The cardinals would take turns at the feeder, one perching to eat while the other hopped around the ground below.

My mom liked to believe—we all liked to believe—that it was Grandpa John and Grandma Mary, reunited as cardinals in the afterlife.

Grandma Alice never remarried, and became less cranky with age. I loved spending time with her, and we used to sit and talk for hours. Actually, let me rephrase that: I would talk for hours, and she would smile and nod. She said she didn't believe in hearing aids, and I don't think she could hear a word I said.

Halfway through my freshman year of college, Grandma Alice passed away.

Back home in Virginia, the same pair of cardinals that had appeared when Grandpa John died was still coming around—they were still regulars at the feeder. Or at least we thought they were the same birds. The male had an especially dark mask, and the female's crest was a bright red—brighter than I'd seen on other birds.

The morning after Alice's funeral—as we were standing in the kitchen trying to figure out what to do with all the leftover food from the memorial reception—a new cardinal appeared. It was another female, and it sat at the feeder alongside the original pair.

This bird was different from the others. She was squat and a little drab, and even appeared cranky, becoming aggressive with birds twice her size when they came too close to her food.

So, naturally, we concluded, these cardinals were Grandpa John, Grandma Mary, and Grandma Alice.

It was fun to imagine that our loved ones had embodied birds so they could come back and look after us. But we never took the cardinal symbolism *that* seriously. I'm not a superstitious person, and for my sister and me, the cardinals were just a coincidence: coincidences happen.

If you pressed me, though, I do have a cardinal story of my own.

It was the winter before I graduated from college. I was driving back to Pittsburgh from Virginia, where I'd spent the holidays with my family. The whole world was gray outside, and it was beginning to snow.

Despite the weather, I was booking it back to the 'Burgh. I was making my way up a long hill when a glint of red came out of the trees along the highway. I could just make out the cardinal through the snow, flapping its way across the road in front of my car.

I slowed and changed lanes to avoid hitting the bird, and as I did, the back tire of an eighteen-wheeler directly in front of me blew out. The truck swerved violently into the other lane, right where I'd been seconds before. If I hadn't hit the brakes to avoid that cardinal, the truck would've crushed me.

A few years later I mentioned what had happened to my mom. She just smiled and nodded. "These things happen," she said.

When I was in elementary school, my mom got sick. Really sick. Nobody could figure out what was wrong. She went to a bunch of different specialists, but they all struggled to diagnose her illness. In the meantime, she was told to rest and drink plenty of fluids.

She spent weeks in bed, exhausted. Moving hurt. Talking hurt. She would break out in rashes whenever she went out in the sun. And then the rash would be replaced by a fever and her joints would swell up. More doctors' appointments, spinal taps, and blood tests all came back inconclusive. At one point she was diagnosed with meningitis, only to have the diagnosis reversed a week later.

We didn't know it yet, but my mom had lupus.

Lupus is a difficult disease to diagnose—and is done so mostly by process of elimination. And, even after it is diagnosed, there still isn't a cure.

When my mom found out she had lupus, little was known about the disease. She was told that the remainder of her shortened life—perhaps only another ten years—would consist of rapid and violent swings of health, and constant joint and intestinal pain.

Instead of resigning herself to her diagnosis, she decided to fight back on all fronts. She proceeded to eat cleaner than a triathlete, tried every immunosuppressive drug on the market, and prayed harder than the pope.

Since her diagnosis more than twenty years ago, my mom's dietary and healthcare choices seem to have been working. To this day, she has remained in reasonably good health.

But lupus is still an insidious disease. At times it acts as though it has a mind of its own.

I went home for Christmas several years ago to spend the holidays with my mom and her sister, Julie. There was a bunch of family in town, and it was lovely to all be together. Christmas is my mom's favorite holiday, so we all went to bed early on Christmas Eve. Everyone wanted the next day to arrive as soon as possible.

Early the next morning, Aunt Jules shook me awake—it was still dark outside.

"There's something wrong with your mom," she said.

I ran to my mom's room and found her sitting up in bed, thumbing her rosary with one hand and taking her blood pressure with the other.

She looked up at me, her body shaking. "It feels like I'm having a heart attack." Her breathing was shallow, forced. "But it isn't a damn heart attack," she said.

My mom worked as a cardiac nurse practitioner for several years—she knew all the signs. And she was right: it wasn't a heart attack. She was having a lupus flare. A bad one.

The paramedics arrived quickly—wearing Santa hats—and they lifted her out of bed and carried her down the stairs.

We spent Christmas morning in the hospital with her, while the doctors ran a battery of tests to see what might have triggered the flare. By that afternoon, she said she was feeling well enough to go home, so they gave her some pain medication and released her.

My mom's recovery over the next few days was painful and slow. She seemed older, frailer than I'd seen her before. I asked if she wanted me to delay my flight back to Los Angeles, but she insisted that I shouldn't change anything on her behalf.

On the morning of my departure, I went for a run to clear my head. When I got back to the house, I heard laughter coming from upstairs. At first I thought it might be Aunt Jules, but my mom's guffaw is unmistakable.

I went upstairs and knocked on the bedroom door.

"Come in," she said. Her voice sounded warmer, stronger.

I stepped into the room to find her rolled onto her side in bed, looking out the window. She waved me over. I sat down on the edge of the bed and we both looked out.

There they were: the three cardinals, Grandpa John, Grandma Mary, and cranky Grandma Alice. They were all perched in the branches of a tree that brushed up against the side of the house.

Grandpa John's mouth was slightly ajar as he looked back and forth between his two cardinal mates. He rubbed his beak against the branch he was perched on.

"You know, cardinals mate for life," I said. "Three isn't a normal number for birds."

My mom nodded.

"So . . . do you think Grandpa John's a polygamist now?"

She laughed. She turned back to me, smiling. She looked healthier, happier, and at least momentarily without pain.

Grandma Mary flew out of sight, around the corner of the house, followed closely by the other two.

We watched them fly off. "That never gets old," my mom said.

I nodded.

She rolled to her other side slowly, then let her head sink into the pillow. As she closed her eyes, she said, "You know, maybe we should change up the birdseed out there. Alice is looking a little chunky."

REDISCOVERING

BIRDS

I've played a handful of different roles in my relatively short career as an actor. I've been a French aristocrat, a jellyfish, a heroin-addicted pornographer, a Roman centurion, a cat burglar, Pfizer trainee #1. At a summer theater program, I once played a pair of haunted cowboy boots.

Most of all, though, I've enjoyed getting to play America's most beloved pedophile.

The role of Ezra Fitz—despite the creep factor and the obvious ethical issues of dating a minor who happens to be one of my students—has been an incredible learning experience. I've played the part for seven years now, longer than any other role I've had, and I've grown substantially as an actor and as a person during my time as Ezra.

The first few seasons were a wild ride. I strapped in and hoped to God that I wouldn't fall off. The show turned out to be a hit—I was even getting recognized on the street. The whole experience was exciting and surreal, and every day was something new. I felt like I'd really made it.

But, as with everything, after a few seasons, the newness began to fade a little. I love my castmates and the crew—they are some of my favorite people on earth—but there were days on set when I counted down the hours until I could clock out and head home to see my girlfriend and play with my dogs. There were days when the job felt like a have-to instead of a get-to.

I knew I was in danger of becoming jaded. I was beginning to act like what Dustin Diamond might have called a "douche nozzle." I knew that I needed to shake the feeling off posthaste or I was going to start losing friends.

Nobody wants to hang out with a douche nozzle.

It was winter. Or the Los Angeles version of winter, elsewhere called "autumn." We were on break from filming, and I was going on a ski trip—a welcome chance to duck out of town for a few days and clear my head.

Every year since we graduated, a big group of my college friends and I have rented a cabin up in Big Bear Lake, a small town in the mountains about two hours northeast of LA. I studied acting at the Carnegie Mellon School of Drama, and I'm still close with a lot of my classmates. It's a tight-knit group, and the annual ski trip is a lot like a mafia summit—except instead of checking on business and figuring out whose knee-caps to break, the major goals are skiing and inebriation.

That year, we'd rented a cabin that could comfortably sleep six. There were two dozen of us, but we'd all gone to school together, so we were used to sharing beds.

The real problem was that it was only mid-December. We'd scheduled the trip a bit early that year, thinking nothing of the suspiciously low rental prices. There wasn't much snow yet. In fact, I'm pretty sure the only powder on the mountain was man-made. There were just two runs open in the entire resort: a bunny run for beginners, and a longer, intermediate-level blue.

The first day, we said screw it and decided to ski anyway. It was shorts and T-shirt weather on the mountain, not a cloud in the sky. The snow was the consistency of a Slurpee.

My friend Jack had never skied before, so I skied down the bunny slope with him a few times to help him with the basics. He got the hang of it pretty quickly, and after four or five times down, Jack decided he wanted to try his luck on the more difficult blue.

About a hundred yards into the run, Jack skidded over a rough patch of snow and went down. Hard. He reached out to catch himself and broke his arm—really shattered it.

I was above him on the mountain and didn't see him wipe out. I came around a bend to find several of my Carnegie compatriots huddled around him. At first I thought he was more shaken than hurt. But then Jack lifted his arm—it was bent at an unnatural angle: something was very wrong.

Jack had to be taken down the mountain in a paramedic snowmobile, and then we drove him to the emergency room in town.

In the ER, an unhygienically musky doctor came up to us. "What seems to be the problem here? Got a hurt arm?" he asked.

Before Jack could respond, the doctor reached out, grabbed his arm, and gave it a hard squeeze, shaking it up and down. Jack screamed and jerked his arm back. The doctor whistled. "That's definitely broken," he said.

"Yeah, you think?" Jack spat back.

For future reference: people with broken arms don't like having them squeezed and shaken. Just so you know.

Eventually a different doctor splinted Jack's arm and loaded him up with enough pain meds to knock out a small elephant. I offered to drive him back to LA, but Jack was a total champ and said he wanted to stay the rest of the weekend with us.

Unsurprisingly, the next morning nobody felt like skiing.

While we all tried to figure out what to do, my buddies Nick and Frank, both from New Jersey, both of Italian descent, made us all a massive breakfast. Nick and Frank are always the chefs on these trips. They never ski. They just come to hang out, drink, and cook, like the Italian grandmothers they secretly are.

My girlfriend Sophia and I loaded up our plates with eggs and pancakes and Italian sausages, and sat down at the breakfast table to feast.

Sophia and I have been together for six years, the longest I've been with anyone. We went to college together but didn't start dating until we'd both moved to Los Angeles. She has the looks of Audrey Hepburn and the comedic timing of Buster Keaton. She's also an exceptional photographer and artist.

One of our group, a friend from Carnegie we all call Wiggy, shuffled into the kitchen, half asleep, carrying an electric guitar and an amp. He was wearing boxers and an American flag T-shirt with the sleeves cut off. He grunted good morning to no one in particular and sat down on top of the table. He leaned over to plug in the amp and then proceeded to strum out a series of death metal arpeggios.

I reached over and unplugged the amp. Wiggy continued to play as if nothing had changed.

After breakfast, I took a couple of people into town to the grocery store. We needed to stock up on provisions since we weren't going back out on the slopes. Mostly I think we were getting beer for a little day drinking. Maybe marshmallows and chocolate bars for s'mores.

On the drive to town, I started feeling irritable. The weekend was beginning to seem like a total waste. It wasn't my friends' fault. It was me.

I'd been craving activity—something to take my mind off everything. Instead, I found myself once again worrying about my work and the ever-lengthening to-do list I'd left back in Los Angeles.

Driving into town, to the right of the car, there was a massive, shimmering body of water. Big Bear Lake is named for a lake, after all. The late-morning light glittered beckoningly off the surface of the water.

Sitting shotgun was a guy named Walter—a childhood friend of my CMU buddy John. We'd just met the day before. He was one of the only people on the trip who hadn't gone to Carnegie—he may well have been the only person there who hadn't studied theater or taken an acting class. For most of the drive he'd been looking out the window, which I assumed was because he was new to the group.

Walter was on the lake-side of the car, and as we drove along, I glanced over to look out at the water. Looking over, I could see that he was focused intently on an object floating on the lake.

I craned my neck forward to look past him. Close to the shore was a duck, floating serenely on the glittering blue. It had a low, sleek profile, and a thin bill. Not your normal duck profile, if that's the kind of thing you pay attention to.

Something about that bird drew me in. For a moment, I was at a loss. I kept driving in silence. A word lodged somewhere in the depths of my brain bubbled up into consciousness: *merganser*.

That's what it was, a type of duck called a merganser.

I braked for a stop sign, then drove on. But I couldn't get the bird out of my head. I looked at Walter. He'd definitely seen that duck. But did he know what it was?

"Merganser," I mumbled. There was a good chance he'd have no idea what I was talking about.

Walter looked over. A big smile spread across his face. "Yeah, dude. That was a hooded merganser!"

"Wait, for real?" I said. "How'd you know what that was?"

Turns out Walter, who'd grown up in Texas, had been a birder since he was a little kid.

I was a birder when I was a kid, too. I just hadn't thought about it in a really long time.

When I was younger—way younger, like back before elementary school—I loved looking at birds. It was one of my childhood passions. Right up there with Pogs and poop jokes.

I was born in Heidelberg, Germany. My parents were both in the U.S. military, and they were stationed there when I was a baby. When I was three years old, they got called back state-side, so we moved from Germany to Springfield, Virginia.

Our first home back in the States was a red-brick town house with forest-green shutters. It was a picture-perfect middle-class suburban home. I had a best friend who lived three doors down, and my sister's best friend lived next door. It was a safe place for kids to play out front in the street. One time some high-schoolers had a knife fight on a basketball court nearby and the cops showed up, but nothing else exciting ever happened.

Behind our house, a path led across a little creek to a playground in the woods. There were swings, a slide, a merry-go-round. And beyond all that, the forest stretched out endlessly.

There were squirrels and deer and foxes. Crawfish in the stream. And lots and lots of birds. I'd chase the robins that were perched on the ground. I don't know what I would have done if I'd ever caught one. But I liked following them. I wanted to get as close as possible.

At some point it occurred to me that instead of going out and chasing them, I could get the birds to come to me.

I went through the trash at home and pulled out all the empty plastic soda bottles. I cut holes in the sides and filled them with birdseed. I then tied strings around the necks of the bottles, and hung them from low-hanging branches in our back-yard. For neighbors walking by, it must've looked like some low-budget human sacrifice cult. The whole setup was pretty *Blair Witch*-y.

Once the feeders were hanging from the trees, I went up to my bedroom on the second floor and waited for the birds to arrive. I had a cheap pair of binoculars with plastic lenses, and over the coming weeks I'd patiently focus them on the nuthatches, woodpeckers, sparrows, and goldfinches that came in to feed. It was like *Rear Window*, except without any murder. Unless you count the murder of crows.

Sorry. That was just—I'm sorry.

The point is, I really liked birds. I had notebooks full of drawings of them that I copied out of an Audubon field guide. And in second grade, I once threw a tantrum when my science project group wanted to build a model volcano instead of a bird feeder.

But then I graduated to middle school. Puberty happened, as it does to many people. I became far more self-conscious and felt a strong need to fit in with the other kids. Birding is often a solitary pursuit. It's not something you need to share with others. For as much joy as it brought me, I was afraid it would come across as weird, outsider behavior.

Also, middle-schoolers think about sex a lot: like, all the time. To my thirteen-year-old mind, birding was the equivalent of a vow of chastity. I couldn't risk it, so I very willfully set birds aside.

There's a book I read recently that reminds me of my middle school experience. Before J. M. Barrie wrote *Peter and Wendy*—the classic tale of Peter Pan and Captain Hook and the wonders of Neverland—he wrote a book called *The Little White Bird*. This book is the first time Barrie ever wrote about a boy named Peter Pan. Before there was a Neverland, before there were pirates or mermaids, there was just a little boy locked in a park at night after the gates had closed.

Barrie talks in the book about how all children used to be

birds: "They are naturally a little wild during the first few weeks, and very itchy at the shoulders, where their wings used to be." Children only become fully human when they forget how to fly. And forgetting how to fly is easy. It just takes doubt. The moment you first doubt whether or not you can fly is the moment you lose the gift of flight forever. The moment when you cease to be a bird and become a human, destined to grow old and dull and unimaginative.

In my adolescence, I took this odd interest I had, and I hid it. Buried it. I was afraid of getting picked on, of getting made fun of by the opposite sex, by anyone really. It was easier to be normal and try to fit in—and wash my face three times a day to prevent breakouts. As long as I tried to be like everyone else—as long as I tried to look normal—I had a chance at being cool. And it's embarrassing to admit it, but being cool meant a lot to me. I wanted to be friends with everyone. Birding seemed like the opposite of all that. If anything, it just seemed like a way to be friends with old people. And everyone in middle school knows that old people aren't cool.

When high school rolled around, I'd forgotten that I'd ever even liked birds in the first place. My attention and interests were elsewhere. I switched from a public middle school to a private high school called Georgetown Prep. I wasn't used to the rigorous academics, and I had to work a lot harder in class.

In high school I also discovered acting, which was a whole new creative outlet for me. I spent all of my free time in Figge, the school's theater building. I would often set up a table in the middle of the stage to do my homework, the auditorium otherwise empty. Sometimes the janitor would kick me out—I would walk around the building and sneak back in.

Now, sitting in the car in Big Bear, looking at the hooded merganser, I felt a familiar excitement rising in my chest, a connection to my childhood—back to when I'd stared out my bedroom window, learning the names of the birds that were eating from the bird feeders I'd made.

I had forgotten that just looking at birds—simply watching them, observing their idiosyncratic behaviors and colorful beauty—could bring me such joy. I felt inspired, light, and totally in touch with a part of me that had been lying dormant for almost fifteen years.

"What the hell is a merganser?" someone said from the backseat.

I looked at Walter: "You want to tell him?"

Walter tried to downplay it. "It's a kind of duck," he said.

I suddenly felt a flash of defiance—not at Walter, but at the entire situation. I'd stopped birding as a child because I'd felt judged by my peers. Here I was, twenty-five years old, an adult, and I was feeling embarrassed by birds again? If I didn't stand up for myself now, when the hell was I going to start?

I half shouted, "It's not just a duck!" I had no idea where I was going with this, but I had to set the record straight. "It's got a serrated bill! It's a fucking awesome duck!"

Yeah, that'd show them. That would make them understand.

From the backseat, a bored voice said, "Whatever," and then went back to what they'd been talking about before the merganser interlude.

When we got back to the cabin with provisions an hour later people were getting antsy. It was downright balmy outside—a ridiculous, global warming–induced seventy degrees. Someone suggested to the group that, since we couldn't ski, we all go for a hike along Big Bear Lake.

A handful of people wanted to stay back to get drunk and eat marshmallows, and Wiggy was still strumming his unplugged guitar, but the rest of us piled into a couple of cars and drove back down to the lake. We parked near a bridge.

As we were getting out of the cars, putting on sunscreen, I noticed that Walter had a small pair of binoculars hanging around his neck.

"Do you always have those around?" I asked.

"Yeah. Actually, I keep them in the glove compartment of my car," he said. "It might be crazy, but you never know. I've seen a lot of birds in places I wouldn't have expected to find them."

The group set off, tromping around the lake. I was suddenly aware again of the world in a different but oddly familiar way. Birds were outlined in silhouette out on the water. They were chirping overhead in the trees and in the bushes along the shore. I was paying attention to every sound.

I wasn't in my head, worrying about work, or thinking about how I needed to watch what I ate over the holidays. It might sound like some hippie California nonsense, but I felt very, very present.

A flock of birds fluttered between trees off to the side of the trail, gorging themselves on tiny red berries. Walter passed me his binoculars. I raised them to my eyes and adjusted the focus knob with my index finger, trying to get a bird to come into view.

The birds were moving targets, and I was out of practice. I lowered the binoculars and looked for them again. I could hear them: their call a single high-pitched note, barely noticeable unless you were listening for it.

Suddenly there was a flurry of wings as one hovered to snatch a berry. I quickly raised the binoculars and adjusted the focus: a little brown crest, a black mask, a dab of yellow at the end of the bird's tail. Very sleek, very elegant. A cedar waxwing.

I made a mental note to invest in a pair of binoculars when I got back to Los Angeles.

In the bushes along the shore, another bird called—it sounded like the avian version of an old-timey phone ring. I could swear I'd heard that call before, but I couldn't place it.

"That's a red-winged blackbird," Walter said, as it flew out and landed in the branches at the top of the bush. It was a glossy black, with red and yellow epaulettes on its wings.

Farther along, coots were paddling close to shore. We scanned the lake—no sign of that merganser. I noticed a bird twisting its way up a tree. A downy woodpecker? It spiraled back around the trunk, coming into view. Not a woodpecker after all, but a white-breasted nuthatch.

It was the same type of nuthatch that had come in to the feeders I'd set up in my backyard in Virginia when I was a kid. Here I was, wandering around a lake in California, the same boy that used to play in the woods, chasing robins.

In the far distance, Sophia and my friend Michele were skipping stones, trying to hit a floating log. The rest of the group was out of sight down the path.

I didn't mind being left behind—it was like I'd found a key to a room that hadn't been opened for years, and I was just beginning to explore what was under all the dust that had accumulated. It was slow work, but I was ecstatic. Yes, that's the word. Ecstatic. It was like reconnecting with a long-lost friend. I couldn't stop smiling.

Walter pointed out birds as we walked along. A lot of them were different from the ones I'd grown up with. I had a lot to learn, and a lot to relearn. There was a childlike sense of wonder to the whole experience: I was a birder again.

Of course, the trip had to come to an end. As I drove back to Los Angeles at the end of the long weekend, there was a lump in my throat. My mind kept jumping back to the merganser, and to all the other birds we'd spotted around the lake. I didn't know when I'd get another chance to go birding like that again.

Later that week, I found myself back on the Warner Bros. lot, wandering past the sound stages where *Pretty Little Liars* is filmed. The show was on hiatus, but I had a casting session for a horror film.

Driving onto the lot, I was feeling irritable again. I wanted to be back in the mountains. And just being in the physical location of where I work made me a little anxious—for something different, for something more. Looking to the mountains in the distance, I felt completely cut off from nature.

I parked and got out of the car. Just then, a pair of swallows darted by, spiraling over and under each other as they shot up into the sky and vanished overhead. I was stunned. I stood there in awe, trying to see where the birds had disappeared to.

An assistant with a clipboard walked up. "Everything okay?" he asked.

"Yeah," I said, still looking up at the sky. "Just trying to see where those swallows went."

The assistant scratched his head. "I know there are a couple of birds that live up in the WB sign," he said, pointing toward Stage 16.

Right above the load-in doors on the soundstage, the iconic WB sign beamed out over the lot. Nestled in the shade below the *W*, a nest made of mud clung to the side of the sign.

"That's it!" I said. "Those are cliff swallows."

I smiled. It felt good to be back. I'd left the mountains behind, but birds—birds are everywhere. I just hadn't been looking for them.

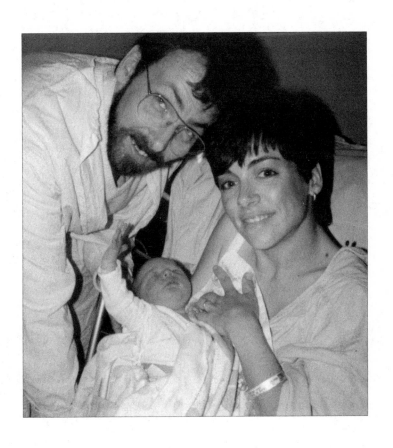

H IS FOR

MR. HAWKINS

They say that second children are easy to raise. After the stress and steep learning curve of the firstborn child, kid number two is supposed to be a breeze.

This was not the case in my family. My big sister Sarah was an easy child, practically angelic. You could give her a book, and she'd sit quietly, entertaining herself, for hours.

I was—as my dear aunt Jules often tells me—a nightmare.

I was a master of tantrums, a great shitter of diapers, and a consummate destroyer of fine china. Then one day I started talking, and the tantrums stopped. To hear my parents tell it, it was all very sudden. The moment I learned to communicate, I stopped lashing out.

I was still a terror, just in different, subtler ways.

We went through a steady stream of babysitters. None of them lasted that long. One time, while my parents were out on a date, trying to remove themselves from the stress of childcare for a few precious hours, our babysitter asked us if we wanted to play hide-and-seek.

This was very exciting for me except for one slight hang-up: I was terrible at hide-and-seek. I was four at the time, and I had a four-year-old's perception of good hiding spots. I hid under the dining table. Sarah found me. I tried hiding behind the couch. She found me again. There is just no winning at hide-and-seek when you are four and your older sister is seven.

That's when it occurred to me: the perfect hiding spot. There was one place where they'd never think to look.

I waited until the babysitter was "it." As she began her slow count to thirty, I watched Sarah sneak up the stairs toward our parents' bathroom. So that's where she'd been hiding.

I turned the opposite way and snuck out the front door, around the side of the house, and into the woods. Brilliant, I thought. They'd never find me in the woods at night.

I mentioned earlier that our house backed up to a forest. The jump from manicured suburbs to wilderness was sudden and thrilling. There was a trail that started just behind our house. Twenty paces in and you were plunged into darkness. The temperature fell, and the sounds of birds enveloped you. The path was edged with moss and Virginia creeper, and it curved its way through the trees for what felt like miles.

My parents would let my sister and me play in the woods on our own. My dad would give us an old Timex watch, and tell us when to be home. The game was to see how far we could get into the forest and still make it back in time for dinner. We'd bushwhack through the undergrowth, hop across stone bridges.

From time to time, we'd pass a playground or a backyard, but gradually those started to disappear. Bit by bit, the neighborhood dissolved around us and we forgot where we were. The path forked again and again, branching out into the woods like blood vessels. Walking along, turning left then right then left again, I felt like I could get lost in those woods for days.

There was a creek that ran through the forest. Ferns lined its edges, and small herds of deer would stop to drink. When my sister and I had friends over, we would all go down to the creek to catch crawfish. One of our friends sometimes brought a net, but the rest of us just used our hands. We never ate the crawfish we caught; the goal was to catch the biggest and to make sure that everyone else saw how big it was before you threw it back into the water.

The best crawfish lived in the spots where the creek got its widest, where the water slowed to a crawl. We would wade in and lift up the biggest rocks we could. In the cloud of dust and leaf litter that got stirred up under the rocks, we could usually find one or two crawfish.

The woods were our second home. And as far as I was concerned, I was Robinson Crusoe.

That night, playing hide-and-seek, I started walking down the usual path, but it was extremely dark outside. Still, I was riding the high of having potentially won a round of hide-and-seek, and I wasn't about to turn back now. I kept on walking.

After walking about a mile, the path sloped up. I followed it until it spit me out on the side of a busy street. As I walked along the road, a four-year-old marching proudly in his Batman pajamas, a white SUV slowed down and pulled up beside me. The window rolled down to reveal a woman about my mother's age.

"Are you lost, honey? Do you need help?" she said.

I shook my head. "No thanks!"

"Are you sure?"

"I'm playing hide-and-seek," I said, smiling.

She let out a nervous laugh. "I'll bet you're winning."

"I am!"

"Listen, you should probably head back. I'm sure your parents are worried sick about you. Can I give you a ride home?"

"I'm not allowed to ride in the car with strangers," I said.

"Good point." She put the car in park and got out. "Come on," she said, reaching out her hand to take mine. "Let's walk."

I told her my address, and we walked home together. When I opened my front door, the first thing I saw was my dad pacing back and forth. Our babysitter had called the restaurant—this was before cellphones—to tell my parents that I'd gone missing. When he saw me, he let out a cry. I'd never heard my dad make that sound. He lifted me up in his arms, a wave of emotion flooding his face, and held me against his chest. He walked me into the living room, where my mom was sitting on the couch with the babysitter, who was crying into her hands.

"Ian, where on earth have you been?" my mom asked.

I smiled. "I won the game."

After that, I wasn't allowed to go into the woods on my

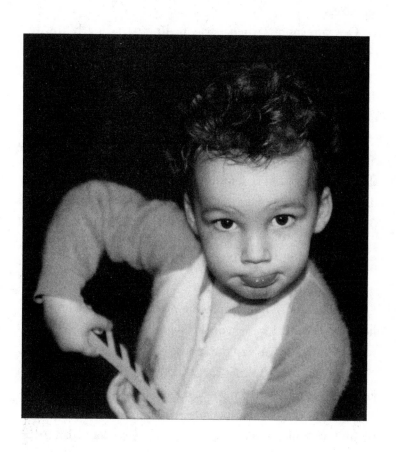

own for a while. But it soon became clear that it wasn't a good idea for me to remain indoors, either. I was a hyperactive kid, like I said, and if I didn't have an outlet for all of my energy, things would get broken and nobody in the house would get any sleep.

One afternoon, when I was feeling particularly rowdy, my dad volunteered to go tire me out. I was up in my room, spinning in circles. My dad stood at the bottom of the staircase and called up: "Ian, do you want to come exploring with me?"

I raced down the stairs, threw some shoes on, and we were off. My dad and I hiked around the woods for the better part of the afternoon. I was so happy to be back outside. I showed my dad all of my favorite crawfish spots, and he told me about the different types of trees we were walking by. When I got home, I was exhausted. I slept soundly that night. And so did my parents.

They had found a way to get rid of my excess energy.

My dad and I went exploring pretty often after he'd get home from work. I, being your average four-year-old, could not pronounce the word "explore," though. So we went on 'splores.

It was on these 'splores that I first noticed birds. I mean, I knew what birds were, I wasn't a complete shut-in. I'd seen the cardinals in our backyard and heard my mom's stories about them. I'd smelled the deathly musk of pigeons outside of the natural history museum in DC. But this was the first time that I ever became aware of their variety, of their nesting habits, their flight patterns, and their distinct, vibrating calls echoing through the woods.

My dad seemed to know all about them. We'd hear a rustling in the trees, and he'd point up and say, "That's a crow, Ian." I'd laugh—because the word sounded funny to my ears—and then I'd try to mimic its call.

I had wanted things before: the previous Christmas, I had really wanted light-up sneakers. So desire was not a new concept to me.

But this was the first time I remember wanting to understand something. I wanted to know everything there was to know about birds. I wanted to devour them with my mind and absorb all of their secrets. The secret of flight, how to perch, what worms tasted like, why they never had to pee . . . I wanted to know it all.

There was one bird in particular that I absolutely loved. I asked my dad what kind of bird it was, and he said it was a hawk. So, naturally, I named him Mr. Hawkins.

Every time we went out 'sploring, I would run ahead of my dad into the woods to see my new friend. Mr. Hawkins would always stare at me with a slightly surprised and cautious look on his face. At the time, I always thought that he was pretending not to remember me, so I would play along and call out to remind him, "Mr. Hawkins! It's me, Ian!"

In retrospect, I now realize that the look on Mr. Hawkins's face was one of deliberation: Do I flee from this screaming child or try to somehow eat him?

When I was in the second grade, we moved from Springfield to Herndon, an even smaller town, which was nestled in the shadow of Dulles airport. A lot of the public schools in northern Virginia have the exact same floor plan, so the transition to a new school wasn't particularly difficult, at least spatially. What I was worried about was saying goodbye to 'splores with my dad.

Despite its proximity to both airplanes and politicians, Herndon still felt rural. My new home was within walking distance of Trailside Park, a perfect place for new and exciting adventures.

Every day after school I would rush home, grab my binoculars, and my dad and I would wander off to the park to look for birds. It turned out there was a hawk that lived in the Herndon park, too. I was convinced that it was Mr. Hawkins, and I couldn't believe his loyalty—he had moved all the way across the county to be with us.

Some friends just last forever, you know.

It was clear to my dad that birds were becoming a passion of mine. One day—I think I was about six—my dad took me into his study. He pulled an old book off his shelves and handed it to me.

"I thought this might help," he said, smiling down at me.

The book was significantly older than I was. The cover was made of fake leather. The white lettering along the spine cracked and illegible. The corners of the pages were all bent with age and humidity. I opened the book and turned to the title page: *The Audubon Society: Field Guide to North American Birds.*

I flipped to a random page. There were row upon row of photographs. In each photograph, a different bird. Birds I'd never seen before. Birds I'd never imagined could exist. Names I couldn't even dream of pronouncing. The book was bursting with information.

I thanked my dad and hugged his knees—I was shorter then. I looked up at him and asked, "Is Mr. Hawkins in here?"

He took the book from my hands and flipped through the pages pensively for a few moments. Then his face relaxed into a grin. He handed the book back to me and pointed to one of the pictures on the page. It was a red-tailed hawk.

I giggled. "His tail *is* red!" I cried, unable to control my glee.

I didn't sleep that night. My mom and dad came by to check on me before going to bed, and I turned off the light and pretended to be sleeping. But as soon as they left, the light was back on and the book was open. There was a whole world of birds out there for me to explore.

The next time we went to Trailside Park, I brought the bird book with me. When I saw Mr. Hawkins perched high up on a branch that day, I opened up the book to the earmarked page with the red-tailed hawk on it and held it up for him to see.

"Mr. Hawkins!" I shouted, "Look! They took your picture. It's you!"

Mr. Hawkins looked down at me, startled, and promptly flew away. My dad told me that Mr. Hawkins was probably just shy and didn't like looking at his own picture.

The Audubon guide was the second book I had ever fallen in love with. The first was *The Velveteen Rabbit*, a copy of which I carried everywhere with me for months. I read it again and again, pressing my finger up against the rabbit's nose, letting him know that I had believed he was real all along.

My dad and I often ran across a little brown rabbit in the woods. I was convinced that it was the Velveteen Rabbit come to life. Every time we saw it, I would unsuccessfully attempt to suppress a gasp, and my finger would shoot out, pointing at the terrified bunny in our path. My dad explained to me that this wasn't the Velveteen Rabbit from the book—it was our Velveteen Rabbit, and we could name him whatever we wanted.

We settled on Sir Hopsalot.

One day in the woods near our house I saw Sir Hopsalot sitting in a field. He was munching on some tall grass and didn't seem to notice my dad and me walking toward him.

My dad stayed behind as I slowly, stealthily crept toward the rabbit. I could see his whiskers twitching with each bite he took. He must have realized I was nearby, because he sat up on his hind legs, alert, his nose twitching. His ears twisted around like a satellite dish.

I had never been this close to a wild animal before. He was beautiful. If I could just get a little closer, I knew that I could reach out and pet him. Just a little tiny bit closer.

Sir Hopsalot pricked his ears up, and became very still. He raised his head and looked at me. I knew it: he was finally ready to say hello.

I took another cautious step forward.

There was a soft thud as Mr. Hawkins slammed into Sir Hopsalot.

Talons ripped open the rabbit's soft belly, spilling its guts out across the field of grass and clover. Wings outstretched, the hawk throttled the rabbit against the ground, making sure it was dead.

I stood there, stunned, as Mr. Hawkins swiveled his head up from his prey and looked me in the eye, daring me to take one more step.

The hawk took off, Sir Hopsalot a deflated balloon of red fur clutched in its talons.

My dad must have carried me back after that, because I don't remember walking home. I was too busy crying.

From then on, I was always decidedly curt—cold, even—when I greeted Mr. Hawkins in the woods. I was scarred. It was the most brutal thing I'd ever seen.

But I did learn a valuable life lesson that day: just because you're friends with two people doesn't mean they'll get along.

MY INNER

ANIMAL

I'd been called in to audition for the role of a Holocaust survivor.

The idea of auditioning for a part like this gave me more stress than usual. There are certain roles where when you portray them, you aren't just a person, you're a stand-in for an entire people. I felt like I could never possibly do justice to the character.

The week before the audition, I spent six hours a day prepping. Every morning, I'd wake up, and read through the scene again, and feel like I had to start over from scratch. I couldn't get a foothold on the character.

I tried out half a dozen different accents—and a physicality for each one—and none of them seemed to fit. Around day three, I stopped drinking water, hoping that doing so might give my throat the sort of rasp I imagined the character might have.

My studio apartment had shag carpeting, and I was pacing back and forth so much every day that I was beginning to wear tracks in it.

I was feeling tired and weak, and more than once I thought about calling my agent and telling him to call off the audition. I just couldn't do it, I wanted to say.

I'd forgotten that I'd stopped drinking water, and one morning, as I was pacing, I felt the room begin to spin around me—once, twice, then a third time. I reached out to grab the back of a chair to steady myself.

When the room finally came to rest, I bent my knees to make sure they still worked.

They wobbled a little. My legs felt weak, fluid almost.

I felt like I was out on the ocean, floating adrift. I felt like a jellyfish.

I hadn't felt that sensation in years, but it was undeniable. Believe me when I say I know exactly what it feels like to be a jellyfish: there was a period in my life where I spent eight hours a day, every day—for months—pretending to be one.

My dad drove me up to Pittsburgh for my first year of college. I was leaving the nest for the first time, and though leaving behind the world I'd grown up in saddened me, I was getting a chance to pursue the one thing in the world I really wanted to do. I was about to begin to study acting at the Carnegie Mellon School of Drama.

Even with all the excitement, it was more difficult to say goodbye than I expected. My parents had gotten divorced the year before, and my mom was selling the house in Herndon that I'd grown up in. When I left for college, it was already on the market, and I knew that when I came back to visit for Thanksgiving, it would be to an entirely different home.

When my dad and I arrived in Pittsburgh, we immediately went to my freshman dorm to get moved in. That year I lived in an all-male dorm called Hamerschlag. My new roommate, Joe, who was a music major, also happened to be there, moving in at the same time.

Joe was from South Africa, by way of Baltimore. He had a big mop of curly hair, thick-rimmed glasses, and he was virtually inseparable from his cherry-red electric guitar.

I remember lying in bed that first night, thinking about this new life I was about to embark upon. It's bizarre being plopped into a new living situation with a stranger for a whole year. Joe and I started talking to each other in the dark, talking about ourselves, seeing how we got along. At some point, he stopped responding.

I looked over: he had fallen asleep in child's pose—a position he ended up sleeping in often. I still don't understand how he was able to fall asleep with his butt in the air. What was not so cute, though, was that he often liked to sleep naked.

That first year at CMU was a blast, but it was also a lot of work. The School of Drama puts its students through the ringer. It's an acting conservatory, so we didn't have any classes that weren't theater-related. We'd spend five days a week, from 7:00 A.M. to 11:00 P.M., studying acting and building sets for the school's plays. Sunup till way after sundown. Then, on

Saturdays, we'd regularly have an additional half day of set-building.

Fall semester was a whirlwind, and looking back, a lot of it is a blur. There were so many new people to meet, a whole new city to explore, and classes were more than a full-time commitment. I had been the only person from my all-boys Catholic high school to pursue acting in college, and I was suddenly surrounded by some of the most talented people I'd ever met. It was intimidating. But over the course of four years of working with the same people, that sense of intimidation—and the natural competition between students—gave way to camaraderie and friendship. Some of my best friends to this day I met during those four years at Carnegie.

We had a month off for Christmas, so I went back to stay with my mom in Virginia. She'd moved into a new two-bedroom apartment, and since my sister was also home for the break, I slept in a little loft that was actually the laundry room.

While I was back home, I met up with a few of my closest childhood friends. We all had one foot in our old Virginia high-school world, and all the shared experiences of that time, and one foot in our college worlds, on the verge of new, independent lives. We weren't twenty-one yet, so we were still in this odd hang-out limbo. We'd play basketball at the Y until it closed, then go to Chipotle. After that, we'd drink at someone's house.

One night, we were all over at my friend Chris's house. There were four or five of us hanging out, shooting the shit, comparing notes on college, bragging about how much we'd partied and the girls we'd met. My other friends all seemed to be headed toward careers in business or medicine or the military.

The guys asked what I was up to. I took a swig of my beer. "I've been doing a lot of physical stuff this semester. It's called Viewpoints. Basically, it's about how you walk around a room and the different ways you can interact with the architecture."

Good. I'd used some big words—I'd even said the word "architecture"—so nobody could deny that I was doing important things.

"That's it?" Chris asked. "You've been learning how to walk around a room?"

"Well, that's not the only thing I'm doing. I have voice class, and speech class, and acting—"

"Voice and speech are two different classes?"

I was starting to feel judged.

"Yeah, speech is all about accents and dialects. This year we're learning Standard American. Next year we learn General American . . ." I trailed off as I realized everyone's eyes had glazed over.

"Anyway, yeah," I said.

Matt tried to be nice: "Have anything fun coming up next semester?"

I took a sip of beer and sighed. "Next semester they want me to figure out what kind of animal I am."

For a while nobody said anything. Then everyone started laughing. Matt grinned. "So, you're in kindergarten."

The first week back after the holiday break, our professors stood us up at the front of the classroom, one by one, and assigned us each an animal.

"Adam, you're a bear."

"Vicki, definitely a catfish."

"Shunan, dear God, could you be more of a penguin?"

When it was my turn, I walked up to the front of the room. The professors put their heads together and whispered. I put my hands behind my back, trying to loosen up my shoulders. After a moment, one of the professors laughed a little, and they all turned back to face me.

"You exude false confidence," one of them said. "Like a mouse with a Napoleon complex." The two other professors nodded in agreement. Behind them, one of my classmates snorted.

The professor continued, "You need to be the complete opposite: an animal that has no ego, no sense of self."

He sat back in his chair and crossed his arms. For a few moments nobody spoke. Then he squinted and leaned forward— "Any ideas?"

I was—to put it lightly—hurt. This assessment of my outward demeanor was tough to stomach. I stood there, trying to shake off what the professor had said, but it was affecting me more than I wanted to admit. Definitely more than I wanted my classmates to see.

I tried to laugh it off. "What, like a jellyfish?" I joked.

The teacher who had issued the critique raised his eyebrows. "Exactly," he said. "You'll be a jellyfish."

We were assigned our animals on a Friday. We were to present them the following Monday. And by "present" I mean act out in front of the class.

That weekend, a number of my classmates went to the Pittsburgh Zoo to research their animals. They wanted to observe their behavior and movement firsthand.

Meanwhile, I did what I had learned to do in high school for research projects: I went to the library.

I wandered into the Carnegie Library and found a librarian.

"Hi there," I said. "Do you have any books on jellyfish?"

"Is this for a research project?" she asked.

"Yes—I have to be one."

She gave me an odd look but didn't press for an explanation.

On Sunday I locked myself in my dorm room and read through all the books I'd checked out. I watched the few jelly-fish clips I could find online—it was still the early days of YouTube.

After exhaustive research, I stood in front of the full-length mirror on the back of the door to the room and did all the things that a human does when they're pretending to be a jellyfish.

I hunched my shoulders forward and let my arms dangle like tentacles. I pulsed my body, as if propelling myself through an invisible ocean. I tried to ride the ebb and flow of the land-locked Pittsburgh tide.

I looked at myself in the mirror—I felt like a crazy person.

I kept at it, though. An hour went by. I continued to wriggle my body in shallow, jellyfish-like convulsions.

A second hour went by, and I looked down at my feet, teth-ered to the ground, holding me back—

Suddenly, the secret to imitating a jellyfish struck me.

The secret to being a great jellyfish—and this is impor-tant—it's all in the ankles.

I wobbled my ankles back and forth, letting the momen-tum wiggle up to my hips. I pushed up on the balls of my feet, heels elevated slightly off the ground, then slowly drifted back down.

Proud of my discovery, proud of how great my jellyfish performance would be, I stood there in front of the mirror and continued to bend my ankles. I felt sure I was bending them just like a jellyfish would.

All of a sudden, Joe was standing where the mirror had just been. I was wearing my skintight drama-school-issued black unitard, and writhing up and down.

"Uh, hey Joe. Just rehearsing for class."

"Don't mind me. What're you working on?"

"You know, Animal Projects . . ."

Joe didn't say anything.

"I'm a jellyfish."

Joe was unfazed. He sat down on his bed and pulled out his electric guitar.

"Keep doing your thing," he said. He plucked at the strings, letting them vibrate in a gentle and meditative deep-sea sort of way. "I'm just going to play us some jellyfish music."

His face took on the expression one gets when deep in prayer. To this day, he's one of the only people I know who sees music as not simply something to listen and dance to, but as a form of communion with something greater.

Monday came, and I walked into the drama building with more confidence than ever before. When it was my turn to present, I strode up to the front of the classroom. I cleared my mind and then focused on my ankles. I whispered to myself, "Mind of a jellyfish. Mind of a jellyfish."

I don't remember what happened next: All I know is that I was a jellyfish. I was born a jellyfish. I could not remember a day when I hadn't been a jellyfish.

After a minute or two of gelatinous pulsating, my professor politely asked me to stop. "Good work, Ian. Very specific," he said.

I smiled. This was one of the first real compliments I'd received in acting class at Carnegie.

"Really good start at your jellyfish," the professor went on. "Excited to see this develop over the next two months."

Animal Projects, it turned out, was not just a few days of research followed by a presentation. It was eight weeks of pretending to be a man-sized scyphozoan. It was the only thing we did in class.

One of the requirements of the project was to construct a costume, so the following weekend I took a bus down to the Waterfront, a strip of big-box stores along the Monongahela River. I had an idea, and I needed bedsheets.

I wandered into Bed Bath & Beyond. On a sales rack I found a set of fluorescent lime-green sheets on clearance. I don't think I'd ever seen a green jellyfish before, but I figured I could take some artistic license. And the sheets were the right price: extremely cheap.

Back in my dorm room, I cut long strips into the flat sheet and tied it around my shoulders. Neon-green fabric reached down to the floor around my body—these were my tentacles. I then took the fitted sheet and taped it over a hula hoop, which created a puffy, human-sized jellyfish bell. I put the sheet-covered hula hoop over my head, holding it up with my arms.

Looking down, I could only see one or two feet in any direction. I could barely make out anything through the sheet around me—the world was a fuzzy green blur. I couldn't make out the costume in the mirror, so I had no idea what I looked like, but it felt right.

I stood there, in the middle of the room, and I did my jellyfish ankles. I felt the tentacles brush up against my legs, the green bell around my head drifting and floating through the air.

Joe said that I was the most realistic jellyfish he'd ever seen in Pittsburgh.

The next two months of class were a little lonely. I couldn't see much because of my costume, and I didn't interact with many of the other animals. Most of my classmates were terrestrial mammals, but I lived in the ocean. We weren't about to mess with the laws of nature.

Every morning, the professor would set aside a little spot for me to wiggle and jiggle and do my jelly-shaking thing. We called this spot "water," and I shared it with Vicki the catfish. Sometimes a penguin or two would jump in, but most of the other animals avoided it. We'd practice our animals, and the professor would walk around, adjusting postures, commenting on the way the gorillas grabbed at their food, reminding the big cats to be aware of their spinal cords.

I would float there, in my imaginary pool of water, counting my breaths—and remembering to lead with my ankles.

Weeks went by like this, which in jellyfish years is . . . a lot.

I spent that winter floating. Floating in the pond. But I also felt like I was floating in life, carried along by forces out of my control. College is about leaving home and growing up, but you're still a kid. And I felt bittersweet about leaving home, anyway.

A lot had changed in a matter of months. I wasn't homesick—I was actually glad to be out on my own. But there was this feeling, somewhere deep, that I'd left a part of me behind along the way.

It wasn't just that I couldn't go back to my old home anymore. There was a part of me that was no longer there. Or a part of me that was changing, transitioning from one set of circumstances to another.

Looking back on it now, I think the jellyfish may have had something to do with it. I felt trapped. I needed an outlet, and I spent my days physically constricted, only able to see my feet and the floor beneath me. Had I been assigned a different animal—a gorilla, or a tiger—I could have lashed out, roared, beat my chest. But I was a jellyfish, subject to the whims of the tides and of the people around me.

I see that my trajectory throughout my college years was borne along by those same tides. I made big decisions then that have affected my future, but I've also had my life determined in many ways by the decisions of others.

This is a big part of being human, and especially being an actor.

Animal Projects culminated in a three-hour event called "Watering Hole." The freshman class had been divided into three sections, and this was a chance for the entire class to come together and sniff and growl and love on one another as animals.

Unfortunately, I was still one of the only aquatic animals—and I couldn't see more than two feet in any direction.

For the first hour and a half, I floated around my lonely patch of ocean as my classmates scampered about. I could hear them playing and rolling around on the ground. At one point, a teacher announced that the "sun had set," and everyone pretended to go to sleep as their animal. Everyone except for me, because I was a goddamn jellyfish. The sun rose again, and the animals awoke with a series of deep-chested growls and loud roar-yawns.

I continued to bob slowly up and down.

Then things started to get tense. I could sense a change in the mood of the room. The animals that had played together earlier were getting more aggressive. The faculty sensed it, too, and one of the teachers—her name was Ingrid—shouted: "Predators, KILL!"

Loud and frantic screeching immediately filled the air. Somebody threw a chair against a wall—I flinched at the crash. Students were clawing at each other, shrieking, running around me. The room was filled with the sounds of carnage.

I continued to float, rising and falling from my ankles. When the room had quieted down, I angled my hula hoop up so that I could look around.

Most of the student-animals were dead, their bodies strewn about the room. The predators prowled about, letting out blood-curdling howls and roars as they sized each other up. The lions growled at the gorillas, who beat their chests with clenched fists in response.

And I just kept floating. Up. And down.

Then, like a hypnotist, Ingrid clapped her hands and announced that Watering Hole was over. We were humans again.

Years later, standing dizzy and dehydrated in my small apartment in LA—trying to figure out the physicality of a Holocaust survivor—I thought back to how I'd felt in my months as a jellyfish during that first year of college.

I became aware of my ankles again. I took a deep breath in and lifted up the heels of my feet, letting my body float a little.

I closed my eyes and ran through the lines in my head. I felt unmoored. Without a home. Adrift. Something clicked. For the first time all week, I wasn't forcing it. I'd found a window into the character—a strange window, but a window nonetheless.

I went in for the audition the following morning, confident that I'd made the character my own.

I got a callback, but I didn't book the role.

COMING TO LOS ANGELES

(TWICE)

The week after I graduated from college, I loaded up my only significant earthly possession—a blue 1994 Toyota Camry affectionately called the "Vomit Comet"—and drove to Los Angeles to begin my life as a film and television actor.

Before the trip, I took the car in for an inspection. The mechanic had strong opinions about the state of the vehicle. "Do not drive this car across the country," he said.

But, with no other car options available, I set off anyway.

I had everything planned out. The AC didn't work, so I rolled down the windows. Since the windows would be down, and the windshield had no UV protection, I'd get a nice bronzy tan in preparation for my new life in California. And the radio only worked maybe twenty percent of the time—that was actually going to be a problem.

I made the trip from Pittsburgh to LA in four days. Every night, I arrived at some out-of-the-way motel well after midnight, my body aching and stomach rumbling. And every single night, the motel clerk informed me that the only restaurant still open at that hour was Hooters. And every morning, I would wake up, brush my wings-stained teeth, and hit the road, praying that that night I would find someplace to eat that wasn't a Hooters.

But my prayers were never answered.

When I finally made it to Los Angeles, I made two promises to myself. One: I would never set foot in another Hooters. Two: I was done with cross-country road trips.

I broke both promises before the summer was out.

Shortly after I arrived in LA, my girlfriend at the time asked me to fly to Florida with her to pick up her car and drive it back to California. Being young, dumb, and extremely energetic, I agreed.

My girlfriend's car had all the amenities that mine had lacked. Actual working air-conditioning, a fully functional radio, tinted windows—and cup holders. We were living the high life.

But, embarking on my second cross-country road trip in as many months, I was again plagued by a series of pit stops in which Hooters was the only available food option. Eyes watering with regret, we gorged ourselves on plate after plate of Hooterstizers—the laziest portmanteau of all time—and prayed for anything, ideally a Denny's, to save us.

On the fourth day of the trip, just after we crossed the border between Arizona and California, I found something interesting on the map.

Just an hour out of the way was a place called the Salton Sea, and judging by the map, it was an oasis—a huge body of water in the middle of the desert. The idea of taking a break from the road, stretching our legs—maybe even jumping in the water—sounded pretty great.

We stopped at a gas station before heading down, bought some prepackaged sandwiches and sunscreen. Not quite speaking from experience yet, I bragged to my girlfriend, "You know, California has a lot of places like the Salton Sea. Little hidden gems. You're going to love it here."

There are a few things you notice as you approach the Salton Sea. The first is the smell. Maybe it was the scorching summer day—it was over a hundred degrees outside—but we could smell the Salton Sea miles before we arrived. I frantically tried to adjust the vents to stop letting in outside air, but it was too late. The stench of rotting fish was so bad you could taste it.

The second thing you notice is that you are the only people there. The few small towns around the eastern shore seem entirely devoid of life. Blocks of buildings are abandoned, relics of their former resort town glory. Once upon a time, when the lake was less salty, less polluted by the agriculture that surrounds it, the Salton Sea was actually a destination for the rich and famous—but no longer. Nowadays, not many people visit, especially in the middle of July.

We pulled into a state park with beach access to have a quick makeshift picnic. I think we got out of the car for about thirty seconds, just long enough to notice that the beach was blanketed with dead fish. Literally, dead fish as far as the eye could see. I'm not even sure we were walking on sand, or if it was just pulverized fish bones.

We ate our sandwiches in the car as we drove away.

I later learned that the Salton Sea is a major migratory pit stop for birds traveling along the Pacific flyway. Birds pass through, moving up and down the continent, and here I was traveling across it—our journeys intersecting at this strange, foul-smelling avian truck stop.

No, I take that back. It's not a truck stop: it's a Hooters. A Hooters for birds.

Sometimes when you're traveling across the United States, you stop there because it's the only place still open.

That afternoon, I arrived in Los Angeles for the second time in as many months. I made the same two promises to myself as before: no more cross-country road trips, no more Hooters.

This time I kept them.

LUCY GOOSEY

A few months after I moved to Los Angeles, I woke up to a call from my agent, Steve. I'd been sleeping in a lot at the time, and I'd slept in again that day. I groggily picked up the phone, still half asleep, and tried to decipher what my agent was saying.

It took me a second to realize he was telling me to hurry up and get out of bed: I'd gotten a last-minute callback for a new ABC Family pilot called *Pretty Little Liars*.

I'd been meeting with casting directors regularly since I'd moved from Pittsburgh. I'd gone out for bit parts in TV, but this was my first pilot, and I had no idea what to expect. There's a difference between acting and auditioning, and I wasn't sure I was a strong auditioner. I could talk to casting directors all day about the quirks of classical theater training, but when it came to actually selling my version of a character to them, I was still very new to the game.

Despite my self-doubt, my representation kept pushing to get me in the room with casting directors all over town. They seemed to believe in my acting abilities, or at least in my bone structure. Their enthusiasm helped keep me motivated.

I'd been in to audition for this pilot once already—for the part of Ezra Fitz, a young high school English teacher. It'd gone decently well but hadn't been anything to write home about. Getting a callback came as a surprise. Steve gave me the breakdown for the *Pretty Little Liars* callback—he told me that I'd be reading across from Lucy Hale this time, the girl that had been cast as Ezra's underage love interest.

Before he got off the phone, Steve said, "Ian, not quite sure how to put this, but look nice, okay? Nice shirt, nice pants, wash your face. Don't mean to sound like your mom, but this one could be good for you."

Unfortunately, I didn't have much in the way of "nice" clothes. Student loans were hanging over my head like the sword of Damocles at the time, and buying new clothes seemed like a waste of money. I'd had to buy a suit earlier in the summer for a wedding, and had left all the tags on it so that I could return it after. About the only thing nice I owned was a blue button-down shirt. That morning it had pasta stains all over it from a raucous Italian dinner a few nights earlier, and I'd forgotten to do my laundry.

I rolled out of bed and surveyed my one-room apartment: all my possessions were strewn about within arm's length. Dangling on a suspicious-looking metal pipe sticking out of the ceiling was a hanger with my only other clothing option: a green V-neck sweater that I'd had since high school.

The sweater was from Hollister, and it had the company's seagull logo on the tag. I always liked that about it. It was like an inside joke between me and myself. Carrying that little bird everywhere with me always felt comforting, like a good luck charm.

Plus, it was also the only item of clothing I owned that didn't have holes in it. I wore it everywhere.

I threw myself in the shower, considered shaving but didn't have time, and tried to dry off as best I could. I didn't have AC, and on warm days the apartment would heat up like an oven. It was early October, and I should have been enjoying something hot and pumpkin-spiced, but it was sweltering outside.

There wasn't time to stand in front of the open refrigerator to cool off, which I did on a daily basis. I grabbed my trusty green sweater off the hangar and headed out to Warner Bros. studios in Burbank, where the audition was being held. Of course, my car didn't have AC either, and I could feel the beads of sweat on my back joining together to form small rivulets. It was as gross as it sounds.

Right before I walked into the casting office, I pulled the green sweater on and prayed that nobody would ask me about my clothing choices.

I walked into the office, which was thankfully cooled to an appropriate temperature for long sleeves.

Then I glanced around the room and started to sweat again.

The waiting area was filled with handsome model types. Guys who didn't own knives because they did all of their slicing and dicing with their razor-sharp jawlines. I recognized a few of them from their stints as sexy werewolves and morally loose ad men from the 1960s. Not only were these actors all phenomenally good-looking, they all had booked serious jobs before.

The only work I had under my belt at the time was a bit part in an indie film and a smoothie commercial I'd done in college.

"Ian Harding?"

A young woman with a clipboard approached and checked off my name.

"You'll be up in just a second."

I'd been to this office once before to meet with casting directors right after I moved to Los Angeles, and I knew there was a bathroom down the hall. I had to get away from everyone for just a second, make sure none of the cold pizza I'd had for breakfast on the drive over was stuck in my teeth.

In the bathroom I looked at myself in the mirror and doused my face with water, careful not to let any droplets get on my festive sweater. I started running through my lines in my head.

When I first started auditioning, I'd listened to music—usually fast-paced metal or hip-hop—to psych myself up. But I realized after a few auditions that I was going in and practically screaming my lines. So, I tweaked my routine to be a bit more meditative. It's been more effective so far than listening to Slipknot.

I closed my eyes, took a few slow and deliberate breaths, and, with my eyes closed, watched as my lines appeared in the dark space behind my eyelids.

The scene I was working on today involved me striking up a conversation with a woman at a bar in the middle of the afternoon. Cut to: we're making out in the women's restroom. It would end up being the scene that introduces my character in the first episode of the show.

The first time I read the pilot, I didn't quite know what to make of Ezra, but I felt like he and I somehow clicked. I felt a warmth about the role, a sort of natural rapport. I didn't want to go in and fuss with the part for this callback. I knew what I wanted to do with it.

From outside the bathroom I heard a door open and a female voice say something. Then a muffled chorus of heys and hellos from all the guys. I didn't want to keep casting waiting on me, so I ran a hand through my hair and gave myself a final once-over in the mirror.

Back in the lobby, the guys were all talking quietly. I sat down in an empty chair.

One of the sexy werewolves turned to me:

"You just missed her. Lucy Hale just walked by. The girl they cast as Aria."

Aria, the girl my character picks up at the bar. The entire room was buzzing about her.

"My friend did a short with her. He said she's single."

"Your friend's wrong, man. She's dating a guy from my cousin's acting class."

"Bullshit."

"I'm serious!"

"She's so hot."

A door opened at the far end of the room, and the casting assistant with the clipboard poked her head around the corner.

"Ian? We're ready for you."

The sexy werewolf called after me to break a leg as I walked across the room.

The shades were all pulled down on the windows in the audition room, and it took a second for my eyes to adjust. The only source of light was a bright lamp mounted on a C-stand. There were half a dozen people seated behind a camera on one side of the room.

"Hey man, good to see you again," a guy called out from behind the camera.

"Yeah you too, bud," I replied, realizing that "bud" might have sounded a little too chummy.

There were familiar faces in the room, but new ones too. The woman to my left—I was pretty sure she was the writer of the show. Or the creator? Both?

The guy to her right—Bob, was it? He had seemed like a nice guy the last time I read for the part. I figured I would try and keep him laughing, maybe crack a joke about all the look-alikes waiting outside.

Gayle, the casting director, whom I'd met a few days prior, gave me a big smile. "Good to see you again, Ian," she said. "Have a seat there and go ahead and slate whenever you're ready."

I sat down, a hand over my eyes to shade the glare of the light over the camera.

"Hi," a voice chirped to my side.

I totally hadn't seen her: right next to me, smiling expectantly, was Lucy Hale.

"Oh hey," I said. "Didn't see you there."

"Hot out, isn't it?" she teased, eyeing my sweater.

"I just like Christmas a lot," came out of my mouth. That didn't entirely make sense.

She grinned mischievously at me.

There was something about her that I recognized immediately, or recognized in her. We'd never met before, but there was something familiar, something comforting about Lucy. Perhaps the way she looked at me in that moment felt open, receptive. Like she was taking me in as opposed to merely appraising me.

It wasn't cinematic: sparks didn't fly, orchestral music didn't well up as we gazed into each other's eyes. It was a simpler moment. Quieter. Two people stuck in a whirlwind of expectation and excitement—we each somehow understood who the other was.

"I'm Ian, by the way," I said, leaning forward to shake her hand.

"Lucy," she said, a slight smile spreading across her face.

"Whenever you're ready," Gayle said.

I sat, took a deep breath, and we began.

Lucy's line went something like, "Oh, I love this song."

I nodded. There wasn't any music playing, but I nodded. I looked into Lucy's eyes, and it suddenly dawned on me what the scene was about. It wasn't a love scene at all. I didn't need to kiss her, or have sex with her, or make her my wife.

I wanted to understand her. It was that simple. I wanted to know everything I possibly could about this woman.

Somebody coughed. I had a line to say.

"B-twenty-six!" I blurted out. It was the number of the song on the jukebox at the bar we were supposed to be sitting in.

Lucy's eyes went wide in surprise. She hadn't expected the line to come out like that—neither had I.

We were both surprised, and because we were both surprised, the moment was suddenly alive. Fresh. We were listening to each other, actually communicating. There was chemistry.

We read through the scene again, the second time the

dialogue rolled out crisper than the first. I wanted to read through the scene once more. I was having too much fun.

But all too soon my time was up.

I looked around at the faces in the room. At the end of every audition, there's a moment, usually no longer than the time it takes to look up from your script, when, for a fraction of a second, you see the next few years of your life align. When you start out as an actor, this is the moment you live for.

Marlene—that was her name!—the creator of the show, thanked me for coming in as she scribbled on the pages on her lap.

"Yup, good job," Gayle said. I think she was smiling.

Headshots were shuffled. Pens scratched paper.

"Thank you!" I threw out to no one in particular.

I grabbed my keys and phone, which I had apparently set down on the floor at some point.

I turned back to Lucy.

"Thank you for everything," I said.

"Oh! You too. Don't die from heat exhaustion in that sweater," she said.

I walked back out through the waiting room, waved to the werewolf and told him something like "go get 'em," and headed for the parking lot. I waited until I got all the way outside before ripping off my sweat-drenched sweater.

On the way home, my phone buzzed. Vikram, my manager, was calling. I pulled over to take the call.

"How'd it go?" he asked.

"I really have no idea."

"That can be good."

"Yeah."

I sat for a moment, mulling over the audition.

"This one was different," I said.

Vikram waited for me to continue.

I put the phone on speaker and laid it on the dashboard, freeing my hands to gesture what my mouth couldn't articulate.

"Lucy Hale was in the room. It was a chemistry read, right? I was surprised at how easy it was. It was like hanging out with an old friend. It was weird."

"Ian, all of that sounds like a good thing."

"Maybe you're right," I conceded.

"No, I am right, because they want you to go in for a network test."

"You already knew!?" I yelled at the phone.

Vikram chuckled. "I wanted to know your thoughts first!"

Several more rounds of callbacks followed. And every round there were fewer and fewer of us in the waiting room. Lucy and I read together in front of different people in different rooms, and we got to hang out a little bit, too. We were becoming fast friends.

Finally, there were just two of us left trying out for the role of Ezra. Me and one other guy. He was Canadian. The pilot, and possibly the entire show, was going to be shot in Vancouver, so my agents had warned me that he was the financially responsible option for the studio.

On the day of the final producer session, I arrived early. I was sitting in my car in the parking lot, going over my lines with my eyes closed, when I heard a tap on the window. It was Lucy. She grinned and waved. I rolled down my window.

"Schmian!" she yelled. Lucy loves nicknames.

"Hey, Lucy Goosey."

"How you feeling?" she asked. "Excited?"

"Nervous," I said. "I'm feeling really, really nervous."

"I know what you mean. Between you and me, I hope you get it. It'd be really fun to work together."

We went inside, shook hands with the producers, and I auditioned my heart out one last time.

I was going to miss this. With all of the other actors I'd met in Los Angeles, acting had felt like work. I showed up and I did my job. With Lucy, it felt like two kids in a sandbox. We were constantly surprising one another.

After the audition, I felt a strange hollowness. It was my last audition for the show. There was nothing else I could do now. And I wasn't ready for this all to end.

I wanted this role.

Back in my neighborhood, I was circling the block looking for a parking space, when my phone started to buzz again. It was Steve, my agent. I put the phone on speaker.

"Hey!" I said.

The voice on the phone was somber.

"Ian, hey," he said. "This a good time?"

"What's up?" I said.

"I've got bad news . . ."

I stopped the car in the middle of the street. It was over. It had been a nice fantasy, but I should have known better than to get my hopes up.

"Let's hear it."

"Yeah. It's just—do you have any warm clothes?"

In the passenger seat next to me was the green sweater that I'd worn to that first callback. One of these days I was going to remember to get it washed.

"Yeah, I've got a sweater or two," I said. "Why?"

"I hear that Canada is cold in November."

"..."

"So you'll need to pack some warm clothes since you're going to be up there shooting for a month. You got the role, Ian. Knocked it out of the park. Congrats!"

"..."

"Ian, are you there?"

"Goddamnit, Steve!" I shouted. "My emotions are not a pipe for you to play upon!"

Steve chuckled and took my outburst for what it truly was: tremendous excitement.

After we got off the phone, I looked back over at the sweater with the seagull on its tag.

When I got my first paycheck, I went and got it dry-cleaned.

IL BUIO OLTRE

LA SIEPE

Every once in a while I'll get a text from a friend asking me to help identify a bird they've seen. Sometimes it's a blurry photo. Sometimes it's a description of what the bird looked like. It makes me feel like an ornithological Google.

Keegan Allen, who plays Toby Cavanaugh on *Pretty Little Liars*, frequently texts me pictures to figure out what he's looking at.

Keegs is an amazing photographer. He's even published a coffee table book of his photographs—so it's always fun when he sends me an out-of-focus picture of a tree or fuzzy telephone wires. Sometimes he'll send me a photo of the sky with a tiny black dot way in the distance and ask me what it is.

I know Keegan's making fun of me. He once texted me a

voice recording of himself cawing. I told him it sounded like a young Woody Harrelson crying in the shower. He texted back to say that I was "extremely bad at bird IDs," then two minutes later texted again to say that birds were stupid and he hoped he hadn't hurt my "widdle birdy feewings."

To his credit, he does send me photos and recordings of real birds, too. He once sent me a recording of a nighthawk that he took while he was visiting his mom up in Northern California. I'm not always able to identify the birds when people ask, but I definitely knew what that one was. His mom now texts me any time she has a question about birds, too.

The most common question I get from people in Los Angeles is: "There's a bird outside my window that sings all night long. What the hell is it, and how do I make it stop?"

It's a northern mockingbird, and they're the worst. If they were human, they'd be telemarketers: always calling at the worst possible time. And, for the record, I don't know how to make them go away.

It's the single males that stay up late—bachelor mockingbirds will sing all night long. Like frat boys, they spend all their time after the sun goes down loudly advertising that they want to have sex. Once they settle into a relationship, they start sleeping again and just sing during the day.

There was one that lived in the bushes outside my bedroom window in my old house in Laurel Canyon. Every night, like clockwork, it'd start singing at one in the morning.

Mockingbirds are known for their ability to mimic other sounds. When they sing, they'll cycle through a bunch of different songs. Besides just other birdcalls, they'll meow like cats and bark like dogs. In cities, they'll loudly imitate car alarms—which is charming.

These birds are easy to hate, but people aren't the only ones who hate mockingbirds. They also hate themselves.

Mockingbirds are fiercely, fiercely territorial. They'll dive-bomb other mockingbirds, shriek at them, flash their wings menacingly—anything to get the other bird to go away.

The problem is, the other mockingbirds they're attacking often aren't birds at all—they're mirrors. Male mockingbirds will attack their own reflections for hours at a time, just bashing their heads against the glass. If you asked a mockingbird to list its greatest enemies, it would probably tell you cats, hawks, owls, and that-son-of-a-bitch-in-the-bay-window-oh-my-God-I-want-to-kill-him-so-bad.

One of my neighbors down the street has to keep plastic grocery bags wrapped around her car's side-view mirrors. If she doesn't, a mockingbird will sit on the side of her car all day, pooping on her windows and periodically swooping down to smash itself into the mirrors until they crack.

They're crazy.

But I get it. I mean, I don't wake up every morning and head-butt my bathroom mirror before I go downstairs to make coffee, but I get where they're coming from. I really don't like watching myself on-screen, either.

Have you ever recorded your own voice and played it back? You probably thought something like, *That's not what I sound like . . . right? That's not actually my voice.* Our voices don't actually sound the way they do in our heads.

Watching yourself act on-screen is the same, except it's not just your voice anymore: you've got to deal with how you look, how you move, how you react. There's that same strange disconnect between what you think you look like and how it all appears on TV.

I've never been able to really enjoy watching myself. It's a little bit eerie and a little bit unnerving. I'll think I portrayed a certain character one way in front of the camera, but then, watching it later on TV, I'll zero in on specific physical quirks or intonations that I wasn't aware of. Body language I wasn't conscious of using.

Still, even if deep down it feels unnatural, I know that watching my own footage is an excellent tool for me as an actor. Sports players watch tapes of themselves swinging bats and throwing footballs to figure out how to improve their form, and actors regularly do the same thing.

When I watch myself, the goal is to put some distance between me and the version of me that's on-screen. I want to judge my performance objectively, so that I can develop as an actor. If I notice that I always react a certain way to a certain type of line, I can take that information and begin to change that habit into a conscious choice. Doing so can give me greater range and control over how I come across. It broadens my acting.

When I first started out on *Pretty Little Liars*, it was even more difficult than usual for me to watch myself. I'd watch new episodes but would find myself squirming when I came on-screen. Occasionally, I got so uncomfortable that I'd have to turn off the TV. Eventually, I stopped watching altogether.

But I really wanted to get better, and I recently happened upon a solution: Italian dubbing.

Turns out, I have absolutely no problem watching myself on-screen as long as I am watching the dubbed version of my show that airs in Italy. The guy whose voice they use for mine is named Francesco Venditti, and his voice is—well, it's just goddamn poetry to listen to. I don't understand Italian, but it's so much nicer than listening to my own voice.

We've never met, but Francesco has helped me get over the discomfort I used to feel watching myself on-screen. He's been like a plastic bag over the side-view mirror for me. Finally, I can relax and enjoy the show.

DEATH AND

LOONS

A lot of people get killed on *Pretty Little Liars*—it's just that kind of show.

Funeral scenes are some of my favorite to shoot. There are one or two each season, and they usually involve most of the regular cast. The scenes when we're all working together are sort of like cast reunions. The mood on set is even more lighthearted than usual.

A lot of the funeral scenes are filmed in a little white chapel on the Warner Bros. back lot in Burbank. It's not an actual chapel: it's only ever used for filming. You can see the same exterior and interior of the building in just about every season. It pops up at the end of season one, for example, when Spencer's brother-in-law Ian Thomas tries to push her off the bell tower.

We actually film almost all of the show on the Warner Bros. lot, and there are a handful of houses and buildings that provide nearly all of the exterior shots. You may recognize some of the same buildings on *Gilmore Girls* or *Heart of Dixie*—they're regularly repurposed for different projects.

There's a courthouse and a fire department, which are two sides of the same building. There are wooded areas for when the girls have to run for their lives through a forest. Some of the trees are real, some are made of plastic.

There's an art museum—or at least the façade of one— where I take Aria on our first real date on the show in season one . . . in a limousine.

Yes, a limo. On a high school teacher's salary.

A few seasons back, the building that was Toby's house got real-life termites. It had to be torn down, so the writers came up with the idea to have "A"—the show's unremitting and anonymous villain—blow it up. I was there for the explosion—and, for the record, it was awesome.

The only thing we don't have on the lot, which you'd think would be useful for a show like ours, is a good cemetery. I'm sure there are plenty of reasons why Warner Bros. doesn't have a cemetery on the lot, but with so many people dying on *PLL*, once in a blue moon we have to leave set to film in a real one.

When you see tombstones on the show, they're usually real.

In season one, for instance, we filmed Ian Thomas's burial at Mountain View Cemetery in Altadena, about an hour east of the Warner Bros. lot.

I understand that sometimes you have to travel to get the right shot, and that sometimes certain locations are off-limits or prohibitively expensive to shoot at. It's still a bit funny to me, though, that we drove an hour off the lot to shoot in a cemetery—because there's another one directly across the street from Warner Bros.

Forest Lawn–Hollywood Hills is a beautiful sight. The cemetery is made up of rolling green hills dotted with towering pine trees, and lush green lawns are manicured to a golf course level of precision.

Once, a few years back, I went to see Torrey DeVitto, who plays Melissa on the show, play violin with the Burbank Philharmonic at a performance space there. Before the concert, I took a stroll through the tombstones. Looking up, I saw a small flock of white-throated swifts far overhead, riding the wind gusting over the mountains of Griffith Park, which the cemetery backs up to.

Dying is big business in Southern California, and I've seen Forest Lawn advertisements at Dodger Stadium during baseball games, and there's even a Forest Lawn kiosk at the Glendale Galleria mall—it's right above the food court.

There are six Forest Lawn cemeteries in Los Angeles. I drive by two of them just on my way to work. There's Forest Lawn–Hollywood Hills, of course, the one directly across the street from Warner Bros., and then there's Forest Lawn–Memorial Park, which is nestled on a quiet hilltop at the southern edge of Glendale.

I've been over to Forest Lawn–Memorial Park a few times. Long, winding roads cut through the graveyard, making their way slowly up the hill. The higher you drive, the more expansive the views of the city become. At the top, there's a gorgeous panoramic vista: Glendale to the east, with Pasadena beyond it; the Los Angeles River to the west; the City of Burbank to the north; and the skyscrapers of downtown just on the horizon to the south.

There's a massive auditorium up at the top, with a 195-foot-long painting of the crucifixion. Next door, in the auditorium's shadow, is a museum. The front half has rotating exhibits, usually contemporary work with a focus on Hollywood. The back half is where they keep the permanent collection—a seemingly disconnected array of artifacts and treasures. You half expect to find a piece of the One True Cross stashed away between the gold chainmail and the paintings of duchess's dogs. It's like a conquistador's messy garage.

I really like spending time at Forest Lawn. Cemeteries can be peaceful, even pleasant, and I don't mean that in a creepy, Edgar Allan Poe–ish way. I don't go over to Forest Lawn to pay my respects, or commune with the dead, or anything like that. There aren't specific gravestones I visit, though it's always fun to see all the weird last names people have. I also don't go to visit the celebrities buried there, of which there are many—Elizabeth Taylor, Clark Gable, Michael Jackson.

I go because there's great birding in cemeteries.

Seriously. In big cities, cemeteries are often some of the best places to find birds. Cemeteries are acres of land unobstructed by buildings or other major human development. They're a lot like parks: well-maintained trees, shrubbery, and expansive grass lawns—perfect for birds.

I don't think I would have ever thought to try birding in a cemetery if I hadn't read about it online. The first time I went to a cemetery to look at birds, it was because of a rare-bird alert. A group of birders had seen a scissor-tailed flycatcher in a cemetery in Santa Monica, and they posted about it on an online forum.

Birding is a solitary hobby. You spend most of your time alone in nature, looking and listening intently to the world around you. There are some birding groups, but for the most part birders keep to themselves.

That all changes when there's a rare-bird alert—they're the ice cream socials of the birding world. Birders come out in droves to see rare birds when they've strayed far from their normal range. Everybody drops what they're doing and hops in their cars and races over to the spot of the last sighting.

I subscribe to a forum that people post on whenever they see rare or unusual birds in Los Angeles. I only learned about it a couple of years ago, and since then, I've been spending way too much time checking for updates. Maybe once or twice a day, somebody will see something unusual and report in. Sometimes it will be a rare-bird alert, sometimes it will be a woman in Hollywood asking for advice on how to get a snowy egret to stop eating the house finches in her yard. Either way, the online forums are an incredible tool.

Birders move in flocks when they get together. A rare-bird alert will go out, saying that an unusual bird has been spotted that morning at such-and-such location. A good alert will be followed by a flurry of confirmations from individuals. Then everybody loads their gear into their cars and drives, all the while dangerously checking their phones for updates, to the site of the last spotting. Once they arrive, the birders gather into a tight huddle, craning their necks this way and that to see if anyone can spot anything. For a while, nothing will happen.

Then, after ten or fifteen minutes, a lone scout on the other side of the park will shout that they've spotted the lazuli bunting or whatever bird it is that day, and the group will clatter together loudly across the park in pursuit. Thirty or forty birders zigzagging about in a binoculared pack. This mass of bodies will inevitably scare the bird away, so by the time the group arrives by the scout's side, the bird will have moved on.

A few years back, I think it was in May, an alert went out that an arctic loon had become stranded in a small town just east of Los Angeles. I expected it to stick around for only a few days, but it was still there in July, and I decided to go find it.

To be clear, arctic loons have no business being in Southern California. It's exciting news when they fly as far south as British Columbia. They have evolved to survive in extremely cold climates—their genetic makeup designed to flourish in the icy tundra of western Siberia, not the rowdy strip malls of West Covina.

The arctic loon had been spotted in a place called Puddingstone Lake. I drove out there one day to try and see it.

Walking around, I passed more barbecues than you'd see in a whole summer of Fourth of Julys. Super-cool lifeguards sat perched at intervals all along the shore.

I pulled out my binoculars to see if the loon might be out on the water. I surveyed the lake. All I could see were mallards and people swimming. Babies bobbed up and down, overinflated floaties manacled to their pudgy little arms. A middle-school boy was trying to convince his girlfriend there were eels in the water. It was exactly what you would expect from a place called Puddingstone Lake: just the cutest stuff imaginable.

I put the binoculars away and decided to walk along the shore to see if I could catch a glimpse of the loon a little farther down.

About half a mile on, I passed a swimming hole where eight or ten kids were splashing around. It was significantly less crowded than the beach I had just left. There was a bored-looking lifeguard sitting up high on his stand.

I wasn't having any luck spotting this arctic loon, and even though I didn't expect anyone else to care about it, I tried my luck and asked him if he'd seen any strange-looking birds out on the water that morning.

"You mean the arctic loon?" he said, his eyes invisible behind his mirrored aviators.

"I, uh, yeah. You know about that?" I stammered.

"Of course, dude. Loon's been here for like a month. It's a pretty chill little bird."

"Do you know where it might be today?"

"I think he's over by Sailboat Cove right now."

"That's not a real place," I said.

He shrugged. "I didn't name it."

Sure enough, about a hundred yards off from a dock with sailboats near it, which I assumed was Sailboat Cove, I saw it: the arctic loon, sitting out on the water.

It looked really lost.

It disappeared underwater briefly, popping back up a few yards away from where it had been swimming. I imagined it was trying to stay as cool as possible given how hot it was outside.

I associate loons so strongly with their call, and just watching the bird, I began to imagine its plaintive wail.

Every summer, my family goes up to New England for a couple of weeks. There's a lake we go to, and visiting it is almost a religious experience for me. The lake is filled with loons— hundreds of them. If you stand on the shore at dusk and listen, the place sounds haunted.

My aunt Jules loves loons. When the family arrives at the lake, before we even unpack the car, she will walk solemnly to the shore and stand completely still, staring out at the loons on the water. She'll stand like that for about ten minutes, then will give the lake a slight nod and return to the car to carry in the rest of the luggage. Other than Saint Peter's Basilica, I've never seen anything else give my aunt pause like that. She is a ball of energy—frantic, kind, and opinionated. But the loons silence her.

As I stood there now, not at the lake from my childhood but on a shore in San Dimas, staring at a totally different species of loon from the ones I'd grown up with, something occurred to me.

Many rare bird sightings only happen when something has gone wrong. Whether blown off course or just extremely lost, somehow an individual bird becomes separated from its flock and finds itself thousands of miles away from home. The land is unfamiliar, the climate sometimes deadly.

When an arctic loon gets lost in a lake in Southern California, it's hard to imagine it's ever going to make it back home to the icy north. And if it doesn't, it's likely going to die. So, in a case like this, the rare bird alert that went out for the loon was also, in a sense, its obituary. It's sad—seeing this magnificent bird and knowing that it probably only has a short while left to live.

There was a voice in my head that told me to respond to this tragedy the way we respond to so many others: to take a picture with my phone and drive home.

But something felt wrong about that approach. Maybe it was that tourism didn't feel like an appropriate response to death. Whatever it was, I didn't feel comfortable standing there and watching a lost animal float helplessly on the waves of a lake that would soon envelop it.

I wanted to swim out and grab the loon, stash it in a suitcase, and fly it up north, as far north as we could go before my fingers froze solid. Then I would fling open my suitcase and shout, "You're free, loon! Free to spend your days swimming in the icy waters of the north!"

But conservation doesn't work like that. In the movies, when you go with your gut, everything turns out okay. You can just go and save the day because it's obvious to everyone around you that what you're doing is inherently the right thing to do.

In the real world there's paperwork, borders, agricultural restrictions, holding periods, smuggling laws. There are ecological standards and conservation rules that change from nation to nation. Ornithologists—and even lifeguards—knew that the bird was there on Puddingstone Lake, and there was nothing anyone could do about it. Sometimes, the best thing to do with nature is to leave it alone.

Driving away from the lake, I kept thinking about it.

As I got on to the highway, I passed another Forest Lawn cemetery—turns out they have one in Covina, right next to the lake.

It occurred to me, as I looked out my window, that the last

few times I'd been to a cemetery, it'd been for a concert or to film the show or to wander around and look at birds. I'd been to a graveyard a couple of times that year, and it'd always been fun.

Getting to see the loon had felt like a funeral.

SPRING

MIGRATION

One of the great things about birding is that you can do it any-where in the world.

In Paris for a fan convention? Head over to the Cimetière du Père-Lachaise, visit the graves of Oscar Wilde and Jim Mor-rison, and see what birds you can find in the trees overhead. Or maybe you're in New York City for a press junket. Easy. Take an afternoon and go try to find Pale Male, a famous red-tailed hawk that lives on the Upper East Side, named for his pale face.

You can tack birding on to any normal trip with the simple addition of binoculars.

Or, you can go all out. Once, on a trip to Seattle with Sophia for a wedding, I hired a birding guide for a morning.

We were out in a marsh, and the guide played a recording of a Virginia rail on a handheld speaker. A little shadow picked its way through a thicket of reeds, was in view for about five seconds or so, and then silently vanished back into the dense stalks. Spotting a Virginia rail hadn't been the point of the trip—they're usually next to impossible to see—but, like I said before, birds are everywhere.

I'd gotten back into birding a few years earlier on the trip to Big Bear, but as of the sixth season of the show, I'd never been on a trip outside of Los Angeles specifically to see birds. I was daunted by the idea.

Sure, I'd look at birds while out walking the dogs. Or I'd go on hikes with friends and wander off when I saw something interesting. On weekends, I'd drive out to the Ballona Wetlands, just north of LAX in Marina del Rey, to see what I could find. There's a path along a swamp there, and you can usually see ducks and herons. In the near distance, double-decker Airbuses take off, on their way to distant shores.

I'd been treating birding as an excuse to get away from work. It was a reason to get outside, not a reason to get on one of those planes.

Last year I decided to go someplace new with the sole purpose of birding my face off. This was big for me. It was springtime: time for new growth, new life. Birds were in the air.

Seriously, birds were in the air. A lot of them. Every spring, millions of birds migrate up from Central and South America to their summer breeding grounds in North America. There are a couple of prime spots to see them, natural bottlenecks on the migration paths, where the chances of seeing normally hard-to-find species are pretty good.

So I pulled the trigger: I booked a flight to Houston.

About an hour and a half east of the city, there's a small bump in the land on the coast—just a little rise, caused by a salt dome that got squeezed up from below the earth's surface. It's a geological pimple. High Island, as it's called, is the highest natural coastal feature from the Yucatán to Alabama. It's a whopping thirty-eight feet above sea level.

That may not sound special, but it is. Imagine you've been stranded at sea for a few days, and you finally spot land on the horizon. Even if that land was Trenton, New Jersey, you'd be excited.

That's what High Island is like for birds. Because it's slightly higher than the surrounding coastal prairie, it's the first speck of mainland that a lot of birds see as they make their way over six hundred miles across the Gulf of Mexico. And once they reach High Island, there's plentiful water and food and trees to rest in. Migrating birds stop here by the thousands in the spring to rest and refuel before continuing their journey northward.

On rare occasions, a strong storm out of the north will coincide with a wave of neotropical migrants flying up over the Gulf. When this happens, birds will come in to land at High Island en masse. It's called a "fallout." Every limb of every tree—and even the ground—is littered with tired birds: warblers, vireos, orioles, tanagers, buntings. All the stunning small birds that pass through ever year but you never see.

And you can't see these birds in such concentrated numbers anywhere else, ever.

All of this is why High Island is a Mecca for bird lovers. Why it's talked about with a kind of hushed reverence—the way your drunk uncle talks about Woodstock. You had to have been there, man.

I booked the trip to Houston for mid-April. We had just started shooting season seven of *Pretty Little Liars*. I only ever know my shooting schedule a few days in advance, but I figured I could change the flight last-minute if there was a conflict.

I tried to cozy up to the producers, hoping they would let me know what my schedule was for the rest of the month. But they didn't know the schedule, either.

The whole process of making the show comes down to the wire every week. I usually don't learn my lines until the day before we shoot. It's not that I don't want to: I can't. Script rewrites happen up until the very last minute, and the head writer on each episode is always on set in case any last-minute rewrites or script changes are necessary. There's an elegant chaos to it all.

I was getting increasingly giddy about the trip, and anxious to get going. It was distracting me from my work. During breaks from shooting, I'd even started studying bird flashcards.

Tyler Blackburn—who plays Caleb Rivers on the show—came up to me one day while I was running through the cards and asked what I was doing. I told him about the trip. He asked when I was going, and I told him the second-to-last week in April, right at the height of the migration.

"So, you're going to High Island for four-twenty?" he asked.

"Yeah, why?"

Tyler grinned mischievously.

"High Island . . . four-twenty . . ."

"It's not like that, man. It's for the birds!"

Not surprisingly, there were last-minute schedule changes, so I had to push the trip back a week. And then I had to push it back again.

My personal and work lives were at an impasse. It looked less and less likely that I would even get to go.

By the time I actually got on the plane at LAX, it was the second week of May. It was cutting it close—the migration was winding down—but I had to go.

In the seat to the left of me was my buddy John. He was in the class below mine at Carnegie, and we've been friends for years. When he was a freshman, he used my home address for his fake ID. To my right was Walter, the guy I'd seen the hooded merganser with at Big Bear. I'd convinced them to tag along. They're both writers, so they can work from just about anywhere.

Sitting on the plane, I was excited. I couldn't contain myself. The small child sitting in the row in front of me kept turning around to glare at my bouncing knee, which was shaking his chair. We hadn't even taken off yet, and I was already vibrating with glee.

"It's okay, dude. I don't like to fly either," Walter said to me, his face a little pale.

"You seem pretty calm," I said.

"Oh, good," he replied. "I'm not." He closed his eyes like he was going to take a nap.

John was straddling an overstuffed backpack. He kept rooting around in it and pulling out snack-sized packages of peanut M&M's.

"John, did you bring anything besides candy?"

"Of course I did," he said.

"What do you have that's not candy?" Walter asked, his eyes still shut.

"Let's find out," John said, reaching into his backpack. He pulled out a king-sized package of Skittles, a gallon freezer bag filled with candy corn, and a tray of Oreos. Finally, he held up a can of Pringles. "See? I've got chips, too."

John is fit, yet has the diet of a hummingbird. He consumes more sugar than should be legal yet still manages to look like a college soccer player.

Walter also looks collegiately athletic, though this is achieved through what he calls "old Russian man workouts"—twenty minutes on the stationary bike, forty in the sauna—and surfing.

This was also not Walter's first trip to High Island, so he knew what we were in for.

As we pushed back from the jet bridge, Walter leaned forward and looked out the window.

"High Island is one of my favorite places on earth," he said. "If we get lucky, the trees will be filled with birds—like Christmas ornaments."

He leaned back into his seat and closed his eyes again. I couldn't wait to see it myself.

I pulled out a magazine I'd picked up at the terminal. It had caught my eye as I passed a newsstand. I don't normally buy *Cosmopolitan*, but this one had my costar Shay Mitchell on the cover—and there was an article about a beach body diet that said I could eat all the pizza I wanted, so I had to learn more about that.

John leaned over, looking at my reading material. "And you're giving me shit for bringing candy?"

It was dark when we got into Houston. Just past 9:00 P.M. We waited for our bags at baggage claim—something syrupy was leaking out of John's suitcase onto the carousel. He grabbed the bag, and told us to ignore it. We didn't press the issue.

Bags collected, we rode the rent-a-car shuttle to the offsite lot. When I'd made a reservation for the car, I'd looked online to find a good price, and a certain vehicle had caught my eye. I hadn't told the guys about it yet—they were in for a surprise.

We all gathered around the vehicle in the lot. It glowed a ghostly white in the darkness.

The minivan's siren song was impossible to resist—for some. Walter was thrilled by the choice of vehicle. John, however, had serious concerns that we would look like a gang of bird-loving pedophiles. That didn't bother me. If you put the two parts of my life together, that's what I am.

Walter and I rock-paper-scissored to see who'd be driving— John claimed the entire back row for himself—and then I drove us away from the airport toward the hustle and bustle of the Houston suburbs.

We stopped on our way into town for bratwurst at a late-night beer garden just east of downtown. It was a shack in the middle of an otherwise vacant lot, with wooden picnic tables and strands of lights strewn between the trees.

Walter was back by the car. I glanced over to see him shielding his eyes, staring up into the inky darkness.

Dipping and looping overhead was a common nighthawk.

Its long, thin wings flapped erratically. It called: a two-tone electronic chirp. Then it vanished into the dark.

"I used to see those after our high school football games," John said, following my gaze. "They'd fly around the stadium lights."

"I didn't know you played football," I said.

"I was the mascot," he said proudly.

"They fired him after one game," Walter said, as he walked back over to join us.

Later, sitting at a picnic table, John put down his bratwurst and shook his head. "This is unbelievable. This modern world, you know? I can wake up in Los Angeles, go to work, meet my girlfriend for lunch, go home to discover that my dog's eaten a condom, and still have time to travel across the country for bratwurst. All in one day. The magic of air travel, man."

Walter and I stared at him.

"John, did your dog eat a—"

"You're missing the point," he interrupted. "The point is that we *flew* here. Just like those birds."

He gestured upward. There weren't any birds. The night-hawk was long gone. "All in one day, you know?"

The next morning, we woke up at 5:00 A.M. We wanted to get out to High Island close to sunrise, to see if we could catch any stragglers that had stayed overnight. And new birds often come in early.

We tried to make coffee at the hotel, but the machine was intimidatingly complex—figuring out which button was "on" was like solving the riddle of the Sphinx.

We stopped at a Starbucks for caffeine, then headed east out of town on I-10. It was the same highway I'd taken in the opposite direction on that cross-country drive from Florida to LA.

The week before, thunderstorm after thunderstorm had wreaked havoc across the region. Houston had flooded. Like take-a-canoe-to-work flooded—and there were still sandbags scattered along the sides of the highway. This rain was exactly what we wanted—thunderstorms equal good birds.

Eventually we turned off the I-10 and started heading south to the coast. The land was flat and swampy. There was agriculture and farmland. Oil pumps were scattered in loose clusters like oversized grasshoppers. We crossed over a bridge that rose high enough to allow tanker ships to pass by in the channel below, and then drove up into the small town of High Island.

By that point, the caffeine had hit. We were raring to go. We pulled up in front of a preserve called the Boy Scout Woods and jumped out of the minivan like a SWAT team. We speed-walked over to the entrance, then speed-walked back to the car when we realized how dense the cloud of mosquitoes following us was. We sprayed ourselves down with bug repellent the way teenage boys use Axe body spray and headed back to the entrance.

Across the street there were a few residential houses. Some of them trailer homes. Directly next to the preserve were more. We were, in fact, just a hundred yards or so from the main road through town.

We walked into the Boy Scout Woods through a gate in a chain-link fence, probably meant to keep out cats. House cats kill more than a billion birds a year in the United States. A billion—that's not a typo.

It was basically an overgrown neighborhood park. One wrong turn and we'd end up in somebody's backyard.

Just past the entrance, a set of wooden grandstands faced a small clearing. At the end of the clearing, a hose hung out of a tree, dripping water for birds to drink and bathe in. I'd seen pictures online of the grandstand filled with birders, all aiming their spotting scopes and binoculars at the drip.

But now, the grandstands were empty. There were only a few people poking around the woods, and nobody was seeing much.

It was still early. It was a Monday. I assumed the birds would pick up as the sun rose a little higher. Or maybe birds just hate Mondays.

Two hours went by and it was still slow. Walter seemed bummed by the low bird turnout, but I was excited. We saw a few different species of warbler: magnolia, black-throated green, and black-and-white. All new for me.

We hopped back into the car and drove over to the Smith Oaks, another preserve about a mile away.

There's a large rookery there, and we happened upon a Japanese tour group all silently taking photos of the nesting egrets and roseate spoonbills. They were all glued to cameras on tripods with monstrous telephoto lenses.

I walked over to see what they were looking at, and the tree next to me moved. I had totally missed a guy decked out head to toe in camouflage standing on a limb right next to my head, and I nearly shit myself when he shifted position.

Farther down the path, we got a good view of a pair of snowy egrets. John perked up. He put his hands around his mouth and did a perfect imitation of their call. The birds looked around, trying to figure out where the sound had come from. I turned to him:

"What the hell was that?" I asked.

"I was an egret for Animal Projects," he said.

"Seriously?"

"Yeah, man. What were you?"

"I was a jellyfish."

"That makes sense."

We walked through the woods near the rookery for another hour or so. I spotted a yellow-billed cuckoo—another new bird—slipping its way through the foliage at the top of a huge live oak tree, but it flew off before Walter or John could see it. Otherwise, it was very quiet. There might have been more birders than actual birds that day. And there weren't many birders.

We stuck around for a few more hours anyway. We kept hoping a new wave of birds might arrive—but it never came. Eventually, we decided to call it quits and took the ferry to Galveston for a late lunch. On the way, we stopped to look at shorebirds on the beach, where I picked up a few more new species: black-bellied whistling duck, gull-billed tern, and magnificent frigatebird.

That night, John dragged us to a Dave & Buster's. As we were standing around an air hockey table, drinking beer and scratching the mosquito bites on our arms, we discussed options for the next day. Walter and I were both in agreement that High Island would probably be a bust again. It turns out, it probably would have been a great place to visit on 4/20. Just not in mid-May. The birds, for the most part, were already farther north.

John took his eye off the puck—

"Guys! I have an idea," he said. "Let's go to the Space Center tomorrow!"

Walter scored on him. He turned to me. "What about trying to find the red-cockaded woodpecker?"

"They have those around here?" I asked.

John cut in: "They also have Space Centers around here!"

"They're endangered," Walter said. "But there's a place not too far away where we can see them," he said.

"Sold," I said. "Let's do it."

Our destination the next morning was the W. G. Jones State Forest—one of the last places in Texas where you can still see the red-cockaded woodpecker. It was directly north of us, about an hour away.

We were on the road just as the sun was coming up.

At one point on the drive, I looked into the rearview mirror and saw John drinking a Red Bull. This was after we'd already stopped for coffee. I asked for a sip and took the can away from him. He was hyper enough already. He pulled another can out of his backpack and popped the tab.

He stared at me in the mirror, not breaking eye contact: "Don't toy with me, Ian," he said.

We were prepared to spend the morning deep in the woods, but W. G. Jones caught us by surprise. It really didn't seem all that remote: like High Island, the forest was bordered by urban sprawl.

We turned off the highway into a dirt parking lot and hopped out of the minivan. It felt like we'd just arrived at a farm. There was a large ramshackle building with aluminum siding. Two men stood leaning against a tractor in work overalls.

Next to the building was a trail, and, not really knowing where else to go, we started walking down it. We quickly arrived at a fork, where a signpost indicated that one way was closed: DUE TO ENDANGERED SPECIES NESTING SEASON AND PRESSURES BEING PLACED ON HABITAT, THIS AREA IS CLOSED.

A pine warbler flew by our heads and landed on a branch over the trail in front of us. I pulled out my binoculars to get a closer look.

I felt a tap on my shoulder. It was John. He pointed up—

"Delta Airbus," he said. The plane was coming in to land.

"Thanks, John," I said.

We walked farther in. No woodpeckers yet.

The main reason that the red-cockaded woodpecker is endangered is that it has very specific habitat requirements: the birds can only live in mature longleaf pine forests with no undergrowth.

Want to know how you get a forest to not have undergrowth? Forest fires. The woodpeckers are susceptible to attacks from predators hiding in the understory, and without forest fires, that vegetation builds up.

For the past hundred years, logging has destroyed a lot of the birds' habitat. But, ironically, so has forest fire prevention. The woodpeckers' population has declined to one percent of its original size.

Even W. G. Jones State Forest has to be actively managed, which is what those buildings by the entrance were for. There are regularly prescribed burns to mimic what happens when a forest is struck by lightning and people aren't around to put out the fire.

Habitat isn't the woodpeckers' only peculiarity. They live in big family groups, and they're the only species of woodpecker to nest in living trees. It can take up to six years for them to carve out a nest—and the longest these birds have ever been recorded to live is twelve years. That's like if you got a flat tire when you were eighteen and didn't finish patching it until you were in your mid-fifties.

And then once they finish building a nest, they often don't even get to live in it. They get bullied out of their homes all the time. Pileated woodpeckers will enlarge the entryway so it's too big for the red-cockaded to live in anymore, and over two dozen other species of vertebrates have been documented stealing red-cockaded woodpecker nests. Even insects will live in the holes. The animal kingdom as a whole has decided to walk all over the red-cockaded woodpecker. It's like the fall guy for the entire forest.

As we hiked on, I noticed that the trees were all evenly spaced. I later learned that this wasn't a real old-growth forest—a hundred years ago the land had been a pine seedling nursery, and the trees we were walking through now had actually been planted during the Great Depression.

The woodpeckers had been attracted to the habitat, which just so happened to be the type of forest that stood here before the area was first logged. The birds were an unintended consequence of reseeding the forest.

Another unintended consequence: gay men. Until recently, the W. G. Jones State Forest has been a meet-up spot for gay men to have anonymous sex. The park rangers have struggled for decades to stop people from having sex in the woods and have closed the forest at times to try to curtail the activity.

Anyway, we were just looking for birds.

There was a buzzing in my ears again. I slapped myself in the face. Despite having brought enough DEET-based repellent to bring about the End Times for mosquitoes throughout the region, I was still getting eaten alive.

There were other sounds, too. We could hear the roar of the highway in the distance. Children were playing and yelling at each other in the backyards of the housing development that bordered the forest just a couple of hundred yards away from us. We could see rows of houses through the trees. A jackhammer started up—literally, a jackhammer—and police sirens wailed by.

Yet despite all of the noise and the close proximity to humans, this tiny strip of land was home to one of the largest groups of endangered red-cockaded woodpeckers in the state.

We crept along the trail, binoculars at the ready, stopping at the slightest sound. Joggers and elderly couples from the neighborhood said good morning as they passed by.

Walter spotted a small bird in the uppermost canopy of one of the trees—it was right over our heads, moving rapidly from branch to branch. I finally tracked it down with my binoculars—it looked like a glowing Cheeto.

"That's a Blackburnian warbler," Walter said. "You see the bright orange throat?"

I pulled out my phone and texted Tyler Blackburn to let him know there was a bird named after him.

We kept walking, our eyes turned upward. My neck was getting stiff from looking up for so long, and I was beginning to go cross-eyed from staring into my binoculars.

I turned to Walter: "I keep seeing creases in the bark of trees and thinking it's a bird," I said.

"That's the Matrix," John said, popping up behind us. He skipped down the trail, stopping from time to time to inspect clusters of poison ivy.

Walter looked at his watch. "Let's keep looking for another hour or so. If we can't find it, we'll take John to the Space Center."

Out in front of us, John started to sing an Irish ballad, his voice echoing through the woods. He was clearly bored out of his mind. Walter looked at me, laughed, and rolled his eyes. John was going to scare all the birds away.

I caught up to him and told him to quiet down. He smiled, shrugged, and stopped singing. He pointed at a tree just off the trail.

"What kind of bird is that?" he asked.

I looked to where he was pointing. A fat, feisty-looking mockingbird was perched on one of the lower branches of a pine about forty feet away from us.

"It's nothing. Just a mockingbird," I said.

"Not that one," he said. "*That* one, right there."

He continued to point at the same bird, which had begun to sing loudly, its throat feathers puffing out as it called.

"It's a mockingbird, John. The same kind we have back in Los Angeles."

As I spoke, a small speckled bird with white cheeks flew in and landed on the same branch as the mockingbird, scaring it off. It moved around the limb, grappling onto the bark with its clawed feet.

"That's the bird I meant," John said, clearly full of shit.

Three other woodpeckers swooped down into the tree to join the first one.

"Those birds too," he said. "Those are the ones I meant."

John, with his loud, stomping boots and his half-remembered drinking songs, had somehow found the bird we were looking for.

We stood there, watching in awe, as the small woodpecker family worked its way around the tree. We crept along the trail to get a better view.

The birds were enchanting. They lived in an area surrounded by golf courses and strip malls—habitats most any animal can't survive in.

I turned to the guys:

"I feel a little starstruck," I said.

"What do you mean?" Walter asked.

"I'm not sure, exactly," I said.

I thought about it as we walked along. For me, finding this woodpecker—even just getting the chance to see it—felt special. Up until that point, I had only seen it in pictures, and here I was now seeing it in the wild.

Eventually the woodpeckers disappeared. We could have turned back, but we decided to push on. We crossed a swinging rope bridge and walked along a creek that was saturated with water moccasins. I counted six of them. The previous day we'd seen more birders than birds. Today we saw more venomous snakes.

We continued walking down an increasingly overgrown path. It didn't seem like we were going the right way. Suddenly the trees parted and we were spit out onto the shoulder of the highway. Eighteen-wheelers honked as they blew by. The sun was beating down and it was getting hot. It was time to head back to Houston.

The next morning we flew back to Los Angeles, and I got back just in time to make it to a table read for the next episode of *PLL*.

That night, lying in my own bed for the first time in days, Sophia and the dogs by my side, something felt off. I couldn't fall asleep. I kept thinking about that tiny forest just outside of Houston.

I closed my eyes, and I could see the woodpeckers again. A few small birds, holding on to the last acres that can support them in this world, because that's all they have left, a scatter plot of managed forests spread across the South. Their world is gone. And what they have left can barely support what remains of their population.

I thought about what it must feel like to be a part of a dying species. To have lost everything that resembles your original "home" and to have your body somehow, instinctually, recognize that.

Part of what I feel as a birder is a sense of urgency. Habitats are disappearing at a sprinter's pace all around the world.

Often, when I see a rare bird for the first time, I know it may also be my last.

I feel lucky to have seen a red-cockaded woodpecker—I know there's a good chance I won't see one again.

PUT YOUR BEST
FEATHER FORWARD

In polite society it's considered taboo to wear white after Labor Day. In the birding community, it's considered taboo to wear white ever.

The color white scares birds away—or so the argument goes—because it's hardly ever found in nature. Red hats or neon-colored sneakers are always acceptable to wear when you're out in the woods, but a good pair of white chinos is a total birding fashion faux pas.

The story I've heard is that the whole "never wear white" rule started when some ornithologist disturbed a rare bird at its nest while he was wearing a white shirt. Frankly, I think he just got too close to the bird and his presence made it uncomfortable. But the guy was wearing white at the time, so now nobody can.

This is, of course, ridiculous, but it's one of those ideas that gets ingrained in a community and then goes unquestioned. Like how actors superstitiously say "break a leg" instead of "good luck," or how they'll never say the word "Macbeth" in a theater.

Really, it's okay to wear white after Labor Day, and it's okay to wear white while birding. (Still, you probably shouldn't say "Macbeth" in a theater.)

A few years ago my girlfriend and I took a vacation to Paris that happened to coincide with Fashion Week, and we received an invitation to attend a Giorgio Armani runway show. I was told that the event would be dressy, and my birding sense of fashion took "dressy" to mean "no white shirts allowed." So I wore all black.

The Armani event was filled with the most insanely trendy people, and Sophia and I had to be careful not to openly stare. Some of the clothing looked like bird-of-paradise mating plumages.

Walking to my seat for the runway show, I passed by actors whom I'd admired for years. Kristin Scott Thomas, Robin Wright, Ben Foster. Seated across the catwalk from me was Anna Wintour.

The show began, and the runway models began their walk. I leaned over to the model sitting next to me and whispered, "What do you think the most common injury in runway modeling is?"

Without missing a beat, she said, "Look at their feet."

Every other woman's toes stuck out over the front of her open-toed shoes, or arched in some anatomically impossible way. My seatmate explained that most shoes in runway shows are sample size, and thus don't often fit the larger-than-normal size feet of models.

After the show, I was ushered backstage to meet Papa Giorgio, the legend himself. He was exceptionally kind, and spoke to me in Italian. I love the sound of the language, as you know, but I don't speak a word of it.

Giorgio looked at me and said "*bello*" a few times. I turned to his niece, who stood next to him. She grinned and said, "He says you're very ugly."

"Tell him I come from a long line of ugly men," I said. Papa Giorgio nodded solemnly.

On my way out of the event, I passed by Juliette Binoche. We made eye contact for the briefest of moments, and she smiled. I smiled back, concentrating all my attention on my knees. I was worried that they might give out in her presence. I've had a crush on her since I was a little kid.

Outside, paparazzi were milling about. One looked up at me from his phone for a moment, then looked back down. Angry Birds was clearly more important. I walked down a flight of stairs and made my way to a car that was waiting.

Right before I reached the car, a young woman broke from the crowd that had gathered outside the event and walked up to me. She asked if she could take a photo, and I said of course. She beckoned several friends over, and one of them shrieked with glee.

The paparazzo who had been playing Angry Birds was the first to look up, but the shriek caught all of their attention. The sleeping photographers we'd passed on the stairs came to life and descended like a wake of vultures. I didn't even get a chance to take a photo with the group of fans. Machine gun–like camera flashes went off as the paparazzi swarmed. "Yan! Yan!" they called out, shouting the French pronunciation of my name.

We smiled for the cameras as we stepped backward to our waiting car and leapt in.

As an actor and an artist, I deeply respect the fashion world and its eccentricities. As a birder, I have no idea what the hell fashion is all about.

Birders don't care much about fashion. The "no white" rule is the closest thing we have to a line in the sand, and it's a blurry line. Birding fashion is pretty laissez-faire. It's mostly earth tones and muted grays. Some people wear nylon fishing shirts and cargo shorts; the very serious wear camouflage. The only real constants in the world of birding fashion are probably our wide-brimmed hats and orthopedic inserts.

Birders aren't fashion people. If anything, we're gear people.

For a hobby that only really requires eyes and ears to enjoy— and for some just one of those senses—people can get pretty into their gear.

Binoculars are the most obvious calling card of a birder and the only major piece of equipment one needs to get started. Some people wear them proudly around their necks, with er-gonomic back straps that keep them from bouncing when they need to walk briskly. Other people palm their binoculars and hold them at their sides, hoping strangers don't think they're Peeping Toms as they walk around the Silver Lake Reservoir at 6:00 A.M.

More serious birders will also invest in a spotting scope, which is basically a miniature telescope designed for looking at birds. Scopes were initially used by hunters to spot game, and by soldiers to spot the enemy. They have stronger magnification than binoculars but are harder to use. Scopes have to be mounted to something like a tripod to keep the image steady, so they're best for watching birds that don't move too much.

Some people take it a step further and get really into bird photography. There are lens attachments that connect cameras to spotting scopes—a type of photography called "digiscoping."

Bird photography is the most gear-intensive variation of birding. I tried to do a little bird photography right after I got back into birding, and one time I got a couple of decent shots of geese by holding my iPhone up to a spotting scope.

But the truth is, it's just not for me. I always feel like the camera separates me from what I'm looking at. That I'm never actually seeing what's right in front of me—it just becomes an image on a screen.

Nowadays, I only bring binoculars with me when I go out birding.

People who get really into bird photography remind me of paparazzi.

A few years back, a rare-bird alert went out for a varied bunting—a tiny red-and-purple songbird not normally found in the LA area. I had the day off from shooting, so I drove out to the park in Duarte where the bird had been spotted.

I arrived to find a flock of bird photographers with their camera kits—camouflaged telephoto lenses, tripods, monopods, the whole nine yards.

One guy was standing at the trunk of his car, changing out the lenses on his DSLR. He pulled an enormous white telephoto lens out of a camera bag.

Aside from the fact that it was white—why risk scaring the birds away?—it was the exact same lens I'd seen paparazzi carry around to take sneaky candid shots of celebrities—the ones where they're looking fat at the beach, fighting on hotel balconies, getting Starbucks in sweatpants, and so on.

In Paris, all of the paparazzi I'd seen had carried smaller, more compact lenses. Those photographers were lining the red carpet—they didn't need telephoto lenses to capture their subjects, who were generally willing to be photographed anyway. The big white lenses I'm talking about serve a different purpose.

Two years before, I'd seen the same type of lens when I was leaving my costar Lucy's birthday party. We'd gone to a restaurant called Beso in Hollywood. As we were waiting for our cars at the valet stand, I noticed a man across the street surreptitiously photographing us from behind a Dumpster. The streetlight above him illuminated his white telephoto lens, giving him away immediately as a paparazzo.

It felt like an intrusion. It's always nice when fans come up to say hi. It's not always nice being photographed from behind a Dumpster—it makes you feel like a Cold War spy whose cover has just been blown.

I wonder if birds feel the same way about having their picture taken.

REHAB

A lot of people who work in entertainment end up in rehab at some point. Drugs, alcohol, anxiety—there are countless reasons to go. I've only been to rehab once so far, and it was just for an afternoon. Also, it was for birds.

As is often the case with this sort of thing, it all started with a party. A few years back, I went to a fund-raiser for the Humane Society in Beverly Hills. My costar Torrey DeVitto had invited me to tag along. Torrey does a lot of volunteer work with animal rehabilitation and is a big animal rights activist. She's also a vegan—I think. I'm pretty sure she is. Every time she comes over for dinner I only cook vegetables, so either she's a vegan or she's convinced that I am. I should actually ask her about that.

Fund-raisers and galas are a pretty big staple in the Hollywood calendar. They bring together celebs and causes to raise money and get the word out about important issues. Whenever I attend one of these events, I spend most of my time by the buffet table. I've never shaken the poor-college-student mentality out of my head, so if there's free food, I stock up.

I'm not always the most graceful of birds at these Hollywood parties. A few years ago, I was invited to a scotch tasting. After I'd tried a number of different scotches, I got cornered by a stockbroker who was complaining that the party wasn't extravagant enough. I excused myself as politely as I could.

In the next room I found a chair and had a seat. It was made of white marble and was incredibly cool to the touch. It felt less like a chair than it did a piece of art, which was interesting, because that's exactly what it was: art. A worried personal assistant soon informed me that I was sitting on one of the host's priceless new acquisitions.

But I've gotten off topic. Back to the Humane Society party: I was standing across the room from Torrey, eating oysters at the buffet table, when a woman came up and introduced herself as Yvonne Bennett. We started chatting, and I found out that Yvonne worked with the Humane Society.

The Humane Society has always had a special place in my heart, and I told Yvonne as much. Growing up, my mom would take my sister and me to visit the cats and dogs up for adoption as an after-school activity.

"That's wonderful," Yvonne said. "Thankfully dog adoptions have gone up over the past few years. But there are certain animals that are hard to get folks to care about."

"Like what?"

"Well, birds, for instance."

"Oh, really? Like, pigeons?"

She laughed.

"No, a lot of what we do involves rehabilitating wild animals and then releasing them back into the wild once they're
better. But birds aren't cute. People don't flip out for rehabili-
tated falcons like they do for Dalmatian puppies. There just
isn't much of an interest in it. Bird rehab to most people is just
'boring but important' work."

I had my hand to my mouth and was midway through slurp-
ing down another oyster when she said this.

"You rehabilitate falcons?" I asked, oyster still in my mouth.

"Falcons, hawks, herons, you name it. We have a red-tailed
hawk we're due to release next week down in Ramona."

I was coughing, choking on the oyster in excitement.

I love hawks. Birds of prey in general are pretty awesome—
I've been obsessed with them ever since Mr. Hawkins, that
red-tailed hawk that lived near my house when I was a kid.

I asked Yvonne if I could come along to see the red-tailed
hawk when they released it. Of course, she said. And, as it turned
out, my possibly vegan costar Torrey was going to be there, too.

Thinking back on it now, I wonder if Torrey had tipped off
Yvonne about my love of birds.

The next Saturday, Torrey and I piled into my station wagon
and drove to Ramona, California. If I haven't said it enough
already, I was very excited. I'd been in Los Angeles for half a
decade, and here I was just now learning that there were regular releases of wild birds of prey. What the hell had I been
doing with my weekends?

We met Yvonne at a rehabilitation facility called the Fund

for Animals Wildlife Center. Yvonne and Ali Crumpacker came out to greet us in the parking lot when we arrived. Ali is the director of the animal rehab center in Ramona. Her general demeanor reminded me of Robert Muldoon—the raptor-obsessed game warden from the original *Jurassic Park*. Before moving to Southern California, she spent twelve years tracking lions in South Africa.

Ali was warm and welcoming, but it was clear that she wasn't particularly interested in photo ops. If you were at the Wildlife Center, you were there to work. And work we did.

The first thing we did was chop up frozen mice carcasses to feed to a couple of crows that were being treated at the center. We hadn't had coffee yet, and already we were chopping off mouse heads. A volunteer showed us her tried-and-true method for efficiently dismembering them.

We fed the mice to the crows and then headed over to the main animal holding area. By the entrance was a massive floor-to-ceiling whiteboard. A grid was drawn on the board—each box in the grid represented a cage, and a number was written inside each of the boxes. The numbers were followed by letters: initials to denote species.

One of the boxes had wso written after the numbers. I decided to hazard a guess.

"Is that one a western screech owl?" I said, pointing.

Ali nodded. "We got him in a few days ago. He's still in quarantine or I'd let you see him."

"What do the numbers mean?"

Ali smiled. "All of the animals here are numbered. It helps us resist the urge to name them." She pushed open the door, and we stepped into the enclosure. On each side of us were pens holding injured animals. Mountain lions that had eaten rat poison, bobcats that had stepped into traps, abandoned baby skunks that were so cute it hurt to look at them.

We passed a cage with a kiddie pool inside it—there was a pygmy hippo splashing about in the water. Yvonne said they'd rescued the hippo from Beverly Hills. Some millionaire's idea of a funny gift for his kid.

As we walked, Ali explained the volunteers' relationship with the animals. "We're all here because we love animals, of course, but sometimes that's the problem. A lot of these animals are here because they got too close to humans. They weren't properly afraid of us. People want to nurse sick animals back to health, but that can actually be really bad for them. The last thing we want is for the injured animal to imprint on us. We're here to help them be independent again. So no names, just numbers. We try to touch them as little as possible, and our attendants are instructed not to talk to them either. We're like ghosts."

"Is that hard?" I asked. "What's it like being surrounded by animals and having to actively ignore them?"

Ali's response came quickly, almost like a mantra. She'd had to answer questions like this countless times. "Part of loving animals—truly loving them—is caring about what's best for them. Often that means removing yourself from the equation."

The red-tailed hawk we were going to be releasing wasn't in the main enclosure. He'd already been transferred to a separate holding area to get him ready for his transition back to the wild. We hopped into a couple of Jeeps and drove out to the field to meet him.

A handful of volunteers were standing in the field. On a table, there was a small blue box—about two feet long and eight inches wide. Judging by the wide berth everyone was giving this blue box, it was clear that the hawk was inside.

As we pulled into the field, Yvonne turned around in the front seat to face me. "So what do you think, Ian?" she said. "Want to release it by yourself?"

I froze. I must have been smiling because Ali glanced at me in the rearview mirror then let out a deep guffaw. Yes. Yes, I wanted to release it. Holy shit, yes.

Then a thought ran through my head. This might all be an elaborate prank—and I'd been pranked before.

A couple of years ago, my costar Lucy fooled the hell out of me. She knew I was really into street art, and she convinced me that she had a connection to Banksy—the famously anonymous graffiti artist. She asked me if I wanted to meet him, and I jumped at the opportunity.

Lucy took me to a parking lot late one night to meet him. I tried to play it cool, doing my best not to let on how excited I was.

It turned out the whole thing was an episode for the show *Punk'd*. I fell for it, hook, line, and sinker.

Sitting in the car now, out in this field on a wildlife preserve, my mind flashed back to that night in the parking lot. I turned to look at Torrey. Was Torrey pranking me right now? Would she do such a thing? With Lucy I'd totally expect it. But Torrey isn't like that. Torrey likes classical music and nature conservatories. But could I be sure of that?

I swallowed and turned back to Yvonne. I nodded. "Yes, please."

"Cool," she said, and we got out of the car.

This wasn't a prank. This was real.

Ali informed one of the attendants that I would be releasing the hawk. He came over and showed me how to handle the little blue box. Hold it at arm's length, he said, with the door tilted away from your body. Then kneel down low, tilt the door toward the ground, and pull this switch to open it.

"The hawk will do all the rest," he told me. "You just hold on tight."

We went over to the table, where Ali was holding the box.

"Have fun," she said and handed it to me.

As I walked out into the open field, the hawk started to rustle inside the box. I glanced through one of the slats on top. A single, massive pupil stared back at me.

The hawk stopped moving. It opened and closed its beak silently.

A couple of months back, the bird had been brought to the shelter after it flew into a power line. Its wing had been badly scorched. It had taken weeks just to get it to move its wing again. But now it was strong. Strong and hungry.

The hawk hadn't been fed that day. They wanted it to be hungry when it was released so that it would immediately fly off to hunt. It was eyeing me like I was food.

I knelt in the middle of the field, holding the box out at arm's length. I angled the door down and away from me. I turned back to look at the small crowd waiting expectantly back by the cars. Torrey gave me an enthusiastic thumbs-up. I waved, took a deep breath, and turned back to the box. I steadied myself, making sure that I had a firm grip. I grabbed the switch, pulled it, and felt the door swing open.

Nothing happened.

The hawk didn't budge. Not even a little bit. It just sat there, at the bottom of the box. I could see the sunlight hitting his beak, illuminating its razor-sharp edges.

I looked back at the crowd of attendants. Nobody moved.

I turned back to the hawk. I tilted the box a little higher and gave it a light shake. This immediately seemed like a bad idea. Who shakes a hawk?

The bird remained where it was, refusing to move an inch.

At that point, curiosity got the best of me. Like Elmer Fudd with a jammed rifle, I lifted up the box and turned the door to face me. The red-tailed hawk and I stared at each other, his face not two feet from mine.

I blinked. The hawk didn't.

Then it let out a bloodcurdling shriek.

I don't know if any of you have ever heard a red-tailed hawk shriek. Actually, I take that back. You definitely have. If you've ever seen a movie that has a bald eagle in it, you've heard a red-tailed hawk. Actual eagles sound like they're whimpering, so, in Hollywood, eagles are always dubbed over with the sound of red-tailed hawk screeches.

It's a majestic and inspiring sound. Unless it's inches from your face. Which this was.

The hawk pushed its feet against the box and rocketed out toward me. Its wings brushed my hair, and it flew out low over the field, flapping to try and gain altitude. I ran back to join the crowd around the table.

The hawk flew about a hundred feet then crash-landed into the brambles at the far end of the field. It stayed there, staring at us. We all stared back.

Then Ali let out a growl. She set off sprinting toward the hawk, arms waving, yelling.

Torrey leaned over and whispered into my ear: "This is always the hardest part for me. They have to scare him away. He still thinks they're going to feed him his dinner."

The hawk looked dazed. It stared at Ali as if confused. She picked up a clod of dirt from the ground and tossed it in the bird's direction. As the dirt landed, the hawk spread its wings and took flight, disappearing over a stand of eucalyptus trees.

Ali slowly walked back to join us, wiping the dirt from her hands on her khaki shorts.

"That's so sad," I said to Torrey. Ali heard me. She smiled and shook her head.

"It's the only way. If we did our jobs right he won't ever see us again. There are no warm goodbyes in this line of work."

LIFE IN

THE WINGS

Probably the least "Hollywood" part of my life as an actor is actually being on set. The press junkets and the parties can be glamorous, but when we're shooting *Pretty Little Liars*, I wake up and drive to work every morning just like most people.

Sometimes work starts early. If my call time is at 6:00 A.M.—which it is if I'm in the first scene of the day—I set my alarm for 5:07. Even though I wouldn't call myself a superstitious man, seven is my lucky number, and I believe in starting the day off right.

I'm usually the first actor to arrive on set. I grew up in a military family, and I inherited my dad's deep, almost panicky respect for punctuality. He believes that unless you are literally caught behind enemy lines, you need to be on time.

Two seasons ago the producers installed a shower in my dressing room. Originally, I thought it was a gift, but then Lucy told me it was put in because I always smelled really bad. I like to think she was kidding, but either way, I make sure to take a shower before work. I almost always use my on-set shower instead of the one at home, because I don't want to wake up Sophia or the dogs.

After I get cleaned up, I usually eat breakfast on set. There's a craft services room at the back of one of the soundstages, complete with an unlimited supply of bacon. Most of the cast and crew stop by in the morning, and it's where I usually run into people at the beginning of the day.

The person I run into most often here is Troian Bellisario, who plays Spencer on the show. Troian, like me, is compulsively early. She's constantly moving and constantly working. She's an actor, yes, but she also writes, produces, and directs. She even directed a recent episode of the show. It's fortunate that she isn't evil—otherwise she'd easily take over the world. In the meantime, she makes a great breakfast buddy.

The only time us actors avoid craft services is when we have to shoot a sex scene. On those days, you'll find me drinking coffee and doing push-ups in my dressing room. When it's a sex-scene day, we'll all avoid craft services so that we look nice and svelte when the cameras start rolling. All of us, that is, except for Keegan, who walks around eating entire pizzas before he has to take off his shirt.

Around my third plate of bacon—it'd be a shame to let it all go to waste—I'll usually get a text from Lisa Hoggett, the set PA, telling me to get my ass over to hair and makeup. I'll grab an apple on my way out so I at least keep up the appearance of making healthy choices.

Hair and makeup is in one of several trailers set up between the sound stages. We call this area "base camp."

On my way over, I'll stop by the PA trailer to say good morning to Matt Buckler. Matt and I have been affectionately trading insults on a daily basis for several years. He and his wife are both lovely. (She had a guest spot in a recent episode of *PLL*.) Matt makes sure all the actors have their sides for the day.

"Sides" are a compact version of whichever parts of the script we're shooting that day, and each actor gets sides for just the scenes they're in. We have to review them carefully: there are often last-minute edits and revisions to the version of the script we were sent the week before.

Sides are handed out every morning, then collected again at the end of the day. The producers are strict about this because the episodes have to remain secret until they air on TV. Nobody wants even the smallest of plotlines leaked. At the end of each shoot day, we hand our sides over to Lisa, and she promptly destroys them. If we ever accidentally took them home with us, I am confident that Lisa would hunt us down à la *Rambo: First Blood*.

Once I get my sides from Matt, I'll quickly read through them to refresh my memory and see if there are any new lines I need to memorize, then walk up the steps to the hair and makeup trailer.

Inside, the first person I visit is Cindy Miguens, who's in charge of the hair and makeup department. Cindy sits me down, closely examines my face, asks me why I can't take better care of my skin, then proceeds to cover my face with a hot towel before I can answer.

Cindy says the towel is good for my pores, but I can't help but think she might just be trying to smother me. I regifted the

NutriBullet she gave me for my birthday a couple years back, and she's never let me live it down. In my defense, I gave the NutriBullet to my mom, so I still use it every time I go visit her. It's still in the family.

Also, Cindy and I share the same birthday, September sixteenth. Apparently we were both conceived after Christmas parties.

Not long after I regifted the NutriBullet, Cindy was planning a whitewater rafting trip, so I gave her a small plastic travel potty. She now uses it as a container to grow herbs in her backyard. I regifted, she repurposed—it all evens out.

After the hot towel, Cindy shaves my stubble to whatever length it needs to be that day. It's a little embarrassing, but I'm not allowed to shave myself. If I happened to nick my face, it could delay the shoot and cost the studio a lot of money. I'm not about to put up a fight on this rule, though: I've been shaving my own face for well over a decade, and I still haven't gotten the hang of it.

After the shave, Cindy puts on makeup to hide any blemishes and make my skin look like I've never had a zit before. Around this time, the coffee kicks in and I (a) wake up, and (b) start sweating, which is my natural state of being. Cindy sighs and begins to powder my face so that I don't sweat off all her hard work.

On mornings when Cindy is working on one of the other actors or actresses, I'll go over to Rebecca Wachtel-Herrera for my makeup instead. Rebecca is extremely efficient. She has a lot of people to get through each morning, usually in quick succession, so she's really good at getting people in and out of the seat quickly. She knows that I am really, really bad about sitting still—I constantly turn my head back and forth to take part in different conversations, and I'll say hi to anyone who walks in—so Rebecca has perfected the art of applying makeup to a moving target.

Also, her husband, Christian, is a fellow bird lover. Once, when I was over at their house for dinner, Christian and I saw a pair of red-whiskered bulbuls fly through their backyard. Red-whiskered bulbuls normally live in Asia, but there's an established population here in Los Angeles, which probably got its start from a handful of escaped pet birds. We sat around outside for half an hour, waiting for the birds to come back, completely forgetting about the food we'd left on the grill.

For hair, I either go to Kim Ferry or Valentino Agundez. My hair naturally forms into a tangled bird's nest, like Jonah Hill's in *Superbad*, so there's a fair amount of taming that needs to be done before they'll put me in front of a camera.

Kim is like a ninja with a straightening iron. I'll be horsing around with Shay or Troian and won't even notice Kim working. All of a sudden, she'll say, "Done," and I'll look up and my hair will be perfect.

If Kim's working on someone else, I'll go to Valentino's station at the far end of the trailer. Her chair is up in a raised side room—it's like a tree house. Valentino and I could talk for hours if they'd let us. We'll go on about everything from our dreams to race relations in America to whether or not humans will ever evolve to lose their pinky toes. It's hard to sit still when I'm talking to her, and I often end up jumping out of the chair to demonstrate a point or act out part of a story.

Once hair and makeup are done, I head to set. We film in the soundstages around base camp, and walking onto the stage

I'll often bump into the head of electric, Eric Forand, also known as E4. I'll say hey to E4 and also to the assistant director, who is almost always around. It varies from episode to episode, so the AD will either be Arthur Anderson, Jenn Anderson, or Laura Sylvestor. The Andersons aren't related.

At this point, we'll do a quick rehearsal of the scene we're about to film. Depending on who the director is—almost every episode has a different director—the rehearsal might be a full run-through of the scene, or it might just be blocking to figure out where we'll be sitting or standing in relation to the camera. Once we all feel like we've got a solid grasp on the scene, the actors are excused from set and they call in our stand-ins.

Tyler Maskell has been my stand-in for years. I pester him, and he plays along, sometimes feigning tears from all the abuse I give him.

The stand-ins are brought in so that the crew can adjust the lights and camera and set pieces around them. When I first started filming the show, I tried to help out. One time, the director said, "We need that lamp moved six inches to the right," and I was standing nearby, so I reached over and moved the lamp six inches to the right. I should've been yelled at, but a producer was nice enough to pull me aside and explain that actors aren't allowed to touch set pieces. It's against union rules. If I try and help out, I could get somebody fired. In college I worked crew on shows all the time, and the "don't help anyone" rule took some serious getting used to.

After the stand-ins are brought in, I'll often swing by Video Village to chat with the writers. Video Village is a collection of chairs and monitors set up directly next to wherever we happen to be shooting. Writers and producers gather there so they can watch the scenes as they're being filmed without bumping into set pieces or peering over the director's shoulder.

The writers on *PLL* are fantastic. They've juggled dozens of storylines over seven seasons. On top of that, they always make themselves available to us, and are willing to answer any questions we might have about the scenes we're shooting that day. There's rarely any improvising on the show, but the writers are open to word or line changes if we've got a solid argument for them.

When lighting and sound are ready to roll, Lucy and I head to stage and find our marks. I say Lucy because, as her on-screen love interest, most of my scenes are with her. Sometimes we'll rehearse again with lighting and sound in place, but we'll usually film the rehearsal. We try to be as efficient as possible with our scenes because we know everyone has families or other things to get to. We've learned that being overly precious with a scene doesn't help the performance—it just takes up time people could be spending with their kids.

Lucy is number one on the call sheet, and I'm number seven—told you it was my lucky number. Lucy's higher placement means she has some say in how we shoot the scenes.

After we've filmed the wide-angle "master"—the shot where you can see both actors at once—we move on to individual coverage, which is basically the same thing as a close-up on one actor. Traditionally, whoever is higher on the call sheet gets to decide if they'd like to go first or second, so they get to either prepare during the other actor's takes, or go first while everything is still fresh. Lucy never seems to care about going first or second, unless it's for a highly dramatic scene that she's the main focus of.

On some productions, after the actor with the higher number on the call sheet finishes their coverage, they'll leave set. This means that their scene partner is left to act opposite a PA with a script in their hand.

This bit of set politics has never been an issue on our show. Lucy has only left set during my coverage once before, and it was because we were running late and she had to hop on a plane for a family emergency. Her focus has always been on whatever makes the day run smoothly.

After we finish a scene and are excused from set, Lucy will always find a place to curl up and take a nap. The girl naps everywhere. She could sleep on a bed made of barbed wire if she wanted to.

If I've got a bit of a break between scenes and need some rest, I'll usually head back to my dressing room.

Shortly after we started work on season four, Marlene King—the showrunner and executive producer of *PLL*—was walking by my dressing room and poked her head in. She took a look around and I think assumed that I was horribly depressed based on the room's general lack of style and cleanliness. I'd never thought about decorating the place, and I'd let it get pretty messy. Marlene was worried, so she had the room redecorated with bright colors, put some art on the walls, and even got me a new mini fridge.

The new décor was actually pretty nice, but the fridge didn't last long. One day I walked in to find Shay Mitchell—who plays Emily on the show—stealing it. When I caught her red-handed, she began to laugh maniacally.

"Don't just stand there, Ian. Help me get this over to my dressing room," she said. I proceeded to help her steal my own fridge.

Shay also regularly takes food that I'm eating right out of my hands and eats it in front of me. She's basically the little sister I never had—the little sister who expresses love through torment.

If I see Ashley Benson, who plays Hanna, I'll pretend to hide. Not a day has gone by when she hasn't tried to punch me in the balls. It's a game we've been playing since season one. Ashley's a good friend, and she'll periodically steal my dogs and take them on adventures.

After we've been on set for six hours, we are released for "lunch." I put lunch in quotation marks because it's not a time-of-day-sensitive meal. When we have night shoots, we'll have a lunch break at two in the morning.

We had one of those nighttime lunch breaks when we were shooting the noir episode at the end of season four. Keegan and I were excused a little early for our lunch break, around 8:30 P.M., and we decided to leave the lot for dinner.

Across the street from where we film is a place called the Smoke House, an old Hollywood watering hole that's been serving actors from the Warner Bros. lot since the forties. We rolled up in costumes that would've fit right in back when the restaurant was founded—Keegan looked like a young Dick Tracy.

The waiter seated us at George Clooney's table—he was a regular at the Smoke House back in his *ER* days—and we sat there, sipping dirty martinis, eating heaping bowls of pasta. I don't usually go in much for Hollywood nostalgia, but it was a memorable lunch.

Similar to how "lunch" is a multiuse term, whenever I finish shooting all of my coverage, no matter what time of day it is, the AD will shout, "That's a goodnight to Ian!" and then everyone on set will call out goodnight. I've been wished a sincere good-night at both three in the morning and three in the afternoon.

Before leaving set, we hang up our clothes—you don't want any enemies, especially in the costume department—then grab our bags and head out.

Sometimes I'll grab a small to-go box of bacon for the road.

NO MORE DUCK

FOR BAILEY

A few years ago, Sophia and I were driving to meet up with a friend for lunch on Wilshire Boulevard. We were running pretty early.

Driving past the La Brea Tar Pits, I noticed that No-Kill Los Angeles, a group that promotes adoption of dogs and cats, was having its annual pet adoption weekend on the park grounds.

When I first moved to Los Angeles, I'd lived practically across the street from the tar pits, and I'd visited the event then. I hadn't seriously considered adopting at the time because my apartment didn't allow dogs—and I didn't have the space.

We had a half hour to spare before lunch, and we decided to stop and look at some of the animals.

Walking up and down the rows of white tents that had been set up to shade the kennels, I found myself thinking about how all these animals ended up here. Families who got evicted and couldn't afford to keep their beloved pets. Nine-year-old ex-fighting dogs. Puppies who proved too energetic for their owners' patience.

The cages were filled with beautiful animals—some friendly, others clearly frightened. It all started to get to me—so many cats and dogs find new, loving homes at these adoption fairs, but then you also know not every animal will be so lucky.

Around the corner of one of the rows of tents, there was a small crowd gathered around a kennel. Suddenly, Sophia let out a yelp and sprinted ahead. She disappeared into the crowd. I squeezed apologetically through several rows of shoulders and elbows to get to the front and catch up with her. When I finally got to where she was standing, Sophia was grinning from ear to ear. She pointed at a kennel. Inside were two labradoodles: Mochi, a girl, and Bailey, her brother.

Mochi was the smaller of the two, with slate gray fur and a chubby face. Bailey was lean and lighter in color, and he had a thin mustache that curled over his upper lip.

Mochi peered from face to face, like she was looking for someone. Her brother was skittishly cowering in a corner, looking over his shoulder to make sure he wasn't about to be surprised from behind.

A girl put her hand up to the metal bars of the kennel to say hi. Bailey, tail between his legs, sidestepped to the opposite corner of the enclosure.

I squatted down next to the kennel and put my hand out. Sophia did the same. Bailey looked over. He cautiously walked over and sat down next to me. He looked up, and we made eye contact. He lowered his head and nuzzled my hand. Mochi wagged her way over to her brother's side and began to lick Sophia's hand through the cage.

At that moment I realized two things: (1) we were getting these dogs, and (2) we were definitely going to be late for lunch.

Sophia agreed to stay with the dogs while I went to find someone who could help us. The adoption counter was in the tent next door, and as I walked over, I heard a man arguing with one of the volunteers. He was trying to adopt Mochi but didn't want to take her brother. The volunteer explained that the dogs were littermates—they hadn't been separated since birth. Ideally, they were looking to find them a home together.

The man took out his wallet and offered to pay extra for Mochi. The volunteer explained that the adoption fee was a set rate, and that they weren't trying to make a profit on the dogs.

Adrenaline took over: "I'll take them both!" I found myself calling out.

The man turned to me.

"I'm adopting the girl now," he said.

"You're offering to buy one, but I'd take them both," I said. I'd only just met them two minutes ago but already I felt protective of these pups.

The volunteer smiled at me—and I knew that we were going to be taking them home.

This was all very unexpected. We'd been on our way to lunch, debating what to do with the rest of our afternoon—and now we had dogs. Plural.

After filling out the paperwork, the volunteer and I walked back to the kennel. She opened the gate and put the dogs on leashes so we could take them to the car. Mochi and Bailey bolted from the enclosure and jumped at Sophia and me. I was wearing a baseball hat, and as I bent down to pet them, Mochi nabbed it off my head, wagging and smiling as she held it in her mouth.

That night the dogs slept in bed with us. I think we may have even shared a pillow.

The next morning they ate a pair of my dress shoes and Bailey threw up in the kitchen.

It's been four years now, and the pups still haven't slept a night apart.

Last year Sophia was spending the holidays with her folks in Florida, so I had the days between Christmas and New Year's all to myself. Los Angeles is especially quiet then—people get together with family, or run from them, fleeing to the mountains or the beach.

The whole town seems to draw its curtains.

The day after Christmas, I was wandering around the house in my boxers trying to find something to do. I'd realphabetized the books on my bookshelf and researched a scuba-diving certification course but didn't sign up for it. I was too restless to commit to anything.

Mochi and Bailey were following me from room to room, clearly frustrated that they hadn't been taken outside yet. I was too lazy to walk them but too lazy to sit still, and they stared at me like I was a sort of inept Judas: the look on their faces less of betrayal than disappointment.

I realized that I couldn't do much more loafing around at

home. I needed to get outside—to get some sunlight and fresh air before the short winter day ran out. I had cabin fever. We all had cabin fever.

I asked the dogs if they wanted to go for a hike. At the sound of the word, Mochi began to sneeze with excitement. She started doing laps around the kitchen island. Bailey ran over to the front door, crying to be let outside.

I loaded them in the car. They ride shotgun—I never said they weren't total divas.

One of the set designers on *Pretty Little Liars* had told me about a hike over in Franklin Canyon that I'd been meaning to explore, so I plugged the location into my phone for directions and set off.

I made my way over to Beverly Hills, and drove up through block after block of almost comically palatial mansions, many of them hidden from the street by towering, multistory hedgerows and security gates. I made a right turn into the park, and suddenly the houses were all behind us.

As I followed a narrow, winding canyon road up into the park, an elderly couple passed by going the opposite direction on a tandem mountain bike—apparently that's a thing people do.

The temperature was dropping outside—it was a whole different microclimate up here. Like a national park had unexpectedly sprung up in the middle of super-fancy suburban Los Angeles.

I passed a sign: COMPLIANCE WITH UPCOMING STOP SIGN SUBJECT TO VIDEO MONITORING AND ENFORCEMENT. And just in case I didn't understand the implications of that sign, another immediately after it stated: PHOTO ENFORCED. Then, a few yards after that, a pedestrian crossing sign.

Franklin Canyon takes its signs very seriously.

I finally got to the stop sign, and after coming to a complete stop and counting to five in my head, I drove around to the right of a small reservoir. It's an idyllic spot, and you may have even seen it before without knowing it: this is where a very young Ron Howard—who at the time went by Ronny—threw a stone into the water in the opening credits of *The Andy Griffith Show*.

The parking lot is at the top of the reservoir. I parked and let the dogs out to do some preliminary sniffing and marking of territory. In the trees above us, a pair of yellow-rumped warblers chased each other in circles.

After poking around a bit, I found a trail that ran along the side of the lake. I took the counterclockwise route, letting the dogs pull me, waiting on them when they found a good scent to work on.

The dogs pulled me over to a small pond filled with mallards and wood ducks. Turtles basked on mossy logs, warming themselves in the oblique winter sunlight. A family with twin girls in matching pink parkas was feeding bread to the ducks—next to a sign forbidding it.

On the far side of the reservoir from the parking lot the trees and reeds along the shore opened up, and I got a great view back over the water. As I walked along, a bird flew in and landed clumsily on the water, skidding to a halt. A wigeon, or maybe a coot.

I thought I'd get a closer look, but juggling my binoculars with one hand while the dogs pulled against the leashes in my other proved impossible. I finally got the dogs to sit.

I scanned the lake again. The duck was still there: a male

hooded merganser! It swam in little loops, the extravagant white crest on its black head fully extended. Beady yellow eyes unblinking. I guessed there was a female around nearby—probably somewhere just out of sight.

And there she was, coming out of the brush hanging over the edge of the lake.

Mergansers have a special place in my heart. It was that hooded merganser at Big Bear that brought me back into birding as an adult. Seeing the pair of them now, I felt my mind begin to relax. The postholiday stress and tension started to melt away.

And then something weird happened. Watching the two little ducks on the reservoir, Mochi and Bailey patiently tolerating my love of birds, a strange feeling crept up on me. It was a feeling I hadn't experienced while birding before, and also one that I haven't since. I was very hungry—starving, in fact.

And what I craved at that moment, more than anything in the world, was duck.

We didn't dawdle on the way back to the car. Hike finished, dogs loaded up, my hat in Mochi's mouth, I pulled out my phone and typed "duck" into Google Maps. The first result was a craft beer spot in Koreatown that specialized in duck and deep-fried Oreos. And to complete the trifecta, it was dog-friendly.

Driving to the restaurant, I thought about my feelings. I thought about how I was going to be eating them soon. As a birder, craving duck while viewing one of the prettiest species of the family is a convoluted and guilt-ridden experience. Here was this animal that I admired—that I had pored over in books—and it also happened to be mouthwateringly delicious. It was a conundrum.

I got to the restaurant, snagged a table, and ordered a duck French dip sandwich and some fries cooked in duck fat. There was a dish on the menu called "Death by Duck," but I couldn't bring myself to order it. The image of a pair of mergansers sitting down to eat me for lunch came to mind.

The waiter brought over a bowl of water for Mochi and Bailey, who were hanging out under the table.

It really had turned out to be a great day after all. And I could see how the rest of the afternoon was going to unfold: I would stuff myself with food. Then I was going to need a nap.

The food arrived, and I sank into duck bliss.

Once I had regained my senses, I noticed that the pups were peering out from under the edge of the table, watching me eat. I was feeling generous—so I handed Mochi my hat. She politely took it and set it on the ground, rejecting my offer—and she and her brother continued to look up at me expectantly.

When it comes to my dogs, I'm a weak man. I slipped them each a piece of duck from my sandwich. Mochi gulped it down, and then put a paw on my knee, trying to pressure me into giving her more. Bailey practically inhaled the piece I gave him and then sat back down, licking the grease off his whiskers.

Mochi growled for more. She's always been pushier than her brother—she's cleverer than he is, too. They love to roughhouse together, and I once saw Mochi feign injury to trick him. Bailey had given her a nip on the leg, and she gave a strange yelp and pretended to limp away. When Bailey turned around, she pounced on him.

I told her to lie down and then gave her another piece of

duck. I gave one to Bailey, too. I didn't want him to think I was playing favorites.

The waiter came over, and I put in an order of deep-fried Oreos.

"You know, your one dog isn't looking so hot," he said.

I looked under the table. Mochi looked chipper enough, but Bailey was wheezing, his eyes closed. He took a long, rattling breath. He exhaled, and you could see he was struggling. I rubbed his back.

"What's going on, buddy?" I asked.

Bailey began to dry heave. Then he threw up.

The waiting room at the animal hospital was playing Christmas music. Obscure *animal-themed* Christmas music. I don't know how many of you know the song "Dominick the Donkey," but, trust me, it's not what you want to be listening to while you're waiting to find out if you poisoned your dog.

After what felt like an hour, the vet stepped into the waiting room and called me back to see Bailey. He was sitting on a stainless-steel table, looking like his normal self. He lifted his head and wagged his tail when he saw me.

"Bailey is going to be fine," the vet said. "He had a strong intolerance to something he ate—my guess would be the duck. If I were you, I'd consider getting him allergy tested. In the meantime, no more duck for Bailey."

In front of me, as I write this, I have a list of all the foods that Bailey can't eat per the allergy testing results. He is allergic to duck (of course), chicken, potatoes (both sweet and regular), eggs, fish (all kinds), wheat, venison, lamb, peanuts, soy, and chocolate (duh).

At my feet, Bailey is smiling up at me while his sister is gnawing at his ears. I've noticed that since I've changed his diet, he's stopped licking his paws as much, or scratching the top of his lip. Some hair has grown in around his nose that I didn't realize was missing. He used to paw at his face and get runny eyes, but no longer.

He's the healthiest dog I've ever met, and he now eats substantially better than I do: a blend of lean pork, quinoa, kale, Fuji apples, carrots, and various omega fatty acids not derived from fish.

Mochi eats dog food.

HOW TO LOOK SEXY

ON CAMERA

The first time Lucy and I ever kissed on-screen was in a bar in Vancouver. We were shooting the pilot, and there's a scene where we're making out in a bathroom.

I flossed at least three times before that scene. I had a bottle of mouthwash with me on set, and I gargled between every take. At dinner that night with the cast, everything tasted minty fresh, and the next day my mouth was numb.

The whole time I was shooting the pilot, I tried to keep in mind a piece of advice a model once gave me. She told me that if you ever want to look sexy on camera, you just have to pretend you're slightly confused about something. Not too confused, she said. You don't want to actually appear befuddled. Just a bit dazed.

That advice seemed to help, but there are a few other hurdles to looking sexy—and most of those hurdles for me involve hair.

I have a lot of stubble, no matter how often my face is shaved. The makeup team on *Pretty Little Liars* has to constantly reapply Lucy's makeup whenever we kiss because my cheeks always belt-sand it off.

Shaving has some consequences. Once, Lucy and I were filming a sex scene, and I had an ingrown hair on my neck from shaving. It was a big red bump—too big for makeup to completely hide. The DP tried different camera angles, but we were romping around in bed in the scene, so he couldn't get a bump-free view.

At one point, someone suggested putting a dab of green paint on it—the same color as a green screen—so that it could be edited out in post. Needless to say, having a crew of twenty-plus people obsessing over a blemish on my neck was a humbling experience.

Whenever I have a shirtless scene, I have to shave off all my chest hair. The network requires all the men on the show to have smooth, porpoise-y chests.

I tried waxing it once. Never again.

The week after I shave my chest, I'm always in agony. Itchy, itchy agony. I've tried everything to help cope with the pain: baby oil, coconut oil—even olive oil, but that just made me hungry. The only remedy that makes any difference whatsoever is Advil, two fingers of scotch, and patience.

If we're shooting a scene where I'm wearing a low-cut shirt or a Henley, Cindy from hair and makeup will use a vibrating mini razor called "the peanut"—I promise it's not a sex toy—and shave a deep "V" around the shirt line in my chest hair.

Strangely enough though, arm hair is always okay on *Pretty Little Liars*. That's how they want the guys to look: smooth in the middle, hairy at the edges. It's a strange formula.

So, I guess what I'm saying here is that, if you want to look sexy on camera, shave your chest and remember to look confused. Just not too confused.

THE BIRDS

AND THE BEES

My sister Sarah entered the world in San Diego, California. I was born three days and three years later a continent away, in Germany. Our parents were in the military, which is why we were stationed overseas. My mom was a nurse with the navy, and my dad was a journalist and editor at *Soldiers* magazine.

Sarah was two when they moved to Europe, so she remembers a lot more about Germany than I do. She's told me about the parks we used to go to, the bakeries and the shops near our home. I don't remember much of it. At the time I was primarily focused on crying and learning to walk.

On days when he didn't have work, my dad would take Sarah and me to the local *Tiergarten*—which translates, literally, to "animal garden." It was a zoo. I was too young to remember, but my dad says I was always drawn to the exotic birds. He says I used to run up and stick my fingers through the chain link of their cages to try to pet their wildly colored feathers. Perhaps the bird-loving die was cast before I even had a choice in the matter.

When I was three, my parents were called back stateside. We moved to Virginia, and my mom started working at a naval hospital in DC, and my dad started his next magazine gig. With both of my parents out of the house, my sister and I spent a lot of time with babysitters—I've mentioned before that I scared many of them off.

During this time, Sarah and I became inseparable. My mom used to joke that I was my big sister's shadow. Anywhere she went, I followed.

Sarah and I would play pretend for hours, lost in worlds of our own creation, and speaking languages nobody else could understand. Sarah would often set the rules of the world, and I would play the part she assigned to me.

We didn't have a dog, and we both really wanted one, so sometimes Sarah would have me run around on all fours and bark at cats. We had to stop that game though after I got carried away and chased a neighborhood boy back to his home.

A lot of our make-believe involved evil nuns. I'm not sure why. Maybe it had something to do with Sarah's love of everything British—and often stories involving British children would also feature a domineering lady of the cloth. Neither of us had ever seen a nun in real life, but we would spend hours pretending to fight them.

When one of us had to play a dreaded nun, Sarah always assigned the part to me.

At the time, my dad was reading Jane Goodall's books, and he would read to us from them. Goodall wrote extensively about chimpanzees and poaching in Africa, and we became obsessed with the settings of her stories. When we played outdoors, we would pretend that we were lost in tropical lands filled with wild tribes of cannibalistic nuns—all played by me.

When I was four, Virginia was hit by a terrible blizzard. Both of my parents stayed home from work for a week. That was the first time my mom and dad ever got to witness the full extent of our marathon make-believe sessions. During the storm, my dad helped Sarah and me turn a couch on its side. We covered it in sheets and created a fort in the living room. When my dad asked us what it was for, Sarah told him that we were defending our keep from a horde of Blessed Sisters.

My parents looked at each other, and my dad suggested, as diplomatically as possible, that perhaps we might want to try fighting something other than the Catholic Church. The idea had never occurred to us.

One day that spring, Sarah and I were spending the day at a babysitter's house, and we decided to run off into the backyard to play "Jane Goodall." We knew that there were poacher nuns everywhere—and rural Virginia was no exception.

In our search for poachers, we came across a large beehive in the trunk of a tree. Naturally, we whacked it with our nunchucks.

This turned out to be a terrible idea.

The hive exploded on the ground, unleashing a cloud of irate bees, hell-bent on revenge. As the first wave descended upon us, our babysitter grabbed her own baby—she was a mother—and ran inside, locking herself and her five-month-old in the bathroom.

Sarah and I ran into the house screaming after her and banged on the bathroom door, shouting to be let in.

"I'm so sorry," she cried from the other side of the door. "I can't. You'll let the bees in."

Just then, another bee stung me. On the eyelid. We had run inside without closing the back door.

The entire swarm had chased us into the house, and they weren't letting up. This was it. The bees had us exactly where they wanted us.

I asked Sarah if we were going to die.

"No!" she said. "I have an idea." Sarah was always coming up with clever solutions to impossible situations.

"Take your clothes off," she said, ripping off her shoes. "The bees won't recognize us if we're naked. They'll just keep attacking our clothes thinking it's us."

My God, she was brilliant. I immediately started taking off my pants. They got caught around my ankles, and I tripped on them and went down. Sarah pulled me up by my shoulders and helped me un-Velcro my shoes.

We hastily laid out our clothes on the floor like flattened scarecrows for the bees to find. What a great idea this was. Surely now, those dumb bees would stop stinging us and attack our clothes instead.

They didn't.

We ran around the babysitter's house naked, screaming, and crying as bees continued to sting us.

Mercifully, my dad came to pick us up early. As he walked

up the driveway, he was greeted by the sight of his two children, naked and screaming, pressed up against the bay windows. Our babysitter was still locked in the bathroom.

This might have been one of the only moments I can recall seeing my dad's military training in action. He took one look at us, ran to the front door, and kicked it in. I don't know if he even tried to turn the knob first.

He rushed to my sister and me, scooped us up in his arms, and sprinted to the car.

He took us home, gave us both oatmeal baths, and put antihistamine cream over all of our welts. We didn't go to the hospital, since my mom was a nurse, but I was still bedridden, waiting for the end to come.

I asked my father for a piece of paper.

"For what?" he asked.

"I want to write my will."

"Who are you going to give all your stuff to?"

"Sarah. For her bravery. And for saving my life."

When I was six, Sarah started taking voice lessons. She would come home every week with sheet music and new songs to learn. She'd lock herself in her room and practice scales for hours. It was the first time that my big sister had gone off to do something that I wasn't allowed to join.

I persuaded my parents to let me take voice lessons, too. I didn't really care about singing, but my sister was doing it, so I had to do it, too. I ended up developing a bit of a crush on my voice teacher, so I kept taking lessons as long as I could get my parents to let me.

Soon after I started taking voice lessons, Sarah and I started going to see local plays. Our aunt Jules worked at a nearby high school called Georgetown Prep—her first and only job: she's been there since 1970. Whenever they would put on a show, Sarah and I would get to see it.

Aunt Jules introduced us to the head of the school's drama department. We told him how much we liked his plays, and he asked us if we ever wanted to be a part of them. Often, the plays would have big ensemble scenes—villagers going about their days, workers in a factory, that kind of thing—and they didn't have enough actors to fill the stage. So my sister and I started acting in the big ensemble scenes of the shows.

Our first big scene was as tavern boys in the play 1776. We wiped down tables and carried around empty beer mugs in the background of the big musical numbers. We were in awe, completely starstruck by the teenage actors dancing and singing around us. Sarah's hair was short then, too, so we both played boys. It wasn't really a big deal for us—when we played pretend in the living room, Sarah and I switched genders constantly depending on the story we were telling.

The first time we acted in a play together, I almost backed out. Sarah calmed me down. She took my hand in hers and said, "It's okay, Ian. I'll be here. If you get scared just hug me and it'll be okay." She was right. Everything was okay. Everything was always okay when my big sister was nearby, and we ended up doing several plays together at the high school.

As is often the case with siblings, things changed when Sarah started middle school. I was still a little kid, but she was suddenly a teenager. She didn't want to play make-believe anymore.

We started to fight—all the time. For the first time in my

life, my sister and I didn't get along. Our status quo became conflict.

Once, when Sarah was babysitting me, I decided to hold her hostage and force her to be my friend again. I snuck up behind her while she was doing the dishes, and I pulled a butter knife on her.

"Freeze," I said, pointing the dull blade at her knees.

Sarah calmly reached into the dishwasher and pulled out a large kitchen knife. I burst into tears and ran to my room.

Over the next few years, Sarah and I grew more and more distant. Sarah was busy with her friends and her writing. I was busy losing the Geography Bee to Danny fucking Gordon.

I moved from elementary school to middle school. Sarah moved up to high school. All along, we were still bickering. By the time I started high school, we were barely on speaking terms.

I was going through adolescence. My body started to grow into my voice. I began going on dates. At school we learned sex ed—awkwardly enough, my sex-ed teacher was my aunt Jules.

In the winter of my freshman year of high school, Sarah asked me if we could go somewhere to talk.

There weren't a lot of restaurants or coffee shops near us when we were growing up. In fact, if you lived in Herndon and you needed to have a heart-to-heart with somebody, there was really only one place you could go. So we headed down to the Dairy Queen on Lynn Street.

Sitting across from Sarah on the red plastic bench in the

Dairy Queen, I found myself unable to maintain eye contact. It was cold outside, but I'd ordered a Blizzard—out of habit, I guess, or defiance. I was pretending to be interested in my ice cream so that I didn't have to look at my sister. I kept turning the cup upside down to see if anything would fall out of it.

Sarah spoke first.

"So, you like mint with Oreos?" she asked.

I was quiet. At first I acted like I hadn't heard her.

"Yeah, I always have," I finally said.

"You're right. I remember you, uh . . . yeah, you love mint."

Our conversation, if you could even call it that, had stalled. Again.

"You doing okay, though?"

I nodded. "Yeah, I'm fine."

She sighed, and covered her eyes with her hands.

"Look, the reason I wanted to talk to you is . . ."

She trailed off. The door swung open and a gorgeous woman in running clothes walked in. She passed by our table and I, being a fifteen-year-old boy, checked her out. I followed her to the counter with my eyes, then caught myself, felt guilty, and turned back to Sarah.

Sarah's eyes were locked on the woman, too. She might have been checking her out even harder than I was. After a moment, she laughed at herself, and turned back to me.

I could practically hear the lightbulb click on in my head.

"That's what I wanted to talk to you about. I'm a lesbian, Ian."

My mouth fell open. I didn't say anything. I didn't look away either.

Sarah and I sat like that for about a minute, just looking at one another in silence.

"I'm going to tell Mom and Dad tomorrow, and I just wanted to come out to you first. It's not a big deal. Just, you know, say something, yeah?"

I sat there for a moment, thinking about what I could possibly say to her.

Then it dawned on me. Sarah had just told me something that she must have been holding on to for years. It couldn't have been easy to share that with me, her bratty little brother, sitting on this cold bench in this small-town Dairy Queen. My sister was incredibly brave. Braver than anyone else I knew in my life at the time.

And I had something of my own that I'd been too proud— or too scared—to admit. When I opened my mouth, it was the only thing my body would let me say.

"I've really missed you, Sarah," I said, trying not to cry. "Thanks for letting me know."

Sarah smiled, and she settled back in her seat. We finished our ice cream, checked out the sexy jogger together one last time, then drove home.

FIFTY SHADES OF

THANKSGIVING

It was Wednesday afternoon. I stood in my backyard, hovering over a raw turkey. This was, in fact, a practice turkey. The next day, my dad, stepmom Mari, sister Sarah, and stepsister Erika would be coming over to spend Thanksgiving with me. Sarah lives in LA, but the rest had traveled across the country for the holiday.

I needed tomorrow's turkey to be perfect. I'd never hosted family before, and this was a chance for me to prove to them just how grown-up and competent I'd become since college. I'd thoroughly cleaned the house, even scrubbing the grout between the tiles in the shower. I wanted to make sure nothing was vulnerable to judgment.

The only obstacle that remained was the bird.

I'd never cooked a Thanksgiving turkey before. Or a non-Thanksgiving turkey, for that matter. I'm not exactly an expert in the kitchen. I was on an episode of my castmate Shay's YouTube cooking show once, and I accidentally brought cucumbers instead of zucchinis for the dish.

Shay, who happens to be Canadian, had a lot of advice about this traditional American meal. She said I should make a smoked turkey—that it would seal in the juices better than roasting it in the oven, and that I could ignore the turkey for a few hours while it smoked so I could tend to the rest of the meal.

I spent a few days looking up recipes online, falling deeper and deeper into a wormhole of culinary message boards. All the information on smoking turkeys was overwhelming, and often conflicting—so I kept reading.

There were websites where commenters made sweeping generalizations about how their way to smoke a turkey was the "right" way, going after anyone who disagreed. One guy got mocked because he only brined his turkey for ten hours. Another guy told him that if he didn't want to listen to Alton Brown, who advocated for a two-day brine, he was a fool. Self-proclaimed experts were throwing around advice for week-long brines and five-day thaws in the fridge. It got to the point where, to have a bird ready by late November, you needed to start planning in April.

I was intimidated—but I was also intrigued. After cross-referencing a number of recipes and YouTube videos, I finally decided on a foolproof plan.

It was time to find out if all that research was going to pay off. I checked the temperature on the grill to see if it was ready to put the bird on. It was nearly there.

When I first moved into my house on the east side of town, Sophia's dad gave me a Big Green Egg as a housewarming gift. The Big Green Egg is the Rolls-Royce of grill-smoker combos. It's substantially fancier than any grill ever needs to be—and it sent an unspoken message to all my friends that I was a substantially better chef than I actually am.

There's a community of Big Green Egg fanatics. They call themselves "Eggheads," and every year they gather in the Midwest for something called "Eggtoberfest." Owning one of the grills put me on the mailing list, but I've yet to attend one of their big annual events.

Smoke was beginning to pour out of the top of the grill. I'd set hickory blocks on top of lump charcoal, and it smelled delicious. I checked the thermometer again—it was hot enough to put the bird on.

I opened up the Big Green Egg and placed the turkey on the grill and quickly realized: my Big Green Egg was not big enough. Perhaps I had a medium Green Egg, or an egg-sized Green Egg. Either way, the lid wasn't about to fit over the turkey. It couldn't. The legs and wings of the bird jutted out over the edges.

I looked down at the turkey—plump from the two-day brine—that I'd trussed up earlier in the kitchen. It was sprawled helplessly on the grill, waiting patiently to be smoked. It looked oddly sexual, with twine wrapped around various body parts. I had auditioned for the lead role in *Fifty Shades of Grey* a couple of months before, and this turkey was giving me flashbacks.

I could cook this bird, I thought, but it wasn't going to be pretty.

I got some more twine and used it to tie the top of the grill down as best I could.

I picked up a couple of bricks off the ground and balanced them on the lid of the grill for added weight. It wasn't fully closed, and it didn't look even remotely safe, but some smoke was getting trapped in the grill now, and it looked like the bird had a chance at cooking.

I cast one last worried look at the precariously balanced turkey and my makeshift grilling solution, and I went inside.

The recipe called for the turkey to be rebasted every hour for three hours. I had time to get cleaned up and answer a few emails. I hopped into the shower.

A few minutes later, I heard a loud crash outside. I put on a towel and ran upstairs.

The bricks had fallen off the Big Green Egg. The top had flown open, and the turkey had rolled off the grill and onto the ground. It was now caked in dirt with a few burn marks scattered across its skin.

Mochi and Bailey rushed over, assuming that this must be their supper. They wagged their thanks to the dog gods and tried to dig in.

I shooed them away and inspected the bird to see if any parts of it were salvageable. None were.

I hauled the turkey back inside and threw it away. I needed a solution, and I needed it by tomorrow morning. The grill definitely wasn't going to work.

I decided to just cook the turkey in the oven. It wouldn't be unusual, it wouldn't be unlike anything my family had ever tasted, but, with any luck, it also wouldn't be a total disaster.

The next morning, most of the fam arrived just before noon: my dad, Mari, and Erika. Sarah was coming a bit later.

My dad is a military historian. He has never not had a beard—I'm convinced that he was born with a goatee. My step-mom Mari is fluent in several languages, knows more about wine than the grapes themselves, and is one of the most supportive, upbeat people I have ever known.

Divorces are hard. They can rip families apart at the seams. But there can be a couple of positives. If you're lucky—and I was—you can end up with some totally badass stepsiblings. That's where Erika comes in. Erika lives on a farm in Northern California, before which she was interning on a small ten-acre veggie operation outside of Portland, Oregon. I went out to help her a couple years ago and was humbled. What gym-carved muscles I had were no match for actual labor, and before we broke for lunch, I had to lie down in a field of shallots and hold my hand over my mouth so the other farm hands couldn't hear me whimpering. Farmers are the strongest people I've ever met.

I helped my dad carry the luggage into the house and showed everyone to their rooms. While they were unpacking, I went upstairs to check on the turkey. I was slow-cooking it—at an extremely low temperature—so it had been in the oven since five in the morning.

I checked the meat thermometer. Everything seemed to be on track. This turkey was going to be delicious. The meal would be a hit. My family was going to be blown away.

I set the oven timer and went to go see if anyone needed any other grown-up items: a newspaper, extra towels, cufflinks, that sort of thing.

Once everyone was settled in, we gathered in the living room to catch up. There's a tradition in my family: pregaming. We've been pregaming Thanksgiving ever since I can remember.

Around 2:00 P.M., various Thanksgiving-themed finger foods are set out on the kitchen island, along with at least three bottles of wine.

A lot had changed since I'd last seen my family. My dad was working on a new book, Mari's wine-importing business was expanding, and Erika had just settled into the new farm in Northern California. All my dad wanted to talk about, though, was *Pretty Little Liars*.

My dad and Mari hold viewing parties at their home in Virginia. Every time a new episode comes out, they gather a dozen or so of their close friends to have dinner and watch the show. I always smile when I think about it. I have this image of a room full of middle-aged professionals—doctors, lawyers, military historians—all dressed to the nines, gathered around my dad's living room TV, watching season after season of this teen drama.

When I was growing up, my dad didn't watch much television. He had a little set, but it was nothing fancy. Then I landed a job on *PLL*, and he upgraded to a state-of-the-art flat screen with surround sound.

They've been hosting their viewing parties since the show started. By now, my dad and Mari's friends know more about the show than I do. They are current on all of the gossip, all of the rumors and fan theories, all of the Easter eggs that the show has to offer.

Recently, I went home for a long weekend, and one of my dad's friends—a 60-year-old periodontist named Phil—cornered me after dinner and told me he'd done the math and he'd figured out who "A" was.

"It's Aria, isn't it?" he said, examining my reactions closely. "You can tell me."

I told him, honestly, "I have no idea who 'A' is."

He frowned, looked me over, then smiled as if he'd worked something out in his head. "I hear you," he said. "NDAs, right?" He winked. "Don't worry. I won't tell." He laughed and strolled back to the table to help my dad put the dishes away.

The smell of turkey was beginning to fill the house.

On the couch, Mari and my dad were laughing. "Should we tell him?" she asked.

My dad shook his head. "He'll be too embarrassed."

"He won't be embarrassed," she said, still giggling. "He'll think it's funny," She leaned forward to get my attention: "Ian, we saw the funniest article about you the other day. Do you read Perez Hilton?"

"No," I said. "Do *you*?"

My dad shrugged. "It's not that bad. Erika, did you bring your laptop?"

She had, and ran downstairs to get it. When I protested, Mari simply refilled my wine glass. Erika came back with the laptop, and we gathered around the sofa to have a look.

"It's really not bad at all, Ian," Mari said. "Steve, what was the title of the article?"

"It's . . . uh . . . wow, I can't remember."

"Here, let's just look up your name." She typed "Ian Harding" into Google and hit enter. On the top of the results page was a row of photographs of me smiling. "Look at all of these nice photos of you!" she said. She clicked an image, and it opened up a page of dozens of photos of me grinning on red carpets.

Erika laughed. "Why do you always look so squinty in these photos? Are the lights really bright, or are you just trying to look sexy?"

My dad chimed in: "I think it has to do with animal instinct. When we squint as humans, we're signaling to a possible mate that—"

"I do it because one eye is bigger than the other," I said, cutting off his evolutionary theory.

All three members of the family crowded up close to my face.

"No you don't!"

"It's not really—well . . ."

"Oh yeah, I guess you do!"

Self-consciously, I turned back to the screen and started scrolling.

And that's when we saw them.

Down at the bottom of the second page, clustered on the right side of the screen, were a handful of terribly Photoshopped images of me completely naked, always with a comically large erection.

"Is that . . . ?" Mari said.

"No!" I shouted. "No, of course not. That's not me!"

The room was very quiet. My dad suddenly became interested in the bookshelves across the room and walked away. Erika stood slightly behind her mom, tears of silent laughter filling her eyes.

"Wait, Mari, do you think that's real?!" I asked.

"Well I didn't look at it long enough to take an educated guess!"

Erika lost it and burst out laughing. I assured Mari that I would only ever do full-frontal for HBO, then excused myself to go check on the turkey.

Erika joined me in the kitchen, still laughing, and began to chop veggies for a salad.

As she and I cooked, I noticed Mari had sat back down at Erika's laptop.

I called over: "Are you still looking for that article? Seriously Mari, I believe you when you say it's funny, but you don't..."

I realized she wasn't looking at me as I spoke. Her eyes went wide and her mouth fell open. She stood and brought the computer over to where Erika and I were standing.

"I ... I googled 'Ian Harding fan,' and this came up ..."

I looked at the screen. I began reading what looked like an interview, but my costar Drew was also part of the interview.

It wasn't an interview.

"Wait, Mari, what is this?"

She pointed, finger trembling, to the middle of the page. I began to read out loud: "He pulled off his boxers instantly, revealing his bare ass. Jason sighed, stepping forward. He dropped his belt, jeans, and boxers as well, and then made Ezra bend over the couch—"

Mari yanked the laptop out of my hands and snapped it shut.

"You know what," she said, "I'm all for loving who you want to love and freedom of expression and all that jazz, but I have to say, I'm not really interested in reading this about my stepson!"

I turned to Erika, who a moment ago had stood by my side but was now crumpled on the floor, convulsing with laughter.

"Is she dead?" My sister Sarah stood at the top of the stairs. We hadn't heard her come in.

"We were just reading some of my erotic fan fiction," I said.

"The gay or the straight stuff?"

"The what now?"

"The gay or the straight stuff? The hetero fan fiction is super dull. You basically just make Lucy soup when she's sick or, like, fix her bike while wearing plaid. The gay stuff, on the other hand, that can get pretty interesting."

"Wait, you knew about this?"

She walked over to the kitchen island and popped a chip in her mouth. "Yup. One of my friends from back home found a few of them and emailed me. I can't believe you didn't know about them."

My dad had had enough of the bookshelves, and came back over to refill his wine glass.

"Are we done talking about my son the porn star?"

Right on cue, the oven timer went off. I donned a pair of oven mitts and took out the turkey—it was perfectly golden. It was time to eat.

The meal was a hit. We ate our faces off, piling on the stuffing and gravy and Brussels sprouts.

As Erika handed me a platter of sweet potatoes, I asked if anyone had gotten a chance to talk with Aren that day. Aren is Mari's son, Erika's brother, and he couldn't make it out to LA that Thanksgiving because of school.

"I did," Erika said. "He sends his love to everyone. He said he wishes he could be here, but he's got a lot on his plate right now."

My dad coughed, and indicated the plate overflowing with food in front of him.

"I've got a feeling he's going to love hearing about your fan fiction, though," Erika continued. "Maybe he can read a passage at the next *PLL* party our parents throw."

It seemed so natural when she said it that it didn't hit me until later in the conversation.

"Our parents."

The first few years after my mom and dad got divorced, the holidays were tense, almost bitter. Sarah and I were angry. Yet now, years later, I find myself looking forward to family gatherings—they are different than before, yes, but families change, and this one is mine now.

THE CALIFORNIA

CONDOR

The California condor once ranged from Canada to Mexico—
and could be spotted as far away as the East Coast—but by
the early 1980s, only twenty-two remained in the wild. Due to
a massive conservation and reintroduction program, the population has since grown to just over two hundred birds, but they
are still at risk of extinction.

Condors are massive. They can soar up to 15,000 feet above
the ground and are often mistaken for small aircraft. With their
ten-foot wingspan, they are by far the largest flying bird on the
continent.

As humans, we have an interesting attachment to big,
majestic birds. We like to tie big, lofty ideas to them. Take the
bald eagle, for example. Really pretty and really big. It isn't just

a bird for Americans. Bald eagles mean freedom. They mean liberty, justice, victory. Bald eagles have become a stand-in for all the values that our country holds dear. That's a lot of pressure to put onto one bird, no matter how big and majestic it may be. Which, in my opinion, is why the turkey would never have worked as our national bird. No offense to Benjamin Franklin, who preferred them over bald eagles, but turkeys just aren't regal enough to support that much symbolism.

Since we love attaching big ideas to big birds so much, I'm going to do the same with condors. Bear with me here, but I'm going to say that—for me, at least—the California condor is a metaphor for great, meaningful acting roles—the kinds of roles you see pop up once, maybe twice, in a lifetime.

Like outstanding roles, encountering a condor is rare, incredibly rewarding, and, often, a huge surprise. Nowadays, California condors only live in extremely remote, craggy, hard-to-get-to locales. So to see one—much like booking a dream role—you have to either put in a lot of hard work or be ridiculously lucky. Usually both.

Last summer, my friend Walter and I drove out to Pinnacles National Park to try to get a glimpse of one. Our friend John was supposed to come with us, but John—who, as I've mentioned before, only goes birding when forced to do so—had said that he would rather get run over by a car than go look at birds with me again.

And that's what he did. John called me the day before the trip to say that a car had hit him while he'd been riding his bicycle and he couldn't come on the trip.

I called bullshit. John had tried to sneak out of birding trips in the past. "Prove it," I said.

John hung up the phone.

Five seconds later, he FaceTimed me. I answered the call, and there was John, holding up his blood-soaked arms. "Enjoy your sky rats," he cackled into the screen. "Have fun without me."

"Go to a hospital, John," I said.

He shrugged and told me he was going to make breakfast first, then signed off.

Walter drove over to my house early that Saturday morning. We loaded my car with camping gear, quickly downed some coffee, and set off for Pinnacles.

Pinnacles is one of the newest national parks in the country. President Obama gave it its park status in 2013. It's a pretty cool spot, and out of the way, so not many people visit.

I had been looking forward to the trip for weeks, but that morning I was particularly happy to be going. I'd had an audition for a lead role in a Netflix show earlier that week, and I'd felt really good about it, but my manager had called me late Friday night to let me know that I hadn't gotten it. I don't tend to get worked up about auditions—rejection is a huge part of being an actor, and I usually don't let it get to me—but I was glad to have an excuse to get out of LA for a couple days just the same.

After driving all morning, we made it to the park. We noticed driving in that the ranger station had its own swimming pool. We thought about taking a dip, but we hadn't come to swim. We drove farther down the road to look for a campsite instead. We needed to get hiking soon if we were going to have any chance of spotting a condor.

The park was pretty empty that weekend, so we had our pick of campsites. We ended up finding a beautiful little spot nestled in the shade of two big oak trees and just a few steps away from a small, gurgling creek.

The first thing we noticed as we pulled up to the campsite was that there were California quail everywhere. Seriously, everywhere. Not flocks, either—they moved in herds. Whole sections of ground were covered, absolutely blanketed in sheets of quail.

We left our tents and bags in the car for the time being and drove over to one of the major trailheads. Condors nest in caves high up in the cliffs, so we had to get some altitude to get a chance to see them. We decided to start out on the Moses Spring Trail—a nice warm-up hike before the vertical trek up the mountainside.

Hiking up the mountain, we crossed through several distinct habitat zones. Occasionally the elevation change can make for some pretty interesting overlap. Normally scrub jays prefer—as their name would suggest—lowland scrub, whereas Steller's jays like a bit more altitude and forest. But, at one point hiking up, we saw both perched side by side.

It was a great day for birds. We saw a big flock of American goldfinches, a few California towhees, a Nuttall's woodpecker, and a black-throated gray warbler—probably getting ready to begin its migration back south for the winter. Off in the distance, we heard a canyon wren, its lonesome descending call echoing across the rock faces, like a cartoon character falling off a cliff.

These were all excellent birds, but they weren't the one I was here for.

None of them were condors.

The trail led us past a small group of rock climbers resting on their crash mats and up to the mouth of a cave. A sign in front of the cave advised us that flashlights were required for entry. I turned on my headlamp and stepped inside.

These caves were not what you might ordinarily think of when you hear the word "cave." There were no stalactites or stalagmites, no glowing insects or crazy deformed cave slugs. The tunnels were created by a series of boulders that were rolled up on top of one another. It looked like the aftermath of a snowball fight between giants, and walking through the caves felt like exploring the underbelly of a rockslide. Light broke through the stones at odd angles and zigzagged its way down to us in faint bursts, giving hints of color to the moss that covered the ground at our feet. It was cooler in here as well.

The rangers were right to put up that flashlight sign. At times, the boulders clustered together pretty tightly, and Walter and I were plunged into total darkness. The path in front of us got narrower and narrower as it got harder to see. I tightened the strap on my headlamp and looked back to make sure Walter was doing all right. He was about ten paces behind me, his flashlight still packed away in his bag.

"Aren't you going to turn your light on?" I asked.

He laughed. "I can see just fine without it."

Moments later, I heard a thud behind me. "Ow," Walter muttered, and then he turned his light on.

The caves sloped up, and suddenly the tunnel was flooded with light. As we stepped out, we realized that we were now on top of the boulder field. We jogged up a couple of flights of stone steps and found ourselves looking out over a reservoir. A thin grove of trees lined the edge of the water at intervals on

the far shore. A snake swam lazily across the water's surface, its black-and-yellow-striped body glistening in the midday sun.

The reservoir was pretty small: Walter pointed out that it was roughly the size of an Olympic pool.

The Olympics were going on in Rio that week. It was all over the news. And for some reason, hearing the word "Olympic"—thinking about sports, about competition and medals—got me thinking about the audition I'd just had again.

Most Olympic sports have clear winners. The criteria for success in a foot race is purely objective. There are no extra points for style, haircut, or music choice. You are the best if and only if you have the best time or the most points. It's simple. There's something comforting about that kind of objectivity.

Acting is the exact opposite. It is purely subjective. Despite the awards given out every year, there are no clear and universally accepted ways to determine what makes one actor better than another. You go into an audition, and you worry about being a good actor, about portraying the role as honestly and compellingly as possible. But you worry about your acting because it is the only thing you have any control over.

A host of other factors can determine whether or not you get the role, and there's nothing you can do about them. Casting often depends on your social media following, on what producers you know, whether or not your previous films made money, whether or not you've been in the news lately, what kind of relationship your agents have with the casting office. And so on.

Just after college I met a casting director at a house party in LA. After we'd introduced ourselves, I asked him to tell me about his job. I wanted to know how hard it was to figure out who the best actor in the room was.

He laughed. "If all I had to do was say who the best actor in the room was, anybody could do my job," he said. "Also, I'd get to go home a hell of a lot earlier at night."

Maybe that's what we like so much about Olympic sports: when there are objective winners and losers, life feels a whole lot simpler and fairer. We can argue until we're blue in the face about whether or not Meryl Streep is the greatest living actor, citing opinions and personal preference, but the whole world agrees that Usain Bolt is the greatest living sprinter because, well, math. It's a rare and fascinating experience to have the entire world agree about something. How often do you get to see that?

Walter tapped me on my shoulder and broke me out of my daydreaming. "What's that over there?" he asked, pointing at a speck in the sky.

I looked up. It was definitely a bird. And it was big. Really big. Possibly even condor big. Reminding myself not to get too excited, I clutched my binoculars and lifted them to my face to get a closer look.

It was a golden eagle.

Son of a bitch.

Don't get me wrong, this was a pretty cool thing to see. It was, in fact, my first time ever seeing a golden eagle. By all accounts, I should have been dancing with joy.

But it wasn't a condor, and so I saved my dancing for later. It's bizarre seeing a bird you've always wanted to see and feeling disappointed by it. I felt bird-spoiled. Like the kid who gets a car for their sixteenth birthday but gets mad because it isn't an Audi.

Seeing the eagle meant that we were high enough up the mountain to start looking for condors, so we scanned the horizon with our binoculars as we walked along the water's edge. We had to be careful not to get tricked by any turkey vultures. Turkey vultures often get mistaken for condors, and condors often get mistaken for small planes. We saw both turkey vultures and small planes flying over the reservoir that afternoon, but no condors.

After a few minutes of scanning the sky to no avail, we heard footsteps on the trail behind us. We put our binoculars down and turned to see a couple in their thirties coming up the path. From the way they waved and greeted us it seemed like they wanted to stop and chat for a bit.

Walter and I introduced ourselves. It turned out the couple was visiting from Germany—the woman was in town for a scientific entrepreneurship conference, and her husband was tagging along for fun. He had a camera with him, and he was taking pictures of everything. He showed us some of his favorites from the day: pretty leaves, oddly shaped rocks, the sweaty T-shirt of a man they'd passed on the trail. He was a photo nut.

"You know, if you're looking for cool things to photograph, we just saw a snake swimming in the reservoir over there," I said, pointing to where we'd seen it a few minutes before.

The man let out an excited yip, grabbed his camera bag, and set off jogging toward the water. His wife looked down and noticed that Walter and I were wearing binoculars.

"Oh!" she said. "Are you two here to see the condor?"

We nodded.

"Have you seen it?" she asked.

"No, no luck yet," I said. "We were thinking we might have to hike up to the top to get a look at them."

She smiled and wished us luck. Apparently they had come to the park with the same goal. As we spoke, her husband came back, a little winded but happy. He'd gotten a good shot of the snake, he said.

Walter and I resumed our hike. As we said goodbye, the German couple was sitting down on a boulder so that the husband could show his wife his snake photos.

We left the Moses Spring Trail and got onto the High Peaks Trail, which would take us up to the summit. The sky was cloudless that day, just a wash of blue with blinding sunlight in the west. We hiked along, spotting birds as we went.

Birding up in the mountains, especially on a day like that, can be difficult. You're staring intently at a tiny black spot set against a sea of blue, and your eyes keep going out of focus, because, naturally, they want to avoid staring directly up at the sun for too long. It's tough to differentiate any clear markings when it's that sunny out and everything you're looking at is hundreds of yards away. If you're not careful, hope and blurred vision can mess with your head—you become convinced that a tiny black dot in the sky is something special, even though you have absolutely no evidence to support it.

The trail sloped upward and broke into a series of switchbacks, cutting its way up the mountainside. As we trudged our way along the second switchback, a merlin flew over our heads. A merlin—aside from being the name of a badass wizard who aged in reverse—is a neat little falcon. Back in medieval times, merlins were the official bird of choice for noblewomen. They called them "lady hawks," and they used them to hunt skylarks.

The switchbacks were getting steeper and steeper. We decided to take a quick break and rehydrate a little. As Walter and I shuffled along looking for a nice spot to sit, we spotted the German couple again—and they were in front of us? When we'd left them, they'd been sitting on a boulder, looking at pictures, and somehow they'd beaten us up the mountain to where we now saw them, also sitting on a boulder and looking at pictures.

They were like lazy teleporters.

When they saw us, they both waved enthusiastically and beckoned us over.

"How—how did you get in front of us?" I asked, still panting from the trek up.

My question seemed to be lost in translation. The wife smiled and shrugged. "Ja, you know," she said, then nudged her husband. "Show them the photo. We saw the condor!"

We were shocked. "Here?" Walter asked. I looked up at the sky. Nothing. Just blue as far as the eye could see.

"Ja," the husband said, cycling through the photos on his screen to find the picture.

"Are you sure?" I asked.

"White on the wings, ja?" he said, his nose still buried in his camera.

Walter couldn't believe it. "Yeah!" he said. "Yeah, white on the wings."

The California condor has an unmistakable strip of pure white shooting across the underside of each of its wings.

"Aha!" the husband cried, finding the photo and handing the camera to us.

On the screen was a perfectly clear, crisp, beautifully captured photo of a turkey vulture.

"See the white?" he said, pointing at the tips of the vulture's wings. They were indeed pale—a light, silvery gray that verged on white—but nothing like the shocking white strip on a condor's wings.

This was awkward. Walter gave me a look. We had a heartbreaking decision to make. Did we tell him the truth, or did we let him go home, thinking he'd seen a condor when in fact he hadn't? Maybe a friend from home would tell him the truth about the bird. Maybe not; maybe he'd never find out. Maybe he'd always believe that he'd seen a condor. He'd go to his grave with that beautiful, happy lie.

I've heard birding described as the last bastion of honesty. We don't have big competitions, rivalries, or races. There is no world's greatest birder. There's no way for us to measure or rate success like you do in sports. If somebody says they've seen a bird, there's no real way to confirm or deny that they saw what they say they did unless they took a picture. The birding community as a whole depends on message boards run by enthusiasts from every corner of the earth. The honor code is all we have.

Most of the time, when you're out birding, it's just you and yourself, and if you can't be honest with yourself, what's the point? Birding cannot exist without honesty.

We decided to tell the Germans that they hadn't actually seen a condor, that it had just been a turkey vulture.

They were crestfallen. We felt terrible. The wife whispered

to me, "Ah, you shouldn't have told us." Meanwhile, the husband began to scroll through his camera, showing us all the photos he had taken of the vulture, trying to prove to us that it had, in fact, been a condor.

We felt bad and decided to get out of there. Walter led the way as we resumed hiking up the switchbacks, and we were quickly out of sight of the Germans.

As we hiked on, I kept glancing up at the sky. Turkey vultures circled overheard, but definitely no condors up there. Not yet, at least. Walter was looking up, too. "I wish we could find some rangers," he said. "They could probably tell us where to look."

As he spoke, we rounded a corner and found ourselves face-to-face with a park ranger. Walter practically ran into him. I think we may have seemed a bit too excited.

"You guys okay?" he said.

"Totally. We're hoping to get a look at some of the condors today. Has anyone reported any sightings of them today?"

He shook his head. "Not my area, guys. You'd have to ask Condor Crew."

"Condor Crew?" Walter asked.

"Yeah," he said, offering no other explanation. "They'd be the ones to ask." Apparently this ranger was not going to be the solution to all of our condor problems.

We walked on. I never did find out what Condor Crew was.

Eventually, the switchbacks ended and we found ourselves on top of the mountain, surrounded by the pinnacles themselves. Pinnacles National Park is named for the sharp, pointy crags that line the top of its tallest mountain, jutting out at all angles like a mouth full of rotten teeth. Despite that description, they are a gorgeous sight, and there are no trees at that altitude, so standing among them you can see for miles in every direction.

We scrambled across the pinnacles and found a nice spot to perch and look out with our binoculars. There were vultures everywhere. I kept thinking each and every one of them was a condor. I can see how the German couple had made that mistake. The two different species look so similar at a distance—they were all just specks in the sky. I kept feeling a small jolt of excitement at each new little black dot, but none of them were what I hoped they would be.

California condors weren't always such a rarity in this part of the country. Hundreds of them once filled the sky. The land surrounding pinnacles is mostly agricultural, so pesticides took out a big percentage of the condor population, but that wasn't the only factor in their decline.

Johnny Cash helped too.

He had a ranch up in Ventura County, and he used to throw sloppy, debaucherous parties up there. Then in the mid-1960s, Cash got really into party buses. He would drive them out onto his property, hook up rows and rows of speakers, and blare out Christmas music as loud as he could into the mountains around him. But then one time his party bus overheated, and he set fire to the entire Las Casitas National Forest. The fire spread across three mountains, and hundreds of acres went up in flame.

At the time of the fire, the area was home to fifty-three California condors. Supposedly, Johnny Cash killed forty-nine of them.

When asked about the fire, he was decidedly unapologetic,

telling a judge, "I don't care about you or your damn yellow buzzards."

I don't think Johnny Cash and I would have liked each other.

Up in the sky, a single bird was flying off toward the horizon. It was just a speck, but it was a massive speck—much bigger than the buzzards circling nearby. I pulled out my binoculars. In the lenses, I could make out its wide black wings. But I couldn't see anything else. It was too far away.

I asked Walter, "Do you think that was it?"

He shrugged. He'd seen the bird, too, but neither of us could get a good enough look to ID it. If it was a turkey vulture, it was the biggest turkey vulture I'd ever seen. But I couldn't be positive that it wasn't.

I was defiant. It must have been a condor. What else could it have been?

I sat down and took out my bird journal. When I first started birding, I hated the idea of keeping a "life list." It felt like I was collecting birds. I thought that keeping track of them—writing down what I'd seen and where—would somehow cheapen the experience. I worried that I was making my hobby competitive. I had this image in my head of two birders comparing life lists, and one of them walking away as the "winner."

I've since come around to the practice, though. A life list is my own personal diary of what I've seen—and it wouldn't be worth anything to anyone else. Also, I have a terrible memory, so I need it.

I opened the book to the first available page and wrote down the date. After the date, I wrote "California condor" and then, to the right of that . . .

I couldn't do it. I couldn't say for certain that I'd actually seen it. I would never really know for sure, and it wasn't something I was willing to lie about. The honor code really sucks sometimes.

I scribbled "Better view needed" into the margin next to the condor's name and closed my book.

Walter squinted at the sun. It was lower now. It would be dark in a couple of hours, and we still needed to set our tents up down below.

As we began our descent, we saw the German couple appear again just over the ridge of the pinnacles. I considered waving goodbye, but they hadn't seen us yet, and I was worried they might still be upset about the turkey vulture. I didn't want to rub salt in the wound. I hope that the Germans had better luck with the condors than we did.

We walked down flights of steps that had been jackhammered into the mountainside by some brave construction crew. The trail home was faster—going downhill usually is. We passed a rock on our right that was absolutely covered in turkey vultures. They eyed us interestedly as we walked by—waiting to eat us in case we didn't make it down the mountain.

"Good ol' Mount Turkey Vulture," Walter said. I scowled. Up by the pinnacles, so many vultures had disappointed me when I'd mistaken them for condors. There was a smug, almost mocking, look on their bald, ugly faces.

If I can stick with the metaphor of condors being a stand-in for big acting roles, then turkey vultures are like auditions. Every time you see one, you think, "Oh my God, this could be it. This could be the big one."

But more often than not what you're seeing isn't a condor at all. It's just a big ol' turkey vulture.

We hiked on in silence for about half an hour. From time to time, a sparrow or a towhee would fly by us, but we weren't really paying much attention to the little stuff at that point. We were tired and hungry, and dinner and sleep were calling.

Near the end of the hike, I heard a light rustling of wings. An American kestrel came cruising along the side of the slope we were walking along. It landed in a tree a short distance in front of us.

I wouldn't say I have a favorite bird, but kestrels are definitely up there. They're hands-down the coolest.

American kestrels are small falcons—and no joke, they're red, white, and blue in color. I've seen one hover in place for minutes on end, then cartwheel through the air to nab some unwitting insect.

Kestrels—and falcons in general—are more closely related to parrots than to other kinds of hawks. I like to imagine they're little carnivorous parrots, though maybe that's not quite biologically correct.

Seeing the kestrel cheered me up. My feet were feeling lighter as we arrived at the end of the trail and began our short drive back to the campsite.

Heading back felt like driving through the opening scene of *Bambi*. There were quail all over the road. We passed mama deer with their fawns trailing behind them. Flocks of turkeys bobbed about in the bushes.

When we got back to the campsite and started setting up our tents, a cheeky raccoon came right up to beg for food. I turned to Walter: "We're trapped in a Disney movie."

It felt good being back at camp, surrounded by animals, feeling like a welcome guest in a wild habitat. I started thinking about my audition again, and about the condor. My mind wandered.

I think the thing about birding—about loving the outdoors in general—is that to do it, you need to find something in nature that is just yours, something that nobody else can touch or take away from you. It isn't about one specific bird. You can't be a birder who only wants to see one bird. That's not birding; that's an obsession. When you become a birder, you do it as a life plan.

Acting's the same. You have to find something you love about it that doesn't depend on anybody else. It isn't about booking one specific role on one specific day. If you just keep concentrating on the things you're not seeing, if you keep focusing on not getting the role, you're kind of missing the point. Nobody has ever seen every single bird on the planet. It would be impossible. No actor has booked every single role—the world would just be one giant monologue.

We had set out that morning to see the California condor. We hadn't seen it, and I'd felt grumpy all day as a result. But I'd seen half a dozen birds that I had never seen before. It was a day of discovery for me. The only choice I had was whether or not I embraced that discovery.

There would be other birds, other days spent outside, other chances to see the skies filled with flying colors. One bad day doesn't magically make you stop being a birder. One bad audition doesn't mean you aren't an actor anymore.

For dinner, we made pasta on a gas camping stove. We hadn't seen any condors, but it had been an undeniably good day for birds. I popped open a bottle of Apothic Red—my mom's favorite wine—and poured it into our metal camping mugs.

I turned to Walter and held up my mug. "To the American kestrel," I said.

"To the turkey vulture," he replied.

After we ate, we sat outside our tents looking at stars. Walter asked me if I knew any of the constellations.

"I know Orion, but that's about it."

"I actually know the bird ones," he said.

I didn't know there were any bird constellations.

He pointed at a big star above us, and I followed him as he traced a cross in the sky with his finger, connecting the first star to half a dozen others. "Cygnus," he said. "The Swan."

"It looks more like a cross," I said.

"Yeah, it's also called the Northern Cross. The Greeks knew it as Cygnus."

Walter pointed up to another star.

"See that one?" he asked.

I squinted. I could just make out a dim star where his finger was pointing.

"Follow it down and to the left," he said. "See it? Now from there, go to the right and a little down."

I got lost. Walter had to trace it out two more times before I could see what he was pointing at: Aquila, Zeus's eagle.

"Aquila carried Zeus's thunderbolts for him when he fought the Titans," he said. "At the end of his life, Zeus placed Aquila among the stars to thank him for his service."

Constellations always seem to overwhelm me with emotions. Looking up at the stars that night, I felt the usual cliché: I was a small and insignificant cog in the larger workings of the vast and limitless cosmos, and it was a humbling experience.

But I also felt the cliché's exact opposite. I realized that I was sitting there staring up at the exact same stars that people had stared at, named, and personified thousands of years before I was ever born. Before my country ever existed. Before my language was first spoken. These stories and these names had come down through an endless stream of shared narratives, shared values, beliefs, and stories. And they had arrived here. At the dawn of the twenty-first century, I was listening to tales and learning names from the beginning of humanity. The name Aquila had not faded with time. Nor had Cygnus. The names had outlived their creators by millennia.

I didn't make it into my tent that night. I fell asleep under the stars. Shortly before dawn, I woke up shivering and crawled into the tent, wrapping myself up like a burrito in my sleeping bag.

I tried to go back to sleep, but I was wide awake.

I pulled my sleeping bag around my shoulders and stepped out of the tent. The sun was poking out from behind the mountains to the east. I sat on a stump and watched it rise. Within half an hour, the campsite was flooded with radiant pink and orange tones.

I walked out into the street to get a better view of the sunrise. As I did, I heard the distant patter of small feet—dozens of them—running along the road. It sounded like a stampede of pygmy buffalo was coming up behind me.

A herd of quail rounded a corner and hustled toward me. They moved as one, curving this way and that like a rushing stream as they overtook the road. Despite their minute size, I was genuinely frightened. A headline flashed in my head: ACTOR TRAMPLED TO DEATH BY QUAIL AT SUNRISE VISTA.

I didn't know where I could run to avoid them, so I stood my ground.

The quail rushed forward, their tiny feet pounding against the asphalt in a muffled din. I closed my eyes as the first quail reached my feet. This was it. Time to get pecked to death.

I felt something soft brush against my right ankle. Then against my left. I felt wind and fluff and dust breezing lightly by my calves. I opened my eyes.

The herd had not stopped, nor even slowed. The quail continued to rocket down the street, but they had parted at my feet like water around a stone, doing their best to avoid this unexpected human obstruction in their path. It was incredible. I felt like the Moses of fowl. Or perhaps I was a quail whisperer.

When the quail had passed, I walked back to camp and sat on a tree stump. I waited for Walter to get up.

When he appeared, we agreed to grab breakfast on the road instead of cooking up something at the campsite. He had a lunch date, and I needed to get back to LA for a fund-raiser that night. We loaded up the car and hit the road.

On the way out of the park, we stopped at the ranger station to use their bathrooms. As we were getting back in our car, a golf cart pulled into the parking lot near us. The park ranger behind the wheel waved good morning.

"Just getting in or heading out?" he asked.

"Heading out," Walter said.

The ranger nodded. "You get any good hiking in?"

"Yeah, we went up the High Peaks Trail yesterday."

"See any condors up there?"

I shook my head. "No, sir. No condors this trip. Just turkey vultures and a couple of falcons."

"And some Germans," Walter added.

The ranger didn't seem surprised. "Yeah, they're up there, but they can be pretty tough to spot." He wasn't talking about the Germans. "Tell you what, if you boys really want to see condors, you might try the Grand Canyon next time."

"To see the California condor?" I said.

"They've got a lot of them out there."

He nodded goodbye and whistled as he lumbered over to the ranger station.

We got back in the car and drove out of the park. The road back to LA was rural at first—and at times there was only one lane going in each direction. We'd been on the road for about fifteen minutes when I saw a flash of feathers dart across the highway and perch on a tree in front of us.

It was a black bird with white on its wings.

I slammed on the brakes. The car came to a screeching halt in the middle of the highway.

"Ian, what the hell are you doing?" Walter yelled. "That's not a condor!"

"I know it isn't," I said, taking off my seatbelt. "It's a yellow-billed magpie. I've never seen one before."

We pulled over to the side of the road and got out. Sure enough, there it was, perched high in the branches of a tree just off the road: a yellow-billed magpie. A gorgeous blue stripe circled its belly like an inner tube. After a few moments, the magpie flew off to continue with its day, and Walter and I got back in the car to continue with ours.

I turned to Walter: "Want to go to the Grand Canyon next week? See if we can spot any California condors in Arizona?"

He smiled. "John'll be better by then so we can drag him along, too."

NOT THAT

KIND OF BIRD

Sometimes it's hard to trust your own eyes. When what you see doesn't match your expectations, your brain can play tricks on you. It's hard to know if you're ever actually seeing what you think you are.

I moved to Laurel Canyon after the third season of the show. I'd spend most Sunday mornings playing with my dogs in the yard. The house I lived in backed up to a hill, which Mochi and Bailey would run all over.

Sometimes we'd play fetch, and I'd throw a ball up the slope. They'd tear after it, then trip over their legs as they raced back to me.

Mochi wouldn't always bring back the ball. Sometimes she'd bring a stick instead—and once she brought me a freshly up-rooted rosebush.

One such Sunday morning, I let the dogs out and went back inside to get some coffee. The kitchen looked out onto the yard, and I glanced out to see Mochi and Bailey hightailing it after a squirrel.

I grabbed some half-and-half out of the fridge, then looked back out the window again to make sure the dogs weren't getting into trouble. All three of them were romping around, tails wagging.

Wait—what the hell? I only have two dogs.

I leaned over the sink to get a better look outside. There weren't three dogs in the yard. There was Mochi. There was Bailey. And there was a coyote chasing them.

I bolted out the door, waving my arms and shouting. I grabbed a shovel on the ground next to a recently replanted rosebush and ran to save my two helpless dogs from this vicious apex predator.

As I crossed the yard, all three of them—Mochi, Bailey, and the coyote—stopped what they were doing and stared at me. The coyote sniffed the air, then ran off into the bushes. Bailey looked at me and whined.

The coyote hadn't been trying to eat them. He had been playing with them!

The dogs had made a new friend, and I had chased him off with a shovel.

I set the shovel down and called the dogs over. I had been right to scare the coyote off. Coyotes are dangerous. They eat cats and maim dogs . . . and they had looked so happy playing together in the yard.

"Come on, guys. Let's go inside." I ushered the dogs into the house, stopping at the door to take one last look around in case their coyote friend had come back. He had totally vanished.

A few Sundays later, I was again out in the backyard with the dogs. The coyote hadn't come back to visit yet, but I'd been keeping an eye out for him.

As I stood there, waiting for Mochi and Bailey to quit wrestling over a ball and bring it back to me, I spotted a small bird perched out on a dead branch of an oak tree. It was mostly black—it looked like a little flycatcher.

Some flycatchers are notoriously difficult to identify. There's a family of about a dozen of them, called the *Empidonax* flycatchers, which are nearly indistinguishable. Early naturalists would kill birds they were studying in order to see them up close, but killing an empid for identification purposes would be nearly pointless—the only way to reliably tell them apart is their song. And, to add to the fun, if *Empidonax* flycatchers aren't at their summer breeding grounds, they don't sing.

Anyway, those flycatchers are mostly gray, and this bird was mostly black, so I didn't need to worry about its song. The bird sallied out from the branch and caught a bug in midair, then returned to its perch.

My first inclination was that it was a black phoebe, a fairly common type of flycatcher that nested in the neighborhood. But the bird wasn't that far away, and with my naked eye I could see it had a crimson breast and patches of white on the wings.

I watched as the bird skated around the trunk of the tree,

flashing white feathers on the sides of its tail. I was looking for field marks—parts of the bird that are characteristic markers to help distinguish it from other species. The bird I was looking at now had what looked like little white bags under its eyes—giving it an oddly sleep-deprived appearance.

Black phoebes don't have any of these features. They're all black with a white breast.

It suddenly dawned on me that I was looking at an extremely rare bird for Los Angeles: a painted redstart.

Mochi dropped a broom at my feet and began whining. Not wanting to take my eyes off the redstart, I tried to shush her as I backpedaled toward the house to grab a pair of binoculars, maybe even a camera. The bird was spiraling up through the branches of the tree.

I got to the door and dashed inside—but in that short interval, the bird disappeared. By the time I got back outside, I couldn't find it again. I'd seen it for just the briefest of moments—so short that I could barely believe my own eyes.

After searching the trees in my yard for a good half an hour, and then walking up and down the street, I gave up and went back inside. I knew what I'd seen, but I pulled out a bird book to confirm it anyway. I found the right page in the book and checked all the field marks. It was definitely a painted redstart. I was sure of it.

Where was Sophia? Out working?! Damnit. I needed to high-five someone.

That night, I met up with my buddy Walter at a bar in Highland Park. I'd told him I had some really exciting news to share, and he was just about the only person I knew who'd understand how excited I was to have seen a painted redstart in my yard.

"Bullshit," he said, putting down his beer.

"I swear to God," I told him.

"I thought exciting news meant you'd won the lottery, or booked a film, or . . . something that was actually true."

"I'm not making this up! Why would I make this up?"

Walter shook his head. "Did you take a picture?"

"I didn't have time—but it had the red belly, the white patches on the wings . . ."

"Maybe you saw a black phoebe and it caught the light in a weird way."

I'd expected Walter to be just as excited as I was, but now he was trashing my birding abilities.

"You're just jealous," I said, exasperated.

"I'm not jealous, I swear. I think you're just a little overenthusiastic about birds—and you thought you saw something that wasn't actually what you were seeing. Painted redstarts only pop up around here once every few years."

"But they do pop up!"

Walter finished off his beer with a big gulp. "When you were a kid, did you tell everyone you'd seen Santa Claus at your house? Did you lie about that, too?" he asked.

We agreed to talk about something else.

Walter and I had that conversation about two years ago, and to this day, whenever he doesn't believe something I'm saying, he'll ask, "Is this another one of your redstart stories?"

It's easy to misidentify birds when they zip by in the woods and you only glimpse them for a few seconds. But it isn't just birds—or coyotes. We do the same thing with people.

Ever since *Pretty Little Liars* started airing, people have come up to me in restaurants and bars to tell me they recognize me from somewhere. They know they've seen my face, but they can't place it. They'll ask if I went to their church, or if we went to high school together back in Minnesota.

One time I was at a restaurant in Los Feliz called the Alcove. It's got a big outdoor patio area under a few giant oak trees. As I was finishing up my lunch, I heard a muffled gasp from the table behind me. I looked around, and out of the corner of my eye I saw two teenage girls staring at me. One of them had her hand over her mouth. The girls were clearly fans of the show, and I heard them start to argue.

"It's him!" one of them whispered, under her breath.

"There's no way."

"It is! It's definitely him."

I turned back to my food and tried to stop eavesdropping, but I could hear the girls continuing their debate over whether I was actually me. Finally, the one who insisted that I was "him" whispered, "Look at his hair. It *is* him."

"Actually," the friend said. "I think you might be right."

"Told you so."

"Oh my God. What do we do? Do we say something? Should we say hi?"

"No! Don't be an idiot. Leave him alone."

The friend, now fully convinced, wasn't backing down. "I'm going to go over and talk to him," she said.

"Don't!" the first girl hissed.

At this point, I was beginning to feel bad. I felt like my presence in this café was becoming an issue. I quickly paid my bill and stood up to go.

As I did, both girls fell silent and pretended to look the other way. They were smiling.

I couldn't resist. As I passed by them, I leaned in and whispered, "It *is* me."

The girls flipped out.

"Oh my God!" the first one cried, shaking her hands by the side of her face.

"Holy shit!" the friend squealed. "You have no idea how much this means to us. I'm like—I'm your biggest fan, Mr. Marsden."

Oh no. Oh shit.

I'm not James Marsden.

I tried to set the record straight as smoothly as possible.

"I'm so sorry," I said. "I'm—my name's Ian. Ian Harding. I am an actor, but I'm not . . . I'm not who you think I am."

The girls' faces immediately fell. Their smiles vanished.

"I'm on a TV show. It's called—you know what, never mind, doesn't matter."

This was not going well.

"Look, I'm sorry for the confusion. I didn't mean to lead you on."

A voice in my head whispered: *Your name is Ian Harding. You are thirty years old. And right now you are apologizing for not being James Marsden.*

I couldn't think of anything else to say, so I excused myself and left the two crestfallen teenagers to finish their meal in peace.

Nowadays, when people come up to me and say they know me from somewhere but they can't quite place it, I tell them I just have one of those faces.

One of those James Marsden-y faces.

'SPLORES
WITH KEEGAN

Keegan Allen, dear friend, costar, and photographer extraordinaire, sat across from me at Dialog Cafe, a small family-run spot in West Hollywood, just down the street from the more intimidatingly named Viper Room and Rockhard Films.

"So how long's this video need to be?" he asked.

"Only like six seconds. You can shoot it on your phone."

"So I don't need any of these today?" He pointed to three cameras hanging around his neck.

I had told him we were going hiking, and that on the hike we would have to take photos that I had to post on Instagram. Keegan dressed appropriately, while I, on the other hand, had opted not to shave or sleep the night before.

We polished off our now watery iced coffees. Looking out the window, I took in the traffic on Sunset Boulevard. Houses dotted the hills above us, and the sunshine was finally cutting through the June Gloom.

In the café, we were surrounded by young parents, all of whom seemed to be shockingly well rested. The shop was crowded with baby strollers, but none of the babies had cried even once. They all just lay there with these eerily serene looks on their calm faces. Can babies get Botox, I wondered? Maybe they couldn't cry.

Several patrons sat with open laptops resting next to half-eaten pastries. Screenwriters most likely. Or accountants. Or anyone really, but I always assume that if you're in a café with a laptop open, you're probably writing the next *Jaws*.

"Thanks again for helping me shoot this," I said.

"Of course, man." Keegan wiped the lens of his Leica. "And don't feel bad about doing this stuff for money. Everyone does it. Besides, you're helping your family, and in a few months no one will remember or care about a little video you shot in the woods."

I'd been having second thoughts about this photo shoot since the moment I signed on. I was beginning to worry that my social media page might someday look like the side of a race car—plastered with ads and logos, having little if anything to do with the personality of the page's original creator. It was a scary thought.

"How are you getting the photos to the company that hired you?" Keegan asked.

"I think I'll probably just email them over. I can do that right?"

Keegan sighed dramatically. "Oh thank God, Ian. I thought you were about to say passenger pigeon."

"Hilarious. First off, those are extinct. Second, you're thinking of a homing pigeon, which are actually still used—"

"Did people ever actually ride those?"

". . ."

"Like, passenger pigeons. Back in the day. Could they ever actually ride them? Like how big were they? Were they—" He spread his arms out wide. "Were they bus-sized?"

"Are you asking me if *The Flintstones* happened in real life?"

Keegan stared at me in silence for a moment then downed the remainder of his iced coffee.

Here's a sentence I don't always like to say out loud: I have a branding agent. Her name is Jean Kwolek, and she's lovely.

Jean attaches her clients—mostly actors—to various commercial campaigns, which supplement their income between acting gigs. Look really good with three-day stubble? She can help you sell whiskey. Never had dandruff? Easy: hair commercials. It isn't always that blatant, either. There are increasingly lucrative ways for people in the public eye to make a little dough on the side without looking like total sellouts.

That's an interesting word, by the way. I struggle with it constantly: sellout. The term has always carried a strange gravity in my mind, and it was echoing back and forth in my head that day. I felt a bit off using my acting for purely financial gain.

But, two months earlier, my sister Sarah had been granted a slot in a highly selective Directors Guild training program in

New York. Both she and I had rejoiced at the news of this opportunity, but our rejoicing quickly came to an end when we began to consider how she would pay for it. Sarah would be working as a PA in New York, and would have a couple of hours here and there to Uber or walk dogs on the side, but she wouldn't be making nearly enough money to support herself in New York City.

For Sarah, this opportunity was a dream come true. I gave it some thought, and I decided to play fairy god-brother. I called my sister and told her I wanted to cover her rent for the two years she would be living in the Big Apple. That way she could focus entirely on learning and working in the field she's always loved. The news brought tears to her eyes, and when I told my accountant about it, she nearly cried as well.

After I told Sarah that I intended to cover her rent, I immediately emailed Jean and my manager, Vikram. I asked them to find me campaign work—anything they could find that didn't involve an actual deal with the devil.

"So how far away is this waterfall?" Keegan asked, holding one of his cameras up to the window and snapping away at the passing scenery.

We were driving along the Angeles Crest Highway as it wound its way up from La Cañada Flintridge through the Angeles National Forest. We were headed to Switzer Falls.

"Can't be more than another twenty minutes or so."

"Did they say why they wanted this waterfall in particular?"

"No, it was my idea. The company just needs me to tape my-self having fun. I told them I wanted to do a hike because it's something I actually do."

A short while later, I spotted our turn and hung a sharp right. We passed some serious-looking road spikes and pro-ceeded down a winding hill toward Switzer Falls.

The last time I went on this hike was in 2014. It had been a wettish winter—not wet enough to break the drought, but it was a welcome change for us—and the falls had taken on the appearance of, well, actual waterfalls. I had hiked out early one morning after a late winter rain with a few friends from col-lege. The falls had bellowed loudly as we approached them at the end of the trail. I had put my head under, and the force of the water blew off my hat.

That was then. This was now. And by "now" I mean it was a Tuesday in July, and the weather service was predicting an-other day of record-breaking heat.

We pulled into a parking spot by a picnic table.

"It looks pretty parched out here. Are you sure there's any water going over the falls right now?" Keegan asked.

I wasn't.

"Push comes to shove, I have a gallon of water in the back of my car and maybe you can just pour that over my head? Then like, throw some leaves at me?"

"Sure, man. I could do that."

We walked over to the trailhead. Ten yards from the start of the hike, a man slowly walked by us, carrying a walking stick. His face was stoic, lost deep in thought. I recognized him. I looked to Keegan, who had noticed him as well. We kept walking, paying more attention than necessary to the trees above our heads, overcompensating in our attempt not to disturb the wistful hiker.

A hundred yards down the trail, Keegan and I, now alone, turned to each other and simultaneously said: "Moby."

I was a huge Moby fan in high school. His music got me through puberty. I've even used Moby songs to prepare for auditions.

"Crazy. Of all the places," I said.

"What are you talking about?" Keegan asked. "Moby belongs in the forest. If we'd bumped into him at, like, Bed Bath & Beyond, that would have been weird."

I turned and looked back up the trail toward the parking lot.

"I kind of wish we had said something."

Keegan laughed. "Well, we can always creep over and watch him from one of those trees with your binoculars if you want."

I stopped in my tracks. I pictured my binoculars, my little Nikons, sitting on my kitchen counter. I'd forgotten them at home.

"Damnit!" I yelled.

My expletive echoed through the canyon, scaring birds from their nests. Birds that I could have seen, if I'd remembered my binoculars.

"Everything okay?" Keegan asked.

"I forgot my binoculars."

"I'm not sure forgetting your binoculars warrants that kind of response." His voice sounded like a high school guidance counselor's.

He was right. I had promised him a short jaunt in the woods.

I hadn't said anything about birding. Still, the anxious bird-nerd in me worried that I might spot something and not be able to get a good look at it.

We continued onward, sans specs.

The trail to Switzer Falls is a four-and-half-mile trek—out and back—with several other paths forking out from it along the way. It starts pleasantly enough: there's a small paved section of the path for the first third of a mile. Eventually the road tapers off into a dirt-and-rock-strewn trail. Several streams intersect the path until roughly the mile-and-a-half marker. Then the trail snakes upward, away from the water. This section continues for some time, rising slowly, before the trail turns back down, leading to a forested canyon.

In the middle of the canyon, there's a sign that states—dauntingly—TRAIL NOT MAINTAINED.

It's not actually that rough. What the sign should say is, THERE'S STILL A TRAIL. DON'T WORRY. JUST FOLLOW THE FOOTPRINTS ON THE GROUND AND THE SOUND OF THE FALLING WATER AND YOU SHOULD BE ALL GOOD. HEADS UP, THOUGH: THERE ARE A COUPLE OF FALLEN LOGS NEAR THE END SO LOOK OUT FOR THOSE.

A lot of people turn around at the TRAIL NOT MAINTAINED sign. But if you keep going, you get to see Switzer Falls in all their glory. And they are worth it. The falls themselves are about fifty feet high. The water shoots out from the top, hitting a landing about halfway down and splashing out in all directions. At the base of the falls is a swimming hole when there's enough water.

Because not everyone makes it past the TRAIL NOT MAIN-
TAINED sign, the falls are usually deserted, especially on week-
days. It's a wonderful place to get away and clear your mind, as
Moby apparently knows as well.

There was a thwack thwack thwack above our heads. Something was making a racket.

Keegan looked to the canopy, scanning bare limbs and
dead branches. "That's a woodpecker I'm guessing?" he asked.

"You're right, though it's a little too high up to see what kind."

"What kinds live around here?"

I couldn't tell if Keegan truly cared or was simply asking
out of politeness.

"There are a few different species. Maybe three or four."

"What are their names? How do you tell them apart—by
the noise they make?"

"Yeah, sometimes."

I don't know why I felt shy. I knew the answers to his questions. I turned and looked at Keegan. He seemed genuinely
curious.

"You're really not supposed to do this, because it messes
with the wildlife, but check this out."

I pulled out my phone and opened the Sibley bird app. I
typed "woodpecker" into the search bar. Twelve options came
up. Judging by our altitude and the type of forest we were in—
and the fact that a few of the dead trees around us had an unmistakable honeycomb pattern running up their sides—I had
an idea of what the racket above might be. I opened the page
titled "Acorn Woodpecker."

"Watch this," I said.

I hit play. My phone emitted a series of shrieks and cackles high into the forest canopy. It sounded like a gaggle of angry clowns at a young child's last birthday party before he embarked on a lifetime of therapy.

The recording came to an end and a few seconds passed. We stood around, waiting for something to happen.

A few feet away, there was an oak tree with a dead branch protruding from its side. Though the sun illuminated the length of it, neither of us had noticed the branch until now. A sudden flicker of shadow fell across the top of it. I blinked, and suddenly there they were: three acorn woodpeckers, perched not twenty feet away from us, their beady yellow eyes fixed on my phone.

I held the phone over my head, then pressed play again on the same recording.

The three birds shot toward us, missing our heads by inches. Keegan's hair was blown to the side by the wake of their flight. They cackled as they disappeared into the woods.

"That was amazing!" Keegan said, slapping me on the back. He was clearly impressed by my cellphone's godlike ability to call the birds down from the treetops.

I suddenly felt silly for feeling shy earlier. Keegan and I have worked through breakups together, the passing of family members, and—perhaps most memorably—the near death of his beloved cat Minin from ingested hair ties. Birds shouldn't have been a big deal.

"Can we do it again?" he asked. "That was sick. Do you have any other animals on there? Like, could we call some deer or something?"

"Yeah, let's get some bears over here while we're at it. Maybe even call in a few rattlesnakes. We'll have a party!"

Keegan's smile evaporated. "Wait, but, not really though, right?"

"No, not really. It's a bird app. It's only birds. And we probably shouldn't do that again, anyway."

We stood there for a moment. Keegan seemed a little disappointed.

I took a few steps down the trail, then turned around. "I didn't know you were afraid of snakes," I said.

"Hate 'em."

"When did that start?"

"When I was a kid. I had few encounters with them, and they were never good. One time, I was driving in the car with my mom, and a snake came up to the passenger side and tried to eat our tire. That was it for me, man. I was done. I know everyone always says, 'They're more afraid of you than you are of them,' but that's bullshit, man. If that thing wasn't afraid of a Chevy, why the hell would it be scared of me?"

We continued to talk as we made our way up the shaded canyon to the falls. As we walked, Keegan snapped a few shots of me. I couldn't remember if the company wanted me to do any other media—all I remembered was they wanted a video— so a few extra pictures of me out in nature looking sexy and mildly confused couldn't hurt.

We heard the falls before we saw them. Magically, there was still some water spilling down to a small pond at the base.

Keegan pulled out his phone. "Get over there, man. Time to sell your soul."

I scrambled around the rocks to the base of the falls, and called back to Keegan:

"You ready?"

"Do it!" he yelled.

I dunked my head underwater and then whipped it back, sending a rainbow of glistening droplets into the air.

Willow Smith has a song about whipping her hair back and forth—it should come with a disclaimer. Whipping your hair back and forth is painful: the result is less fun and fancy-free and more dizzy and neck pain-y.

Keegan, standing about thirty feet away, called out, "Do it again, man. I didn't catch that one."

Time for take two. I doused my head in the pond and let it soak for a moment. Then, really selling it this time, I whipped my hair back up and out of the water. I felt something pop—in my shoulder, of all places—and I rolled sideways into a pile of rotting wood.

Keegan remained where he was, squinting at the screen of his iPhone.

"Did you get it?" I asked, still lying on the ground.

He shook his head. "Let's try it again."

I resumed my position on all fours above the puddle at the foot of the falls, and whipped back once more. And then again. After a few more takes, Keegan stopped me.

"Can I ask you something?" he said.

"Shoot."

"Why are you so set on this? They said you can do anything, right? Why not do something that doesn't involve soaking your head in giardia?"

He had a good point. I stood and brushed off my knees. "I

don't know. It's like a ritual, I guess. I have this thing that I do whenever I go on a hike—I've done it since I was a kid. If I see a body of water at the end of the hike, I just have to dunk my head into it."

"Like a baptism?" Keegan's face looked a bit incredulous.

"I guess. Like a cleansing thing."

Keegan squinted at the phone again then looked back at me. "Dude haven't you already been baptized enough?"

"I don't know. I want to make it at least seem authentic. I don't want it to look like I'm not trying. If I have to sell something, I at least want to make it matter. So I want to do my little ritual, and I know it's stupid, but I want to pay homage, I guess, to the woods. Or something. But looking at it now, I realize we're in a drought, and bathing in a waterfall when there's a drought doesn't really seem right."

Keegan looked serious.

"I hear you, man. But honestly this is as authentic as you're going to get. You freaking hiked here. You made me hike here. For a four-second video for—what does the company do again?"

"Online music sharing."

"Yeah, for online music sharing. That's not half-assing it. That's full-assing it. I mean that's a whole lot of ass, Ian. You've got more ass than I'll ever have."

"Because I'm fat?"

"Yeah. Because you're fat," he said, smiling. "Now get your fat, horrible face back into that waterfall and let's send your sister to band camp."

"It's not band camp, Keegan—"

"Back in the waterfall!"

I dunked my head back into the pond, and Keegan circled around, trying to find the best angle for the shot. After a few more takes, I started hopping around the rocks, striking super-hero poses for the camera and trying my best to balance on one leg.

"Try to look thoughtful. Like high school yearbook-y," Keegan hollered over the sound of the falls.

I raised one leg and put it on a rock in front of me. I tilted my head a little and tried to look pensive. My back leg started to slip, and I looked down to catch myself. As I looked down, I noticed that I was not the only thing basking on the rocks that afternoon. I jumped backward and jogged over to Keegan.

"What's up?" he said, putting down the phone.

"Want to see something cool?"

His face fell, and his voice grew small. "There's a snake in those rocks, isn't there?"

"Yes. Yes there is."

He closed his eyes and took a deep breath. His fists were clenched, knuckles white. We stood in silence for a moment, listening to the soft patter of the falls behind us. The birds in the trees around us were quiet, seemingly awaiting our next move.

I looked back at the rocks to see if there was any movement. The snake seemed to be lying low.

"It's not in the path," I said. "We can easily go around—"

"Nah, let's do this."

Keegan swung a camera from around his back into his right hand. He looked like a gunslinger from the Old West. He approached the rocks with a steady pace, showing neither apprehension nor glee.

I tried to stop him. "Hey Keegan, I'm pretty sure this was like day one of Boy Scouts. You know, 'Hi Ian, nice to meet you. You'll be in Rabbit Troop. Don't touch snakes!' "

He kept walking, completely resolved to the task. He placed his foot on top of the small boulder where mine had been moments before, and peered over, raising his camera to his eyes as though the lens were a shield.

He looked over the top of the stone and saw the snake.

At this point, several things might have happened. One option—a very viable one—was for Keegan to see the snake, let out a bloodcurdling scream, and run for the hills. Another option was for the snake to bite Keegan. Or perhaps he could have stomped on the snake in a fit of fear-fueled rage.

What I absolutely did not expect, though, was to see Keegan's face go from slight fear to unguarded sadness. His brow furrowed, and he lowered his camera as he stepped over the rocks.

I walked up and looked over his shoulder as he knelt before the motionless reptile.

The snake was dead. When it was alive, it had been a California kingsnake, a beautifully patterned nonvenomous snake native to this part of the world. People keep them as pets, and they're supposed to be quite affectionate.

There were several wounds around the kingsnake's head and neck. It had been in a fight with something, maybe a rock squirrel, and it had lost.

Keegan couldn't take his eyes off it. "Maybe it's a good sign that this actually makes me really sad," he said. "You know what I mean?"

I nodded. We stood there for a few moments, arrested by

the sight of the gentle-looking snake. Keegan slowly rose and turned back to the falls, leaving the snake where it lay.

After a moment, he regained his composure. "How about you jump over the pond like you did when you saw that snake and I'll try and take a video of it," he said, smiling again.

I walked back to the tiny pool, rubbing my neck at the thought of my previous video attempts.

"Do you think I could look sexy jumping?"

Keegan put the camera down. "Ian, no one looks sexy jumping. Just do it."

The route back to the parking lot was the same as the one we had taken to get to the falls. It took longer getting back, though. I stopped to examine every chirp and drum in the trees above— despite having forgot my binoculars. Keegan scaled the hillsides, cameras swinging from the straps across his shoulders, in search of the perfect nature shot. I felt like I was back in the woods behind my house in Virginia, playing with my friends and making up stories about the world around us.

Our conversation, like our journey back, wandered to and fro. We talked about relationships, about altruism, about what it really means to love somebody more than you loved yourself. We talked about butts, too. And how they're awesome.

As my car came into view, Keegan turned to me.

"So we're going to be done in October," he said. "No more *Pretty Little Liars*."

"Yup," I said. "It's almost over."

I opened the back of my station wagon—a car Keegan at first ridiculed but now adores—and sat under the lift gate. I took off my damp boots, allowing my feet to dry in the mountain breeze. Keegan sat next to me.

"You know what I'm looking forward to?" he said.

"What?"

"Having someone come up to me and say, 'Hey, weren't you that guy from *Pretty Little Liars*?'"

"Why are you excited about that?" I asked.

"Because that will mean the show is done. I like the show, don't get me wrong. I don't want it to end, but it will be nice to finally get to look at it in hindsight, you know? Try and wrap my mind around the whole thing. You can't do that when you're in it."

I hadn't thought about it like that. Saying goodbye to *PLL* had never felt like an opportunity to me. For me, it had always felt like an ending—and as I often do with endings, I tried not to think about it too much.

But now, in a parking lot in the middle of the mountains, in wet socks and sweaty clothes, I actually began to think about this chapter of my life coming to an end.

It's difficult to describe. It's similar to the pain you experience when reading a book that has really moved you. You feel the pages thinning as you near the back cover. You love the book, so you want to keep reading, but you know that the more you read the closer you are to being finished, to not getting to read that book for the first time again. I began to choke up.

We sat there for a moment. Sweating. Thinking.

Keegan turned to me. "We should do stuff like this more often. Especially when we're unemployed in a few months."

I closed the trunk and got into the car. Keegan climbed into the passenger seat.

"Yeah," I said. "I'd like to hike a whole lot more. It's like meditating, but, you know, with more birds."

"No. I mean we should do more social media posts for money. I want to stave off having to do porn for as long as possible."

AND ALL

THE BIRDS AT SEA

Late last June, I had the morning off from shooting, and I
wanted to get out of the house.

I called up John and Walter the night before, hoping they
were both free. Walter was wrapping up a writing project but
said he could take the morning off. John huffed at me over the
phone—he said he'd been planning to color-coordinate his
massive book collection the following day.

"What did you want to do?" he hollered over the Chopin
that was booming in the background.

"Let's go down to the beach in San Pedro, find a local brew-
ery..."

"I'm listening," he said.

"Maybe we could even peruse a bookshop or two," I said,
trying to rouse the bibliophile in him.

"Fine," he said. "I'll make an exception this time, as long as we stop at a bookstore."

Before I got off the phone with him, he had one last question. I couldn't hear him over the music he had playing, so he had to repeat it a few times.

"There aren't going to be any birds on this trip, right?" he finally shouted into the phone.

"Nope, not at all. It's a beach day," I hollered back.

It wasn't a beach day. There'd been reports of a brown booby down in San Pedro—I'd never seen one before, and I thought it would make a good half-day trip to try and find it.

Yes, that's right, I was hoping to get a good look at a brown booby.

Despite what you might be thinking, boobies aren't named for their pendulous breasts. The word "booby" comes from the Spanish *bobo*, meaning clown or idiot.

Most birds, when humans get too close, fly away. Boobies are different. They're curious, and they're clumsy. Boobies will land on sailing ships and toddle around the decks like buffoons—they'll even wander up to people to see what *Homo sapiens* are all about.

Because they land on ships, they're particularly easy to catch and eat—so humans took the birds' innate curiosity as an opportunity to brand them as stupid. It's a little bit like what happened to the dodo: when animals aren't overtly aggressive or fearful, humans assume they're slow in the head.

I had to keep the purpose of the trip to myself when I picked up John. I swung by his house a little before six the next morning, and he came outside in a bathrobe. I thought he'd just woken up, but he tried to get into the car and insisted he was ready to go—I refused to unlock the car doors until he changed into regular clothes.

After he did so, we grabbed Walter, who was waiting outside his apartment with a thermos of coffee and extra paper cups for the road.

As we coasted down the highway to San Pedro, the three of us still slowly waking up, Walter piped up from the backseat:

"I wonder what our chances are of seeing the booby first thing in the morning."

John's whole body swiveled to face me.

"The booby?" he asked. "Like the blue-footed booby?"

"Oh, so you know what we're talking about then," I said.

"Yeah, I know. The last time I saw one was in the Galápagos."

"Well, that's pretty cool," I said.

"A sea lion tried to mate with me."

Hesitantly, I offered, "Well, technically, we're trying to find the brown booby today—they're closely related."

John was not pleased.

"I thought you said there wouldn't be any birds—"

"We'll be on the beach, it'll be beautiful and sunny, and we can jump in the water. After that we'll go find a bookstore," I said, not sure if any of the things I had just promised were true.

San Pedro is technically a part of the City of Los Angeles, but driving in, it felt like a different world—it was originally a small fishing village but is now a part of the Port of Los Angeles, the largest port in the United States. Massive cranes line the channel that juts inland just east of the city, and cargo ships stream in and out, loaded to the brim with shipping containers.

As we got closer to the coast, it began to get cloudy, then very cloudy, then completely overcast. It didn't look like weather for sun-tanning, or even beach-going. That morning it'd been sunny back home in East LA, but now it was clouds as far as the eye could see. It was at least ten degrees cooler outside, too.

John told us he had spent some time in the town before when he was auditioning for the role of Creon in an immersive production of *Oedipus Rex* put on by a band of local fishermen. He said he knew a good spot for breakfast.

As we sat around eating bagels and sipping our second cups of coffee for the day, Walter pulled out his phone to see if there were any new rare bird alerts about the booby that morning. It was still early, and there weren't any.

After breakfast, we headed to the coast—to an overlook people had seen the booby from before. Watching the frothing waves of the Pacific wash up against the rocky shore reminded me of New England.

The sky was the same distinctive gray you get on the East Coast. Like dull smoke, it blended seamlessly with the waves on the horizon—a wash of ashy steel as far as the eye could see.

The three of us walked along the overlook, gazing out at the water. There wasn't much going on bird-wise. The only thing of interest was a group of sad-faced fishermen bobbing up and down on a ship called the *Monte Carlo*. Way off to our left was the port, where cranes were speedily transferring shipping containers off vessels.

There were a few seagulls. Terns. Pelicans flying low over the water. The usual.

"There's a Jesus egret out there," Walter said. He'd been scanning the water with his binoculars.

"What? Where?" I asked. "What's a Jesus egret?"

Walter pointed out toward what may have been the horizon—I couldn't quite tell where the water ended and the sky began.

"That speck of white out there, way in the distance—check it out," he said.

Sure enough, way, way out I could see an egret standing on a raft of kelp and seaweed. The bird took a cautious step forward—it was hunting for small fish or crustaceans.

"See, it's walking on water," Walter said.

Behind us, John groaned loudly.

I looked at the egret for another second or two, then turned back to the guys.

"What do you think?" I asked. "Seems pretty slow out there—definitely no boobies."

John pointed a little up the coast at some spray-painted structures on the side of a cliff.

"Want to check over there?" he asked.

As we walked toward the spray-painted buildings, we passed an old woman on a park bench who was feeding stray cats like they were pigeons. Five cats gathered around her, meowing and vibrating with feral purrs.

As we passed her, I wondered, would that be me someday? Would I end up an old cat lady, too? It was a definite possibility. But she seemed happy enough—and so did the cats. Maybe being a cat lady would be fun.

We walked through the neighborhood and wandered behind the houses to see if there was an open gate somewhere. Nothing.

About a hundred yards away, a man was walking around inside the fenced-off enclosure. He climbed up onto what appeared to be a partially collapsed roof. I took out my binoculars to get a closer look.

The man bent down and adjusted the cuffs of his pants. Then, slowly, the man sat down to face the ocean and began to meditate. I could see his back rising and falling with deep, mindful breaths.

I felt a tap on my shoulder. It was John.

"Check it out," he said, and he carefully pushed my binoculars down and to the right so that I was suddenly making eye contact with a mostly bald, mostly angry Chihuahua seated just next to the man on the roof—keeping guard while his master meditated. The Chihuahua glared unblinkingly at me from across the fence, daring me to even consider interrupting his master's solo time.

We kept walking for a few minutes and eventually found a gap in the fence. Someone had pried off one of the iron bars and replaced it with a bit of iron-colored wood. We squeezed through the fence and stepped into what I would later learn was San Pedro's Sunken City.

The Sunken City was a real estate development that started with a visionary's dream in the early 1920s but ended with a landslide less than a decade later. The landslide was gradual, but devastating. In January of 1929, the pace picked up considerably. The ground underneath the entire development started shifting down toward the water at a rate of roughly eleven inches per day. Residents paid to have their houses moved farther inland, but a few of them weren't moved in time. The houses began to slide off the muddy cliff and into the waves below.

Nine months later, the stock market crashed, plunging the country into the worst depression its ever faced. Any plans of salvaging the quickly vanishing development were abandoned, and the remaining structures were left to slide into the sea at their own pace.

Nowadays, high school kids and local gangs take over the Sunken City at night. But during the day it's just a sad collection of collapsed rooftops and empty concrete structures with dirt paths winding between them.

We shuffled down a steep incline and into the center of the Sunken City. Walter and I headed to the cliff overlooking the ocean while John hung back to look at graffiti. We didn't see many shorebirds, and definitely no boobies, but we did pass a group of seven or eight teenagers who looked like they were straight out of the movie *Warriors*. I don't know if they were actually a gang, but if they were, I have to say that they were remarkably cordial, and I'm impressed that they hold their gang meetings at 8:30 on Wednesday mornings. It's not every gang you see that can really master the breakfast meeting.

We walked past the roof where the man had been meditating a few minutes before. He was gone, along with his guard Chihuahua.

Walter was scanning the horizon for shorebirds. John was trying to read a graffiti-ed love note on the underside of an old roof. I decided to go off on my own for a moment.

The man I'd seen meditating on the rooftop had looked so peaceful, so serene, that I wanted to take a crack at it myself. I climbed up on the same concrete rooftop he'd been on, crossed my legs and closed my eyes. I started to take slow deep breaths.

I listened to the waves, to the sound of John's voice as he tried to decipher the spray paint on the walls, to the sounds of a well-organized gang meeting in the distance. I heard footsteps nearby, and I opened my eyes.

Walter stood below me on a precarious-looking slab that angled downward toward the sea. His binoculars hung from his shoulder, a sign that there was little to see.

We began to wonder if it was legal for us to be wandering around the Sunken City. Squeezing between the bars of a fence tends to fall under the header of "trespassing," so we started walking back to where we'd snuck in. On our way, we found a different break in the fence that spit us out into a park. We walked along the perimeter, which had views to the ocean, and observed a couple of bored-looking seagulls and two more feral cats. A group of old people threw some bread their way as we walked by.

San Pedro needs to stop treating its cats like pigeons.

Finding nothing but cats and seagulls, we headed to the car.

"Sorry about the waste of a morning, guys," I said, as I turned the key in the ignition.

"We could still go somewhere else," Walter said. He didn't seem ready to give up quite yet on the booby.

"What about the shipwreck?" John said from the backseat. He was looking at his phone.

"What shipwreck?" I asked.

"Apparently there's a shipwreck thirty minutes from here. It could be cool."

Walter looked at me and shrugged. "Let's check it out."

When we got to Palos Verdes, the closest town to the wreck, the first thing we noticed was the view. The sky had parted, and the sun illuminated the beach.

We got lost in a neighborhood trying to find the path down to the shipwreck, finally parking along the ocean across from a few palatial estates. On the other side of the road, the ocean sparkled in the light. We had arrived on the edge of a cliff, and a picturesque beach lay a hundred feet below. Wave-smoothed rocks lined the shore—and there didn't seem to be an easy way to get down to them.

We agreed to split up and try to find a trail down. Walter went to the left and peered over a ledge. Then without much fanfare, he jumped.

John and I, wondering if our friend had just casually killed himself, sprinted over to see what had become of him. Walter had landed roughly ten feet below, on a rocky outcrop on the cliff face. He waved to us, then skidded down on his heels to about the halfway point of the wall. He motioned for us to slide down and join him, but neither John nor I liked our odds of survival on the near-vertical cliff face, so we kept walking to see if there was a slightly more gradual trail available.

As we walked along, John started humming a tune that I quickly recognized as "One Headlight" by the Wallflowers.

"Please stop that," I said. I tried to walk faster so I could get away from him.

It was too late. Certain songs are earworms. They enter your ear, innocently at first, then get stuck in the core of your brain, and nothing can shake them out.

By the time we found a trail down the cliff, John and I were both several verses in, belting out Jakob Dylan like our lives depended on it.

John started laughing. "He really was the better of the two Dylans," he said.

"Whatever happened to him?"

John shrugged. "I don't know, man. Whatever happened to any of the nineties pop stars? He probably settled down and opened a bike shop somewhere in the Pacific Northwest."

The path we were going down was treacherous, and rocks crumbled beneath our feet as we scrambled our way down to the beach below, where we found Walter patiently waiting.

Sailors can be superstitious folk. To this day, many of them still refuse to set sail on Fridays. They avoid bananas and redheads. They don't like whistling—and not because it's annoying, but because they say it causes storms.

For all of the superstition of sailors, the people who actually name the ships clearly don't buy into the idea of bad luck. I don't know who it was who first spread the rumor that the *Titanic* was unsinkable, but trust me, it wasn't a sailor. Openly advertising that level of hubris is flirting with disaster.

Similarly, naming a ship the SS *Dominator* begs for the

ocean to destroy it. And that is exactly what happened to the SS *Dominator*, a freighter bound for Los Angeles in the spring of 1961—it got dominated.

Nobody died in the wreck. Bad weather drove the ship aground, battering it into the rocks, where it remained. Attempts to pull the boat back out to sea were fruitless. The *Dominator* was then auctioned off, but the new owners weren't able to salvage much.

The coastline is now littered with bits and pieces of rusted freight ship. The larger pieces are bright orange with rust or covered with multiple generations of graffiti. Here and there around the wreckage you can see spiny lobster traps, dented by sea lions that have tried to break through the metal grates in hopes of a free meal.

We stayed down by the shipwreck for a little under an hour. We watched some crabs fight, cast bets on our favorites, hung our heads in disappointment when they reached a truce, and decided to hike back up to the car.

As we walked back up the cliff to the car, I started thinking about the SS *Dominator* and its terribly ironic name. Once a ship runs aground, nobody remembers what it did or what its purpose was; we just remember that it crashed. All we think about is how it ended.

This got me thinking about endings. I was a few months away from ending what, for the past seven years, had been my life. *Pretty Little Liars* would soon be over—I was less than four months away from the end of filming—and I'd been mulling over the coming changes in my life ever since my hike with Keegan.

A few weeks before the trip to San Pedro, my mom had

emailed to ask if I wanted her and Aunt Jules to fly out to LA to celebrate the end of the show—sort of a small family wrap party. She had also asked how I was feeling about the show ending, and I told her I didn't really know yet.

I read somewhere that, when Shakespeare was alive, nobody really liked the plays that we now consider to be his classics. Nowadays, we remember Shakespeare for plays like *Hamlet*, *Macbeth*, and *Othello*. But in his lifetime, those shows weren't the favorites. Everyone kept asking him to write more plays like *Titus Andronicus* and *Pericles*—violent, sex-filled crowd-pleasers.

If someone as gifted and hardworking as Shakespeare didn't get to have any say in the trajectory of his career, what chance do the rest of us have? You could spend thirty years working on Greek tragedies, and all anyone would remember you for was a smoothie commercial.

Thinking all of this, I started to feel guilty. I was lucky to be where I was. It's a rare enough thing to get to make a living as an actor—I knew I needed to stop overthinking it all and just be grateful.

But you can't turn off thoughts like that. They're like Jakob Dylan songs—they just get stuck in your head for hours and hours.

We got back in the car and debated about what to do next.

About a mile down the road, I pulled off at another overlook. Living in LA, I don't get to see the ocean nearly as often as you might expect, and I wanted to get one last look before we headed home.

There was a trail near the turnout, and Walter suggested we go down it a ways to see if there was anything to see.

As we walked, a thought struck me. I turned to Walter. "There are about ten thousand species of birds, right?"

"God, I hope not," John said.

Walter nodded, "Yeah, just about ten thousand."

"Nobody's ever seen them all, have they? Like, that's not possible. Nobody could ever do that."

"You're right," Walter said. "It's probably not possible."

"Because that's not the point of it, right? I mean, even though we try to see as many as we can—and we keep life lists and call each other whenever we see a new bird, it isn't about the numbers. Not seeing every last bird doesn't diminish the joy of birding."

"When you guys *have* seen them all, will you please stop tricking me into going on these birding trips?" John asked. I'd completely forgotten that I'd promised to take him to a bookstore.

We arrived at a bench on the side of the sea, and we sat down. Walter took out his binoculars and scanned the coast. I thought I saw a loon in the distance, but it was too far out to be sure. I thought about my aunt Jules.

A gray blur shot by us. I tracked it with my eyes and turned to follow it but wasn't fast enough. I didn't see where it landed. It had disappeared somewhere in the bushes.

"Did you guys see that?" I asked.

John pointed to some brambles about a hundred feet from us. For someone who claims to hate birds, he's pretty good at spotting them.

Walter perked up. "That's a California gnatcatcher. They're a coastal specialty."

It was the first time I'd ever seen one.

We drove back to San Pedro for fish and chips, then headed home.

As we sped along in my station wagon, we talked about taking another trip. John told us he wanted to go to Oregon to do some white-water rafting, and he invited us to join him. I told him it would depend on when I was filming—as the show got closer to ending, my schedule was becoming more erratic.

"Oh yeah," he said. "I forgot about the show ending. How are you feeling about that?"

"You know honestly, I don't know," I said. "Everyone keeps asking me that, and I wish I had a better answer to give. But I'm still in it now. Filming these last couple of episodes hasn't felt any different from filming the rest of the show. I don't feel a loss, or an absence in my life, or anything like that. When I stop filming, then I know I'll start to feel something, but as long as I'm working on it I can't really imagine what it will feel like to say goodbye."

In the backseat, John pulled a pack of Twizzlers out of his backpack and offered them around.

"And I know that once it's done there will be some big changes," I said. "Like my hair. I've been contractually obligated to have the same haircut for the last seven years. Whenever it gets long, I text Kim to see if I can come in during my lunch break to get it trimmed—I'm not supposed to go to anybody else. It will be strange to not have her cut my hair anymore. Or when my chest hair grows back and I don't have to worry about shaving it again for work, then I'll be reminded that the show is really over. That might be when I start to feel nostalgic. Then I'll be sad. But right now, I'm still busy with it. My mind can't be here and four months in the future at the same time, you know?"

Walter nodded. John was quiet for a moment. Then he spoke up.

"When the show's over, can you do me a favor?" he asked.

"Yeah, what's up?"

"Shave your head and grow a mohawk."

When I was a kid, I couldn't count to thirty.

My brain would always skip the number. I'd try really hard to count correctly. I'd start out: "Twenty-eight, twenty-nine . . . forty." Every time. Something about the number eluded me.

When this book is published, I will be halfway through my thirtieth year—a number I could never imagine. It isn't frightening. It isn't thrilling. It doesn't feel that different at all.

The thing about uncharted territory is, once you get there, it just becomes familiar terrain.

I dropped the guys off at their homes in LA. Walter went back to his writing and editing, and John returned to his library and his beloved Chopin records.

As I drove home—my car winding through the hills of East LA—my mind returned to the ocean. We hadn't seen many birds, but I had found myself looking out at the horizon all morning. I was looking for something. I knew, even though I couldn't see them, that there were birds out there.

There's a set of birds called the pelagics. They're the first ones in most birding books: the albatrosses, petrels, shearwaters, and so on. The thing about these birds is most people will never see them. Every bird book starts with pages and pages of pictures of birds that most people will never lay eyes on.

The reason nobody sees these birds is because they never come to us. If you sit in your yard and wait by the feeder your whole life, you'll never spot a pelagic bird. If you want to see one, you'll have to hop in a boat and actually leave the land to meet them on their own turf.

Pelagic birds live at sea, and some species will go five years without ever seeing dry land. Their life is constant movement. They eat while flying. They sleep while flying. When the wind stops, they float in the sea and wait for the next gust, but there's no stopping. They hatch out of their eggs, and once they fledge, they're up in the air for life. An albatross or a shearwater will live for forty years, and every day of that life is spent either floating or flying.

As humans, we tend to crave solid ground. We want stability, comfort. Some of us live our whole lives waiting for that moment when we can say, "Now. Now I'm here. Now I'm where I need to be, and everything's okay."

But not all of us are the same kind of bird.

Some people need to nest. They need to make a place that they can call home, and that's what makes them happy. Others are like falcons: they live for the hunt, for the rush of competition and moments of intense, beautiful conflict.

I think I may be more like one of those pelagics. I can't look forward and say, "There. There is the place where I want to land." My show is ending soon, and with any luck I'll book something new—or I'll just keep flying, waiting for the next gust of wind.

If the goal is to find a comfortable place to perch and watch the world go by, I know that doesn't exist for me. At least not now.

I think the secret to a happy life is to keep moving, to keep trying to do the things you love.

And maybe—just maybe, if you're really lucky—while you're out there flying and flapping for years and years, you'll see some pretty incredible things.

Acknowledgments

Publishing a book and starring in a television show are shockingly similar; both involve the creation and telling of a story by hundreds of people, for which the lead of that book/show gets all the credit.

Here I wish to thank the many, MANY people without whom this book wouldn't have been possible.

For my ever-loving and ever-supportive family: I owe you all. Thank you for encouraging my imagination over the years, and for showing me that a life on the stage is not only a career, but also a calling.

John McKetta and Walter Heymann, for your support, wisdom, and deep love of all things avian. Especially you, John....

For the Herndon fellows: I miss you all daily. Thank you for the childhood from hell/heaven.

For my *PLL* family: Thank you for an epic seven years. It was an honor to grow with you all.

Scott Mendel, for pushing me to write the book I wanted to write, and for the attentive ear.

Vikram Dhawer, Steve Gersh, Nick Collins, and Kyetay Backner, for your guidance and for giving me the opportunity to chase my dreams.

St. Martin's Press, for taking a chance on an actor with a crazy idea. Most especially thanks to Sara Goodman, for your keen eye and ability to clarify everything I've written. For the rest, Alicia Clancy, Anna Gorovoy, Olga Grlic, Jess Preeg, Laura Clark, Jessalyn Foggy, Meryl Gross, Eva Diaz, and Jim Tierney: thank you for your hard work.

To those of you who have watched *Pretty Little Liars* with the same passion I had in making it: thank you. I would not be half the person I am today without you.

Lastly, but oh, so importantly; Sophia: What we have cannot be reduced to the written word or a token of thanks. I do not know where I end and you begin.

Jacket photo outtake. Apparently, posing makes me sneeze . . . (photograph by Sophie Hart)

Last day, taking it all in with Troian Bellisario. We began the journey together as two kids fresh out of drama school. Now we're old. Just. Old.

This photo was taken by yours truly on Keegan's last day. Oddly, I didn't cry in any of the farewell moments with the rest of the cast. The only time I shed a tear was right after this photo was taken. Keegan looked me in the face, sighed, and said, "Well, I guess we're done man. . . ."

Church *in* Crisis

The Gay Controversy and the Anglican Communion

OLIVER O'DONOVAN

CASCADE *Books* · Eugene, Oregon

CHURCH IN CRISIS
The Gay Controversy and the Anglican Communion

Cascade Books
A Division of Wipf and Stock Publishers
199 W. 8th Ave., Suite 3
Eugene, OR 97401

www.wipfandstock.com

ISBN 13: 978-1-55635-897-5

Cataloging-in-Publication data:

O'Donovan, Oliver

Church in crisis : the gay controversy and the Anglican communion.
/ Oliver O'Donovan.

x + 124 p. ; 23 cm. —Includes bibliographical references

ISBN 13: 978-1-55635-897-5

1. Homosexuality—Religious aspects—Anglican Communion.
2. Anglican Communion—Doctrines. 3. Anglican Communion—
Doctrines—Sermons. I. Title.

BX5005 .O36 2008

Church *in* Crisis

CONTENTS

PREFACE

THE SEVEN CHAPTERS of this book were originally published at monthly intervals between June 2006 and January 2007 on the London-based Fulcrum Web site under the partly ironic title, "Sermons on the Subject of the Day," borrowed from Newman's last published collection in the Church of England. They were never sermons in the proper sense of the word, but polemical essays, contributions to the now long-running struggle of the Anglican Communion for its future existence, a struggle that entered its latest and possibly mortal phase with the consecration of a gay divorcé as bishop of the Diocese of New Hampshire in 2003, but which can be seen to have been in preparation for years previously. Events have moved fast since these pieces were written, and for up-to-the-minute event-watchers, they will have the feel of the day before yesterday. Moments of hope and moments of despair have come and gone. The task of drafting an Anglican Covenant is well under way, and now we are on the threshold of the 2008 Lambeth Conference, which will certainly mark a point of no return for better or worse. The reason for putting them now in this more accessible form is that the diagnosis they present still seems to me persuasive. Certain older assumptions and ways of coping that served Anglicans well in the past have now failed. Nothing will do but that we bend our minds to the task of thinking deeply together, asking basic and open-ended questions about the challenges we face and the authority we acknowledge.

Prompted by a reminiscence of that earlier crisis in Anglican identity that evoked a book from Newman, the designation of these essays as "sermons" was ironic, but also hopeful. Even church polemics, unpleasant a form of communication as they are, can be, and at moments of need sometimes have been, elevated to achieve the effect of good preaching, setting stubborn issues within a new and more radically Christian framework, to be addressed in a spirit of evangelical faith and hope. I am well aware that it is difficult to align the polemical aim with the homiletic one. Only, perhaps, as criticisms are seen to bear upon all and encouragement to exclude nobody, can they transcend the incessant exchange of misunderstanding and misrepresentation. And that is what is done when the cross and resurrection of Christ are faithfully preached. The reader alone can judge how close I have come to achieving this goal.

New College, Edinburgh
Lent 2008

ACKNOWLEDGEMENTS

THE AUTHOR AND publisher wish to acknowledge the leadership and generosity of Fulcrum—the network of evangelical Anglicans dedicated to renewing "the centre of the evangelical tradition and the centre of Anglicanism." Fulcrum first published these *Sermons on the Subjects of the Day* on its website: http://www.fulcrum-anglican.org.uk. We are grateful to Graham Kings for granting permission to republish them in book form.

1 THE FAILURE *of the* LIBERAL PARADIGM

> *Your treaty with death will be annulled, and your pact*
> *with Sheol will not stand.*
>
> (Isa 29:18)

EIGHTY YEARS AGO the poet Robert Frost penned an affectionately mocking portrait of his home state: endowed with every feature and advantage, it was proud of having nothing to sell, nothing "in commercial quantities." But did it perhaps have "an idea to sell"—like the man who once tried to persuade him to write a political pamphlet in verse? No, Frost declares—unpresciently, as it now seems. "It never could have happened in New Hampshire!"[1]

In 2003 New Hampshire had an idea to sell. On all sides it was agreed, it was the *principle* of the thing. No one pleaded in defense of the consecration that, after all, the Anglican Communion could surely wink an eye at *one* gay bishop! What

1. Frost, *Collected Poems*, 200.

1

was on trial was quite simply a proposition: a divorcé in an active homosexual partnership may be a worthy chief pastor of a Christian flock. Two years earlier a diocese in Canada had stepped forward, probably outside its legal competence, to enact another proposition: the church may solemnize a same-sex union with a rite of blessing. In the subsequent row, the two propositions have become inextricably associated; in the future, if the Anglican Communion has a future, they will need to be disentangled again.

What was implied in the propositions? What did they mean to say about the creation of Adam and Eve, about Natural Law and history, about principle and pastoral accommodation? The difficulty was that we did not know, and still do not. They had the virtue and the weakness of all political propositions: they could be read in many ways, with different interpretations put on them and different inferences drawn from them. In defending them the North American churches followed the counsel that it was wiser not to be too explicit. They spoke to the world about a "discernment" they had been privileged to make over a long time and from the grassroots up, leaving the ontology of the question strictly to one side.[2] *The Windsor Report* thought it surprising that the actions of the Canadian and US churches were so unaccompanied by theological explanation or interpretative commentary.[3]

2. ECUSA presiding bishop's statement to the 2005 primates' meeting at Dromantine.

3. Lambeth Commission on Communion, *Windsor Report 2004*, 30: "Neither the Diocese of New Westminster nor the Episcopal Church (USA) has made a serious attempt to offer an explanation to, or consult meaningfully with, the Communion as a whole about the significant development of a theology which alone could justify the recent moves by a diocese or a province."

The North American initiative presaged a worldwide drought of trust and understanding in the Anglican churches, in which every spring of traditional affection seemed to dry up and the communion seemed near to death. At the Dromantine meeting of 2005, the Primates themselves declined to receive communion together. Responding to the emergency, the Primates' meetings of 2003 and 2005, together with *The Windsor Report* (2004) which they commissioned and endorsed, attempted to create a new kind of worldwide conciliar process such as Anglican churches had never had before and had never needed. It has moved painfully slowly, so slowly that some have wanted to declare it stillborn. The Archbishop of Canterbury's measured statement of June 27th, 2006, however, still showed a resolve to carry it forward in the wake of the resolutions of the 2006 General Convention of the Episcopal Church of the USA (ECUSA). As Lambeth 2008 approaches, there may be a cloud no bigger than a man's hand to be seen on the horizon. It is too early to be sure.[4]

The task these essays address is that of sketching in outline the content of a consultative endeavor still very difficult to conceive in detail. If the "miscarrying womb and dry breasts" with which Newman reproached his mother-church in his valedictory sermon, "Parting of Friends" were a rhetorical extravagance on the part of one who had lost his sense of proportion, there are plenty who, with greater or less exaggeration, repeat the charge today.[5] Can we find an answer to it? That will certainly depend on the Anglican churches' ability to sustain a disciplined common deliberation about Christian life in the world. But to pave the way for that, we must engage with the

---

4. Williams, "Challenge and Hope."
5. Newman, "Parting of Friends," 460–62.

situation to which the churches have come in a manner that will strike some as polemical. To sketch broad lines of opinion, to subject them to broad lines of criticism, is a rough-and-ready business at best and inevitably a contentious one. If the sketch is any good, some will see their opinions reflected in it; if it has any breadth, they will complain that justice has not been done to their subtleties. How can it be otherwise? I know no way of escaping the problem but to ask for as much charity and fairness in return as my reader may think I have offered.

For it has to be said at the beginning: the crisis in Anglican Christianity is quite specifically a crisis in its hegemonic tradition and the manner in which it has managed and controlled differences in the past. The church's old habits of negotiating stubborn oppositions by synthesizing them within a central, undogmatic stream of opinion—let us follow the convention and call the paradigm "liberal," without prejudice to any person or group claiming that title as their own—seem to have fallen away. When from as early as Queen Victoria's day British prime ministers preferred liberal bishops, it was because they seemed to be able to stop the church from falling apart; they seemed to have made a covenant with death and a pact with Sheol. They mediated effectively between antithetical dogmatic poles, catholic and evangelical, that marked the extremes of Anglican identity since the Oxford movement in the 1830s. In the late twentieth century, it began to be apparent that this traditional spectrum might be reconfigured; what the New Hampshire crisis announced was that this had finally occurred. The historically centripetal middle had become a new centrifugal pole.

Recent essays advocating a revisionist approach to homosexuality afford an interesting perspective on the present state of liberal Anglican thought.[6] It appears to be in deep denial: denial about the record of the past, denial about the traditional role of the Lambeth Conference and its authority, denial about the crisis of the present. (One theologian actually counsels us to deal according to the old proverb "If it ain't broke, don't fix it!") In deploring what the Primates have done, it offers little acknowledgment that the Anglican Communion is in sore need of doing something. There are times, of course, when it is the higher wisdom not to produce answers to every practical dilemma others thrust on us. Like a breach birth, a moral crisis may present itself from the wrong angle and need rotation before it can be brought into the daylight of a sensible answer. It may be that before the problems of the post–New Hampshire churches can be solved, a *pas en arrière* is required, a reopening of some questionable assumptions. But that defense is not available to liberals who oppose that very strategy when it is pursued by the Windsor-Dromantine process. Stepping back, untangling the skein, reconciling conflicting views, toning down exaggerated positions, forging coalitions, squaring circles, finding commonsense ways through: the whole stock in trade of a tradition once defined by opposition to enthusiasm of every kind, seems to have been mysteriously wiped off the software. In its place are radical postures, strident denunciations and moralistic confessionalism. Here we are at act 1, scene 2, on the opening night, and the production is already going badly: the scenery has collapsed; the villain has fluffed the lines that should have struck terror into the Upper Circle; the curtain has been down too long; the audience is restive. Surely it is time for the hero to appear, and the lovely heroine whose courage and beauty draw the crowds back to see the play

6. Linzey and Kirker, *Gays and the Future of Anglicanism*.

a dozen times? And where are the well-drilled extras who will keep them on the edge of their seats with a stunning display of hand-to-hand fighting? The producer looks around, nervously. Good Lord! There they are, up in the gallery, booing and cat-calling along with the audience!

Religious liberalism is not an Anglican phenomenon alone, but a pan-Protestant one. "Pan-Christian," one might say, since Roman Catholicism has had two difficult engagements with its own liberals in the course of the twentieth century, one in the early years with the so-called Modernist Controversy about historical biblical criticism, the other in the postconciliar period about the direction of moral theology. But the hegemonic character of liberalism in the Protestant churches has given it a distinctive profile, which deserves to be treated on its own terms. "Liberal" is a word with many uses, both intellectual and political, and its protean polyvalence can create misunderstanding. Political liberalism and theological liberalism are animals of a single genus but different species. When qualifying a religious posture, "liberal" suggests independence in relation to spiritual authorities—scriptural, hierarchical, or congregational. This distance may be no more than a questioning habit of mind, an independence of judgment that may lead back to a new and clarified recognition of authority. It may, on the other hand, be a deep alienation that fosters resentments which never quite proceed to an open breach. There is no way of telling a priori where on the spectrum of distance any "liberal" proposal will turn out to lie. It may be renewing; it may be subversive. The tree will be known by its fruits, and by nothing else. Yet in the lowering gloom of the Liberal Christian evening, we ought to begin by acknowledging the good that has been wrought in its day. No major theological voice of our age has failed to have its intonations deepened by what the Archbishop of Canterbury describes as its "habit of cultural sensitivity and intellectual flexibility that does not seek to close down unexpected questions too quickly."[7] For what we have received may the Lord make us truly thankful!

The story of theological liberalism could in principle be taken back a long way—certainly to the fission of the established Protestant churches in the seventeenth century, and perhaps to Renaissance humanism, even to Abelard. To understand the twentieth century, however, it makes sense to begin from the nineteenth-century attempt to reconstruct the expression of Christian doctrine by reference to ethics, the program of "the primacy of the ethical," drawn from the Ritschlian school of post-Kantian theologians in Germany. The interests of this school lay with dogma, which needed adaptation to the scientific climate of post-Enlightenment civilization. Ethics had "primacy," but only in the sense of being *presupposed;* it was the starting point of the dogmatic inquiry. To the intelligentsia of this period ethical judgments seemed very much more certain than creedal formulations. Predestination, resurrection, the omniscience and omnipotence of God, each chapter in the catechism could be interrogated as to its expression of the noblest and highest ideals, and rewritten as necessary. Ethics afforded a criterion by which the truth of doctrine could be verified: "belief in truth of a special and practical kind . . . as life-truth, in its central and creative reality for our person, and not in its congruity with other truth. . . . Christ did not come to teach us truth, but to make us true."[8] The ethical conception of truth was the essence of the modern; and this program was *ex professo* "modernist," taking for granted that the highest and noblest

7. Williams, "Challenge and Hope."
8. Forsyth, *Principle of Authority*, 4, 18.

ideals were being grasped and realized in contemporary history. Standing in no need of independent inquiry to verify them, they were immediately available to verify Christian dogma.

It has often been claimed that liberalism implied no special doctrines but was merely a critical temper of mind. This claim was never quite untrue; but it is an important aspect of our current situation that it was never quite true either. Liberalism related itself to the traditional dogmas of the church and aimed to modulate them. Inevitably, its methodology was reflected in an account of Christian belief with a distinctive shape. The inner shrine of the liberal gospel was its attitude of respectful attentiveness to the world as it is. The term "incarnation," used without an article, speaks of this embrace of the world. This is something different from *the* incarnation, the historical birth of Jesus the Son of God from Mary, which is now reconstructed as a paradigm or model for a conjunction of the human and divine to be effected in all times and places. The incarnation of the Word takes place continually. Being party to the positive conjunction of God and world is the distinct form of theosis offered to believers in liberal theology.

In making this conjunction its object, liberalism assimilated a Protestant construction of Christian existence in missiological terms. In assuming it already present and needing only to be affirmed, it assimilated a Catholic, doxological one. Yet the conception is neither Protestant nor Catholic. Both the eschatological frontier between this world and the next, important to Protestants, and the ontological frontier between the Creator and the creature, important to Catholics, are collapsed. This world being the sanctuary of God's full self-disclosure, talk of a reign of God can only be talk of this world projected to its logical term. The present harbors no ultimate antithesis; it faces no final judgment. God's worldly self-disclosure may be seen as the dynamic of world history, as in the confident progressivism of an earlier liberalism, or simply as a series of disjoined intuitions, as in the existentialism that replaced it. But one way or the other the theological liberal looks to "see the hand of the Lord in the land of the living" (Ps 27:13), and knows that when seen it will be stretched out in blessing, not in judgment.

A prime candidate for reconstruction among the classical doctrines was, of course, sin and judgment. Original sin, the understanding of the human world as lying as such under divine judgment, is replaced by resistance to mediation and reconciliation, tardiness over the opportunities of the present; judgment as the destiny of this world is replaced by a patience of divinity that can outwait the longest delaying tactic. And here we encounter one of those important, but possibly misleading, intersections of theological liberalism with the political stance bearing the same name. "Sin is conservatism" is a thesis on which the two liberalisms could converge. Yet their approaches to the common thesis are actually quite different. "Conservative," for the political liberal, designates a determinate social order, authoritarian and nonreciprocal, inhibiting individual initiative and freedom, which merely happens to have prevailed at some point in the past; if the ebb and flow of history were to yield a new flood tide for such an order, the political liberal would resist it just the same. For the theological liberal, on the other hand, the substantive content is indeterminate, and what is wrong with conservatism is precisely that it clings to the past, holding back in reserve from the God-destined character of the present cultural moment. At which point the distinctive character of liberal ecclesiology comes into view; for what can it be that holds us back, if not the stubborn antithesis of church and world? The self-validating ethical convictions of modern civilization are the final criterion for

judging all else; they are the very image of God that it bears
anonymously as its birthright. Resistance to the image of God
may come from any source, but most typically it comes from
where the antithesis is most upheld, which is to say, the church.
All that is institutional and naturally sluggish about the church
is a standing problem, a regressive obstacle in the way of its
incarnational mission. Ecclesiology begins and ends with the
semper reformanda, the casting off of the fossilized deposit of
an outworn past.

Of this thumbnail doctrinal sketch it will rightly be said
that it shares the limitations of all thumbnail sketches. It rep-
resents an "ideal type," tending to caricature and corresponding precisely to the views of no one in particular. When this
is conceded, however, it can play a useful heuristic role; it can
help us diagnose the problem that has drained the hegemonic
tradition of its strength. For there certainly has been strength
in the program of reviewing doctrine critically in the light of
ethics. Hopeful attention to the present as the theater of God's
action has proved to be an absorbent and reconciling cata-
lyst. Liberal thought in Anglicanism has woven itself in and
through other strands of thought, balancing and qualifying
angular postures and attitudes and so negotiating institutional
Anglicanism's self-effacing way through the world. When the
thread was strong, it knit the church together. Why, then, did
it snap? Was it because of a one-sided emphasis on reason, as
critics have often said? Did it promote rationalism rather than
faith seeking understanding?

My own analysis is rather different. If the antecedent for
the program of the "primacy of the ethical" is Kantian, it is not
the Kant of the *second* critique, the critique of practical reason,
into which liberalism never really ventured. Here lies the point
of truth in the accusation that liberalism, far from being over-

serious about reason, treats it "all too blithely."[9] If it is necessary for reason to think the true in the light of the good, it is no less necessary for it to think the good in the light of the true. An apriorist "intuitionism" in ethics which, as one critic has well said, "wants to know too much about values, and to know it too quickly," cuts short the disciplines of discursive practical inquiry.[10] The liberal compact with modernity was ratified in the court of Hegelian idealism, and "Hegel," as Kierkegaard already observed tartly, "had no ethic."[11] Kierkegaard's account of the downfall of poor mad Pastor Adler, persuaded by Hegelian dialectics to think of himself as a prophet, might serve as an account of the crack-up of the liberal tradition as a whole. In the interests of finding the modern world God-enchanted, it closed down on the serious deliberation with which Christians ought to weigh their stance of witness in the world. Potentially world-critical questions were suppressed. Liberal moral commitments, though sometimes urged with a passion verging on outright moralism, were not steered from the helm of discursive inquiry but set adrift on the moral currents of the day.

Among the early passages of arms between the sinking catholic and rising liberal powers in the second decade of the twentieth century, one minor but interesting one is recorded by Hastings Rashdall, a liberal of some note as a moral philosopher. "I was requested to give evidence before the Royal Commission," he wrote, "which has recently been investigating the question of the Divorce Laws in England. I ventured to suggest that the question was one upon which the moral consciousness had

9. I borrow the happy phrase from Benedict XVI. See Ratzinger, "Church's Teaching: Authority, Faith, Morals," 52.

10. Lacoste, "Du phénomène de la valeur au discours de la norme," 123.

11. Kierkegaard, *On Authority and Revelation*,129.

something to say. Thereupon I was severely cross-examined by eminent ecclesiastical authorities as though I were a setter forth of strange gods . . ."[12] And from the vantage point of nearly a century later, one can only comment that Rashdall's gods look very strange indeed. *The* moral consciousness? By what right does the definite article, carefully detached from the incarnation, attach itself to the collective moral judgments of the human race? Are we to listen out for a single decisive judgment of the human conscience, so pronounced and so unanimous that only crabbed churchmen and cantankerous academics will dare raise questions about it? That is a pretty remote proposition for the world that has come to supervene in the past ninety years! Here, as often, the conservatives of a past age had greater premonitions of the deeper currents, since they were more skeptical about the shallow eddies. That the twentieth century saw the recovery of a discipline of ethics in the Anglican theological tradition (absent more or less since the seventeenth century) was due not to liberal but to Catholic impulses. [13]

The relation of liberal Christianity to the modern world, then, contains a paradox. Turning, as all Christianity must, from contemplation of past and transcendent realities to consider how it must behave, it orients itself to a present world

12. Rashdall, *Conscience and Christ,* 5

13. The story deserves quotation as a moment full of symbolism for the transition of an age: Rashdall's was the ecclesiastically rising star, but intellectually his style of moral philosophy was at the end of its influence, while the work of my Oxford predecessor Kenneth Kirk still lay in the future. One should, however, quote it with a frank admission that it hardly does justice to Rashdall's contribution. Can we keep our anger forever against someone who was prepared to devote such careful attention to the moral teaching of Jesus of Nazareth—even if he seriously imagined himself (and everyone else) capable of estimating its true worth by the inner illumination of a moral a priori?

that has its primary meaning as *our* task, the challenge to *our* action. (That is the primary meaning of the present for us who live in it, at any rate; what meaning it may have for our grand-children, who will look back on it as their past, is not ours to comprehend.) Yet liberalism fails to bring a critical practical reason to bear on the present world. In its pursuit of doctrinal reconstruction, it treats the moral questions of the age as moral certainties; it views the indeterminate shapes of the present as sharp outlines. It may even imagine that in the present it can find some kind of speculative counterweight to correct a bias in past and transcendent reality. Instead of looking to the world as a frame within which to serve God and neighbor, it looks to it for a demonstration that in the past reality was misunderstood. Thus is crystallized the "modern world," an artificial entity with no existence in real time, achieving its dominion over thought only as we allow the world of *action*, for which we should have our loins girded ready for adventure, to be permafrosted into a world of pseudo-fact.

The tragic fault of liberal Christianity was to have no criti-cal purchase on moral intuitions comparable to the purchase it had on doctrinal judgments. Precisely for that reason liberal-ism proved vulnerable when twentieth-century society began to be riven through with deep moral fissures. In affirming the world, liberal theology condemned itself to shipwreck on the same rocks where a unified modern civilization broke up. Decolonialization left it without a dominant moral tradition that it could claim as forerunner of the kingdom of God. When economic self-interest and the emancipation of the senses be-came the solvent forces of the new West, unhappy Christian liberals struggled to keep the smile on their faces and suppress their instinctive repulsion. Comparatively late in the story, the tradition of theological liberalism reached for narratives of emancipation to give its cause fresh energy.

The older political-liberal narratives told the story of Western history as a story of constitutional complexification, dissolution of privilege, taming of autocratic government, and the economic and political equalization of the classes. Their tone was complacent and gradualist. It was the postwar conflict with communism that first imparted a crusading note to political liberalism. As though to drown out the revolutionary trumpets of the East, Western society began to proclaim itself the site of an ongoing series of conflicts over sectional emancipations and inclusions. It was natural that this style of civilizational apologetics should have an appeal for Christians. There were some very good stories of emancipation to be told, testimonies to the liberating implications of the gospel and the pastoral involvement of the church, the enormously influential struggle for civil rights in the USA, for instance, and the Latin American base ecclesial communities that gave new sharpness to Catholic witness in the face of poverty and economic injustice. These threw a lifeline to a floundering liberal imagination, offering a matrix by which the present could be seen as standing in perpetual judgment on the past, allowing the Western hegemonic tradition of modernity to rebrand its anticonservative appeal. Whether the pastoral and missionary endeavors that inspired this rebranding were helped forward by being put to this use, is a question we may leave aside. In grasping the lifeline, however, Western liberalism paid its price. From that point on, it became identified with one kind of moral cause to the exclusion of others. It became a church-party proper, a specific agenda to pit against other agendas.

Whether, if prevailing fashions of thought had been different, the emergent gay consciousness would have presented itself to the church as an excluded class in search of inclusion, is not a question it is possible to answer. What does deserve comment, however, is a persistent lack of fit between what gays find important about themselves and the role they are given to play in the emancipatory narrative. Gays do not always present themselves as natural liberals, since they represent a sectional rather than a universal vision. The *specialness* of gay experience is important to them. It was an insight into this logic that led the late Michael Vasey to insist that the natural discussion partners for gays who took their own experience seriously were Christians of a more conservative stamp, for whom sex was also a matter of interest as such.[14] The gay cause is grist for the liberal mill while it is in militant mode, for the mill processes victim classes in want of a fair deal. But Proudhon's "Justice, nothing but justice!" is as restrictive on one front as it is empowering on the other.[15] It allows not the slightest observation on the aesthetic or emotional timbre of gay existence. To demand justice is to make this class like every other class, for justice is thought's weapon against arbitrariness. But when gay experience starts attracting interest and interrogation in its own right and for its own sake, its usefulness to the liberal project is at an end. For that raises questions that were supposed to have been settled long ago; it draws attention to the fragmentation of the modern moral world, and therefore to its insufficiency as a measure to judge the performance of the church.

Gays also pose existential questions. They interest themselves in the riddle of gay existence. *Anexetastos bios abiôtos,* said Socrates; the life that is unexamined is intolerable to live. And much of the gay angst is to do with the difficulty of raising

14. See Vasey, *Strangers and Friends.*
15. Proudhon, *What Is Property?* 15.

questions in public that seem overwhelmingly pressing when
they directly concern oneself. The pastoral challenge that the
gay phenomenon presents to the church, then, is not primarily
emancipatory, but hermeneutic. And that is the supreme justification for a conciliar process that will take up the experience
of homosexual Christians as its leading question. How is this
form of feeling to be understood? What are the patterns of life
with which it may appropriately clothe itself? As far as I can tell,
it is deeply in the interest of gay Christians, men and women,
that their experience—by which is meant not merely *sexual* experience, not merely *emotional* experience, and not merely the
narrative of experience, but the whole storehouse of what they
have felt and thought about their lives, should become a matter
of wider reflection, reflected on by those who are called to live
this experience, by those who are called to accompany them in
their living, by all who share their understanding of living as
something they owe an account of to God.

Ten years ago an abortive attempt was made to open such
a discussion by the authors—antirevisionist in their assumptions—of the "St. Andrew's Day Statement."[16] Various aspects
of the document ensured that its intentions were not well understood: its confessional structure, meant to provide an ecumenical rather than sectarian framework, deterred those more
used to experience-based discussions; its reticence in saying
things it wanted to treat as secondary encouraged critics tri-
umphantly to uncover what the "real" point was, and so on.[17]

16. See "St. Andrew's Day Statement," in Bradshaw, *Way Forward?*
5–11.

17. Foreseeing their risk of this fate, the authors hoped to avert it
by warning readers not to read "between the lines." That, however, is
where current fashions of "unmasking" have taught a whole generation
of readers to begin and end their reading!

What remains important about the attempt, however, was that it addressed questions quite specifically *to gay Christians*, not to liberals, and *about the essentials of Christian faith*. Long as the way might seem, these authors thought there was an exploration to be had, which, if undertaken in good faith, might yield a common discussion over what it could mean to be both homosexual and Christian. It appeared that Christian gays were not prepared for that discussion at that time. Fruitful gay self-interrogations in the secular world had not yet prompted gay believers to embark on a comparable course. What is the situation today? Is the gay Christian movement still attached to the wheels of the liberal chariot, content with the victim mentality that the liberal program prescribes for it? Or can it present itself as the bearer of an experience of the human that is, at the very least, of irreplaceable importance for our understanding of our own times? Is it of age, able to speak for itself? On the answer to that a great deal may depend.

2 THE CARE
of the CHURCHES

*And apart from other things there is the daily pressure
on me of my anxiety for all the churches.*

(2 Corinthians 11:28)

AT THE STILL center of the storm in the Anglican Communion stands the isolated, scholarly figure of the current Archbishop of Canterbury—the first holder of that office since the Reformation, it is worth recalling, to have come to it directly from outside the Church of England, and probably the only one to have received appointment by something close to acclamation. It is necessary to recall the circumstances.

In 2001, on the verge of the British-American invasion of Iraq, the British prime minister must surely have had some qualms about placing in the seat of highest spiritual authority in England a figure known both for antiwar and disestablishment sympathies. (His theological credentials as a critic of liberalism were, perhaps, less in the prime minister's mind.) Popular demand in England for the appointment of the reluctant

Archbishop of Wales was, however, widespread, and embraced all the traditional party emphases. This harmony was disturbed at the last minute by a vigorous press campaign in his favor in the pro-gay interest, signaling an expectation in some quarters that he would promote a change of attitude on the subject; this produced a panicky reaction of hostility from some evangelicals. But most, even of these, knew well enough that the press portrait of the "radical" Archbishop revealed only a fraction of the sympathies of a complex mind, and reckoned that he would make it his first business at Canterbury to seek a common judgment and pursue a common policy. The lengthy personal statement of June 27th, 2006, confirms what was evident from the beginning: that the Archbishop's own comportment in relation to the crisis is indissolubly identified with the conciliar policy of Windsor and Dromantine. And that is not the least cause of his present isolation, for conciliarity has been his practice, not merely his theory, at a time when many have wanted high-profile personal gestures. Such gestures used not to lie outside his repertoire: his appointment to the Lady Margaret Professorship at Oxford was greeted by John Macquarrie, his predecessor, with the unforgettable words, "He'll do fine—if he's out of jail at the time!" But they do lie outside his very Anglican understanding of church authority. "The idea of an Archbishop of Canterbury resolving any of this by decree," he writes, "is misplaced, however tempting for many. The Archbishop of Canterbury presides and convenes in the Communion, and may . . . outline the theological framework in which a problem should be addressed; but he must always act collegially, with the bishops of his own local Church and with the Primates and other instruments of communion."[1]

1. Williams, "Challenge and Hope."

The Anglican Communion was not the first major family of churches to be caught up in the throes of a divisive moral disagreement; the Roman Catholic Church after Humanae Vitae found itself in just such a state of disarray. In that case, however, the ecclesiological tools needed to confront the disagreement lay to hand; for the Anglicans they did not. The most important feature of The Windsor Report was an attempt to forge them. The serendipitous character of Windsor's achievement was to combine the somewhat ill-defined commitment of the 1998 Lambeth Conference to an ongoing "listening" to homosexual Christians' experience with a project for which the churches of the Southern hemisphere were eager, "mending the nets," i.e., constitutional reform of the Communion's institutions that would have the effect of weakening Northern, and especially US influence. A surprising amount of Windsor's attention was given to longer-term prescriptions for what it called the "instruments of unity," i.e., the primacy of Canterbury, the Primates' meeting, the Anglican Consultative Council. and the Lambeth Conference, including the proposal of a common canon-law framework to define their roles. This caused some dismay among Northern Hemisphere Anglicans, which might have shipwrecked the proposals from the outset; but it also tended to win the confidence of the churches of the South, more likely to be suspicious or lassitudinous about the listening process.

Windsor looked to find a point of reference in ecclesiology, borrowing aspects of the "communion ecclesiology" elaborated in Anglican-Roman Catholic discussion. The irony of this should not pass without notice. The historic stress lines of the Anglican self-consciousness were ecclesiological; yet at the beginning of the twenty-first century the one point offering some hope of purchase on an intractable disagreement was a doctrine of the church worked out in conversations with ecumenical partners. Almost everything else that might have served as a point of reference was in contention: the ethical a prioris to which liberalism habitually appealed; the authority and hermeneutic of Scripture, to which evangelicals appealed. More than an irony, it was in its way a triumph: a triumph for the ecumenical movement from an unlikely source, and even, since the ecumenical movement itself owed much of its early impetus to liberal antidogmatism, a triumph for the liberal hegemony of the century just closed. Yet antidogmatism alone could not have produced communion ecclesiology, and at the close of the twentieth century liberal Christianity, increasingly suspicious of doctrinal agreement, by no means looked on the ecumenical movement as its favorite child. Another case of Newman's "miscarrying womb," perhaps?

For one church to wish it of another "that you may have communion with us" is framed by a daring and demanding conviction: "our communion is with the Father and with his Son Jesus Christ" (1 John 1:3). No communion can possibly be claimed within the church of Christ on other than these gospel terms. But to claim evangelical communion is a statement of faith in God's gift of himself, a gift that cannot be proved empirically, but must be believed in and witnessed to. In the divided state of the Christian churches, no witness to it will be perfect. Yet it is not unwitnessed to. Ecumenical encounters between the churches witness to it; so do attempts to make existing institutions and structures more serviceable within the churches. What makes a structure serviceable? It is serviceable when it secures communion within the church on its gospel basis; for "one holy, catholic and apostolic church" cannot live apart from "one faith" and "one baptism." In order to do this, structures must be equipped to exercise judgment, to draw a line, where necessary, between true and false communion. To have structures capable of doing that is to enjoy an institutional communion that witnesses to, and safeguards, evangelical communion.

Evangelical communion is never merely synchronic; it is always also diachronic, involving a communion with past Christians in receiving from them the faith they have witnessed to and handing that faith on again to further generations. This is what is meant when we speak of the need to preserve "tradition." Traditional communion does not imply that there can be no radical correction of the tradition as received, such as was undertaken in the Reformation. Tradition is founded upon the authority of the prophets' and apostles' testimony to Christ, and so has a principle of self-correction built into it with the authority of Scripture. It does imply, however, that when there is a question about authentic terms of communion, tradition has a significant role in helping us answer it. Anglicans have understood the authority of tradition as running much wider and deeper than what has been thought and done by Anglicans. They have aimed to interpret and regulate Anglican practices in the light of an ecumenical tradition running back to the apostolic age.

Only in this wider context can the role of the instruments of unity within the Communion be understood. The significance of the See of Canterbury, in particular, lies in its service to the tradition of Christian faith and practice. The Archbishop has authority; but, like all authority, his is subject to the authority of God the Holy Spirit speaking to and through the churches in the process of faithful receiving and transmission of tradition. It is not invested with discretion to abolish existing terms of communion and replace them with others. And what the Archbishop cannot do, neither can others by using communion with his office as a kind of wrench to split the church apart from its historic practices. "Communion with the See of

Canterbury" is an institutional function in the service of communion among Anglicans, and, through them, in the service of the communion of the *una sancta catholica ecclesia*. A claim that someone is in communion with Canterbury is not valid merely by being asserted, nor even by the acceptance of the Archbishop of the day. Such a claim must be open to evaluation, submitted to the theological test of whether the Anglican tradition of Christian faith and practice has in fact been sustained and renewed by the communion that is claimed. Just as Christians are not admitted as Christians by other Christians, only recognized as Christians on the basis of the Holy Spirit's work in them, so it is with Anglicans—for being an Anglican is simply a specific modulation of being a Christian. The heart of the Archbishop's role in the Communion is to give voice and effect to judgments the churches have reached about the work of the Spirit in their midst, to speak and act on behalf of their common mutual recognition. This is complicated by his special role within the Church of England, for the Anglican Communion is constructed on the historic relationship of its member churches to the English mother church, its senior primacy vested in the primate of all England. But that does not give the Church of England a deciding voice in defining the Communion's direction. The historic relation between the English church and the Communion is entrusted to the harmonious way the Archbishop exercises his authority in the two concentric spheres.

One way of describing the focus of the Windsor Commission is to say that it was asked to render a service to the exercise of *episkopē* within the Anglican churches, not a service of *didachē*, the teaching of the word. Its more immediate prescriptions, then, were aimed at achieving the minimum steps backward necessary to get a conciliar process on the road, a process within which the *didachē* of the church could be examined, refined, and strengthened. Minimum steps, however, did not mean "minor steps," especially in the case of the North American churches, which were asked to accept responsibility and express regret for initiating the disruption, "breaching the proper constraints of the bonds of affection" as it was portentously expressed, in the consecration of the New Hampshire bishop. The non-American bishops, on the other hand, who had intervened in the North American churches in reaction, were to express regret for the unfortunate consequences of their response to the challenge. To these proposals of the Windsor Report the Primates gave flesh in their Dromantine meeting in 2005. The heart of the action they took there was not their decision to request that ECUSA and the Anglican Church of Canada (ACC) voluntarily withdraw from the bodies of the Communion "up to the next Lambeth Conference." That was only intelligible when set beside the preceding resolution: "In order for the recommendations of The Windsor Report to be properly addressed, time needs to be given to [ECUSA and ACC] for consideration . . . according to their constitutional processes."[2] In other words, the Primates intended to begin the conciliar process in the churches that had made it necessary, allowing these churches to be heard to speak as a whole—lay, clerical, and episcopal—apart from the decisions of their leaders. It was a daring strategy, which may yet turn out to have led nowhere, depending how the ambiguous resolutions of the ECUSA General Convention finally appear on consideration. But it opened the way to those North American Anglicans who believed the measures taken were right in principle to reevaluate their policy of "never explain, never apologize," and it opened

2. Communiqué February 2005 §13. Cf. §14.

the door to those who believed the new steps misconceived to turn from impotent protest to serious synodical argument.

Shrewd observers have remarked that the Primates' response transformed a polarized situation, revisionist against antirevisionist, into a quadrant of views, where conciliarists of different judgments over the moral issue had to come to terms with anticonciliar revisionists and anticonciliar antirevisionists. The emergence of a strong conciliar front, more or less the official position of the Communion and most of its constituent churches, was what the process was supposed to achieve. An anticonciliar revisionist resistance loyal to the North American initiatives was only to be expected. But the emergence of an antirevisionist strand of opinion that was cool, to say the least, about the conciliar process was, perhaps, more perplexing. With the North Americans on the back foot, it might have seemed that antirevisionist sentiment only had to cling tight to the conciliar project. How is this development to be accounted for?

By a conjunction of two factors: the first was a confidence in the immediacy of moral judgments, such as underlay, also, the development of liberal Christianity. Where there seems to be nothing to discuss, there can be no discussion. But "in the beginning is the half-light," as one philosopher says about the foundations of ethics.[3] A process of moral reasoning is needed if we are to reach well-founded concrete moral judgments. By its very logic moral intuitionism will be indifferently radical or conservative. Once the moment of moral insight is detached from the discursive project of reflection and deliberation, it can rebound off the wall at any angle whatever. The intuitionist appeal to a "discernment" on the revisionist side called forth an equal and opposite move—all the more so since an antire-

3. Lacoste, "Du phénomène de la valeur au discours de la norme," 124.

visionist "discernment" could claim, with much greater prima facie plausibility, to be in line with the unwavering testimony of Scripture. To some reflections on how Scripture is to be approached in this discussion we must return later. It is enough to remark in passing that, on this side as on that, the immediacy of the insight tends to make the interpretation of Scripture seem superfluous. The contrast with the rather careful hermeneutic of scriptural teaching on divorce and remarriage is striking; to this interesting, if teasing analogy, too, we must return.

But there was a second cause that reinforced the intuition-Scripture conjunction. That was an interest in communion structures, the "mending the nets" agenda that had reacted in wrath to the challenge to the authority of Lambeth. This quite separate cause of offence went back to the unhappy inconclusiveness of the 1988 Conference's reflections on the consecration of women bishops, when churches supportive of that initiative made it plain that the authority of the Conference was not, in their view, sufficient to prevent it. This was a new theme in the Anglican fugue, and one with serious implications, just at the point when bishops from the developing world had achieved a majority in the Conference. In the postcolonial era, racism is necessarily a sensitive issue. The innovating churches not only failed to appreciate the wider resonances of their tough-minded pitch of 1988; some of them came back in 1998 apparently resolved to repeat the offense. Those who claim special powers of moral discernment can hardly afford such moments of massive insensitivity, to which a great deal of the bitterness is attributable. Certainly it accounts for strands of opinion that have wanted to ram the Lambeth Conference Resolution forcefully down the revisionists' throats. Hooker's *causa finita est* has been invoked in support of the view that, Lambeth having spoken, nothing remains to be said.

Yet a reading of Resolution 1.10 of Lambeth 1998—with whatever sympathy and appreciation—does not quite support the view that it was meant to bring the whole discussion to a close.[4] The attempt to treat this text as a point of closure, rather than a disciplined overture to explorations yet to be conducted, puts excessive strain on it, and tends to frustrate, not further, its goal of shaping the practices of the Communion under the authority of Scripture. It meant, certainly, to set some fairly tightly drawn parameters: faithfulness in marriage between a man and a woman in lifelong union; sexual abstinence as the

4. Let the reader judge: "This Conference: (a) commends to the Church the subsection report on human sexuality; (b) in view of the teaching of Scripture, upholds faithfulness in marriage between a man and a woman in lifelong union, and believes that abstinence is right for those who are not called to marriage; (c) recognises that there are among us persons who experience themselves as having a homosexual orientation. Many of these are members of the Church and are seeking the pastoral care, moral direction of the Church, and God's transforming power for the living of their lives and the ordering of relationships. We commit ourselves to listen to the experience of homosexual persons and we wish to assure them that they are loved by God and that all baptised, believing and faithful persons, regardless of sexual orientation, are full members of the Body of Christ; (d) while rejecting homosexual practice as incompatible with Scripture, calls on all our people to minister pastorally and sensitively to all irrespective of sexual orientation and to condemn irrational fear of homosexuals, violence within marriage and any trivialisation and commercialisation of sex; (e) cannot advise the legitimising or blessing of same sex unions nor ordaining those involved in same gender unions; (f) requests the Primates and the ACC to establish a means of monitoring the work done on the subject of human sexuality in the Communion and to share statements and resources among us; (g) notes the significance of the Kuala Lumpur Statement on Human Sexuality and the concerns expressed in resolutions IV.26, V.1, V.10, V.23 and V.35 on the authority of Scripture in matters of marriage and sexuality and asks the Primates and the ACC to include them in their monitoring process." 13th Lambeth Conference (1998), Resolution 1.10, "Human Sexuality."

right course for those not called to marriage; homosexual practice as incompatible with Scripture. At the same time it recognized the existence of church members with a homosexual orientation who were seeking pastoral care, moral direction and God's transforming power for their lives and relationships; it committed itself to a process of listening to their experience; it called for pastoral and sensitive ministry to them, but it declined to "advise the legitimising or blessing of same sex unions nor ordaining those involved in same gender unions"—the change of term may possibly mean that the pastoral problems of transsexualism were also at the back of bishops' minds. It condemned irrational fear of homosexuals, along with one or two other causes of indignation that tend to turn up at every party; it affirmed that baptized, believing, and faithful persons, regardless of sexual orientation, are full members of the Body of Christ and loved by God, and requested a means of monitoring work done on the subject of human sexuality. It was, notoriously, a resolution improvised and hammered out on the floor of a plenary session, and a variety of entertaining and only partially reconcilable narratives soon came into circulation about how the procedural debacle arose. But three things are crystal clear: it was generally conservative in posture; it was overwhelmingly supported; it was open to further exploration. And exploration must be meant to make some difference. Even if Lambeth would not envisage a major reorientation of its approach, it must have envisaged, in the light of greater pastoral experience and understanding, possibilities for considerable further nuance of detailed practice.

When The Windsor Report posed, as the alternative to its own approach, that "we shall have to begin to learn to walk apart," it clearly did not mean this as a choiceworthy alternative, one that the church of Jesus Christ could opt for with integrity.

It was to be viewed as a horizon of total failure.[5] Unhappily, it seems to have underestimated the capacity of Anglicans to think the unthinkable. The immediate effect of the hardening of the antirevisionist position was to make the breach more likely; indeed, some voices, however little representative, did not hesitate to suggest that this was something to be welcomed. On the revisionist side, the idea of an amicable separation of the ways had long been mooted—just another example of liberal otherworldliness, unfortunately, since the only separation ever to be looked for was bound to be far from amicable. To the antirevisionists looking in this direction it was to be a solemn exercise of church discipline. A curious combination of ecclesiological influences, Calvinist and patristic, had already encouraged a number of bishops to raise their voices and announce the several combinations of churches and bishops with whom they were and were not in communion. The resulting untidiness in the Anglican world communion began to make some think that a shoot-out would be the desirable curtain-fall.

But this severely underestimated its difficulties. Such an occurrence would, for one thing, destroy the Anglican identity. The Anglican churches are not, and do not claim to be the whole Christian church as comprehended in its Augsburg-derived formulae.[6] They are a particular communion of churches that mediates the gospel in a shared tradition deriving from English history and the network of global relations springing from it.

5. Lambeth Commission on Communion, *Windsor Report*, 75–76. Indeed, its final words, building on a statement of the 2000 Primates' meeting, embody a decisive condemnation of this option: "'to turn from one another would be to turn away from the Cross,' and indeed from serving the world which God loves and for which Christ died."

6. Thirty-Nine Articles, article 19: "The visible Church of Christ is a congregation of faithful men, in the which the pure Word of God is preached, and the Sacraments be duly administered according to Christ's ordinance. . . ."

The Anglican identity is constituted by its particular continuities, and cannot survive a decisive breach in them. Even if we were to accept this as the price to be paid for a purer church, however, there is a more profound obstacle in the way of achieving purity by these means. The new configurations could not possibly be formed along the lines of the division over homosexuality. Separating evangelicals would not carry with them all, not even perhaps the majority, of those who sympathized with their antirevisionist views. Many of their sympathizers are not evangelicals, and would certainly look for other alternatives. Many, not least evangelicals, would think such an act of separation wrong in principle. Not the new true ex-Anglicans, but the Roman Catholic Church, already recruiting evangelical intellectuals by the dozen, would be the great winners (if we can speak of winners in this dismal scenario) from the disorderly explosion of Anglican forces. The idea of a united antirevisionist Anglican church is as fantastic as the idea of an amicable parting of the ways.

The point of principle can be explored by posing the theological question: in the view of the New Testament, what grounds justify a deliberate breach in communion within the church? Two contradictory answers press themselves on us, each with apparent inevitability. On the one hand, we are never justified in breaking communion within the church of Jesus Christ, for schism is sin; on the other hand, communion implies and requires fundamental agreement in the gospel. Those who "go out" from the church of Christ declare that they were not of it (1 John 2:18). Yet disagreement is not something we are free to relativize or set to one side. So unity in the truth turns out to be a commitment that may pull us in opposite directions to opposite conclusions: there is no communion-breaking moral disagreement, on the one hand; on the other, any disagreement is potentially communion-breaking. The one answer we cannot find is the answer we set out to find: this, rather than that, is the specific cause that will justify a breach.

It is worth pausing to make a comparison with a similar moral antinomy, much discussed in the Scholastic period: Is it right to obey a mistaken conscience? On the one hand, obeying one's conscience is, apparently by definition, something it is always right to do. On the other hand, a mistaken conscience is, again by definition, a conscience that instructs you to do the wrong thing. So doing what a mistaken conscience tells you is to do right and wrong at the same time. There is a lesson to be learned from the deft way Aquinas, confronting this paradox of "perplexity," thrusts it aside. "One can withdraw from the error," he tells us.[7] Commentators have expressed bewilderment at this, for it is, of course, not an answer to the question, but an evasion. It does not tell us what to do when our conscience is mistaken; it tells us not to have a mistaken conscience. Is Aquinas merely saying, "If that was where I wanted to go, I wouldn't start from here"—always a bad answer to a practical question, since "here" is where all practical questions start from? No: he means that there is something that the framing of the question has left out of account; the alternative is wrongly posed.

It beguiles us into imagining a helpless innocent pathetically trapped between the devil of dutiful wrongdoing and the deep blue sea of guilt-ridden right-doing. Moral reality is simply not like that. The perplexed actor always has a further recourse: she or he can reconsider. The conscience is not a fixed and unnegotiable natural force, but precisely "the mind of man making moral judgments." It can therefore be made use of, and if it leads to bewildering conclusions, it can be made

7. *Summa Theologiae* II–1.19 ad 3: "potest ab errore recedere"; here, as elsewhere, unattributed translations are my own.

use of again, to reflect on the validity of its own deliveries and hold them up to reflective scrutiny. On the best scenario further thought will correct the initial mistake; even on the worst scenario the effort of critical reflection will break up the illusory appearance of conscience as a moral dictator, imposing just one course of action upon us, perhaps the wrong one! The very possibility of moral thinking transforms our experience of the conscience, which is directed to forming judgments, not delivering commands.

Just as Thomas cuts the Gordian knot with the proposal, "one can withdraw from the error," so we may suggest, "one can address the disagreement." Communion should not be broken, but that does not mean disagreement can be ignored. There are ways of addressing serious disagreements that affirm and renew communion by proven willingness and determination to resolve them. And the very attempt to reach a resolution transforms our experience of the disagreement. Disagreements are no more unnegotiable natural forces than deliveries of the mistaken conscience are. They are openings for those who share a common faith to explore and resolve important tensions within the context of communion.

This kind of proposal is, of course, easy to mishear. It can be taken to mean that parties to disagreements must be less than wholly convinced of their position, ready to make room for possible accommodation. When really serious issues are at stake and talk of a *status stantis aut cadentis ecclesiae* begins to rumble like thunder, urging the search for resolution can seem like an invitation to capitulate, to concede essential points before beginning. It can seem as though Scripture is deemed to be inconclusive and ambiguous, so that either side is free to concede the possible right of the other's interpretation. It can seem as though what is needed is an indefinite irresolution about everything important, in which there is no need for, and no possibility of, a decisive closure. But that is all a trick of the light. None of this is implied in the search for agreement. The only thing I concede in committing myself to such a process is that if I could discuss the matter through with an opponent sincerely committed to the church's authorities, Scripture chief among them, the Holy Spirit would open up perspectives that are not immediately apparent, and that patient and scrupulous pursuit of these could lead at least to giving the problem a different shape—a shape I presume will be compatible with, though not precisely identical to, the views I now hold, but which may also be compatible with some of the views my opponent now holds, even if I cannot yet see how. I do not have to think I may be mistaken about the cardinal points of which I am convinced. The only thing I have to think—and this, surely, is not difficult on such a subject!—is that there are things still to be learned by one who is determined to be taught by Scripture how to read the age in which we live.

Every approach to resolving disagreements may turn out to fail. In the end God may have so hardened our hearts that we can see no way through our difficulties and simply find ourselves apart. God may in his judgment scatter a church that lacked the common will to search for its unity in the truth of the gospel. And then there may come a point at which this situation has to be given some kind of institutional expression. Nothing can exclude a priori the worst possibility that certain persons or groups, or even whole churches, may be declared to have left the communion of Jesus Christ. But it must be a declaration, a formal statement of what has obviously come to pass. It cannot be an act to produce a result. The problem with the notion of separation is its expressive, self-purifying character. It will not wait for God to purify his own church in his own time.

Schisms may come, but woe to that church through whom they come! There is no right, or duty, of schism. As unity is given to the church as a gift, so it is taken away as a judgment. But on no account can disunity be a course of action that the church may embrace in pursuit of its mission or identity. The only justified breach is the one we have taken every possible step to avert, the one that lies on the far side of every conciliar process that can be devised.

3 ETHICS *and* AGREEMENT

Can two walk together unless they are agreed?

(Amos 3:3)

THE CREED-MAKING labours of the churches of the fourth and fifth centuries left a series of statements to measure orthodox Christian belief, but no authoritative moral concepts or norms. For the classic liberal theology of the nineteenth and early twentieth centuries this feature of its legacy was disturbing. The concerns of the first-century Council of Jerusalem, the concerns, indeed, of Jesus's own teaching, spoke loudly enough, it seemed, for the priority of ethics. The kingdom of heaven lay not in the iota of difference between *homoousios* and *homoiousios,* but in righteousness and peace and joy. The best that could be said for the creeds, perhaps, was that moral definitions might prove intrusive. The principles of behavior pleasing to God were perfectly well known, to unbelievers as well as believers, but the circumstances of each age required fresh applications of them not to be hampered by decisions of past ages.

Recent mutations in the liberal tradition have effected a re-positioning. We now hear it urged that the grounds of Christian communion are simply creedal, not moral at all. A universal morality, once the solid rock on which the liberal critique of theology was built, has been swallowed up in the shifting sands of change; moral differences can, and should, be accommodated.[1] This is a fairly radical shift of view, and it might seem that the only thing to connect the new liberal pluralism and the universalism it replaced is that they both challenge a reigning ecumenical consensus. The consensus holds that doctrines and moral practices are deeply intertwined, and to agree on the one is to agree on the other.[2] Communion is itself both a moral practice and the *idiōma* of the third person of the Trinity. It would be hard to imagine a morally pluralist Christianity that had not lopped off the Third Article of the creed—which would mean lopping off the church, that common life in the harmony of God's will which is better than toleration. Civil societies are necessarily tolerant to a degree, and intolerant to a degree; they punish what they cannot afford to tolerate, tolerate what they cannot afford to punish. But the communion of the Spirit is harmony; and a church that understands its identity embraces the gift and task of moral agreement from the start. The very concept of *belief,* moreover, involves moral commitment. "Fully to grasp Christ's teachings and to relish them takes an effort to

1. For this point of view, see M. Adams, "Faithfulness in Conflict," 70ff.

2. Cf. Breidenthal, "Disagreement as Communion," 190: "communion names our willingness to embrace unity within the household of faith . . . not so much a formal relationship as a moral practice."

conform the whole of life to him," as Thomas à Kempis says.[3]
Belief is never neutral in respect of practice; the Epistle of James
declared that faith without works is dead. With whatever lati-
tude or rigor, a Christian communion must surely have *some*
idea of its specific moral shape: *these* works are of a kind that
attests living faith, *those* indicate that faith is dead.

The two liberal poles seem to oscillate on either side of
this ecumenical consensus, the one insisting that morality is
primary and universal, reaching even beyond the community
of belief, the other that it is plastic and diverse, even within the
community of belief. But they have more in common than at
first appears. Both maintain a distance between moral and doctrinal belief; both insist that ethical judgments are subject to a
certain variability. In each of these two respects, it would seem
to me, they have a measure of right on their side. But so does
the ecumenical consensus. To reconcile them effectively, to secure the ecumenical consensus and to restore the lost strengths
of liberalism, we need some further clarity on the underlying
issues: the relation of ethics to doctrine, and the kinds of difference that can be sustained within an underlying agreement.

This demands a short digression into the formal charac-
teristics of ethics. And here is a call for patience. But it will have
its reward at last.

"Ethics" is not the name of a descriptive science, like
"chemistry" or "sociology." There is no slice of reality in which
it specializes. Ethics is the explication of the logic of practical
reason that directs our conduct, individual and collective. It
terminates not in a descriptive judgment about how the world
lies, or a slice of the world, but in a practical judgment on how

3. Thomas á Kempis *De imitatione Christi* 1.1.2, echoing John 7:7:
"Qui vult plene et sapide verba Christi intelligere, oportet ut totam vi-
tam suam illi studeat conformare."

we shall conduct ourselves. But since any practical judgment belongs to the same "here and now" as the thinker does, its conclusions may differ from one day to the next, even though the train of reasoning is essentially the same. The historian who told us on Tuesday that the Battle of Hastings took place in 1066 is expected to say the same on Wednesday, barring any new evidence that has come to light in the intervening hours. But the *same* train of practical reasoning by which on Tuesday I decide to post a letter may lead me on Wednesday to pay a personal visit rather than post another one. This implies no revision of my thinking; it is simply that the successive situations require their own decisions.

But that does not mean that the practical reason by which we direct our conduct is *independent* of description. St. Thomas Aquinas spoke of practical reason having its own independent starting-points, its own "axioms"; but that is a misleading picture. Practical reason is more like an *extension* of descriptive reason, going beyond telling how the world lies to judging how we may find our way through it. It builds on descriptive judgments, and if the descriptions it builds on are false, its judgments will be misconceived. The fool who says in his heart "there is no God" will be corrupt and do abominable deeds (Ps 14:1). That is why practical disagreements may sometimes be very perilous. Not all differences of practical judgment can be accounted for in terms of different situations.

Here are three formal coordinates for mapping differences of practical judgment, followed by a brief commentary on each:

1. Some differences of practical judgment are not *ethical* differences, others are.

2. Some ethical differences of judgment do not indicate *underlying moral* disagreements, others do.

3. Some ethical disagreements do not reflect *doctrinal* disagreements, others do.

1. Practical judgments differ *concretely*, simply as distinct events in history. Different judgments are made in different situations by different actors simply because the same river never flows under the same bridge twice. In one sense, then, *any* two moral judgments *must* differ. But that level of difference is quite banal and does not constitute an ethical difference. By "ethical difference" we mean that two judgments have features that can be *contrasted*. This can only occur when they can be classified in kinds. Our deeds fall into *moral* kinds: there are honest deeds and dishonest deeds, resolute deeds and hesitant deeds, impetuous deeds and long-considered deeds. They also fall into *material* kinds: some deeds concern financial transactions, some faithfulness in love, some the telling truth or falsehood, and so on. An ethical difference arises when two deeds alike in material kind differ in moral kind. Deeds of different material kinds are not contrasted ethically. If Renate gets married to her boyfriend this Saturday afternoon while Michelle is busy filling out her tax return, we can draw no conclusions about a difference in moral outlook between Renate and Michelle. There is a variety of things people properly set out to do, and the fact that different people are pursuing different projects at any given time does not imply that there are ethical differences among the agents or their acts. But if Sven and Kostas both their submit their tax returns, and Sven's is truthful while Kostas's is untruthful, then, though everything else about the two acts may be different—different place, different laws, different time, different circumstances, different sums of money

involved—we are also forced to recognise a difference which we can only think of as an ethical difference.

Of course, an apparent difference of this kind may, on further inspection, melt away. Two contrasting decisions may be like one another in material kind, but have different specific features that make, as we say, "all" the difference. In 1939, when both Greece and Denmark faced invasion from fascist powers, Greece, believing it had a trained army, defensible borders and reliable allies, offered forcible resistance; Denmark, knowing that it lacked all these things, capitulated. We may at first assume that the Greek decision was courageous, the Danish uncourageous, or perhaps that the Danish decision was prudent, the Greek imprudent. Yet we will probably be right to hesitate over these judgments, since the question the two nations faced was the same question *only in general terms*. Their differing answers were explained, and perhaps entirely justified, by the specific differences between their situations. We can quite reasonably think that each acted courageously, and each prudently, "in the circumstances."

2. An ethical difference is one that can be expressed in binary terms as contradictory answers to the same practical question. In practical decisions there comes a point at which the multitude of options is reduced to two. The twenty-five possible houses we found on the estate agents' websites are reduced by patient elimination and we have settled on our favorite; what it comes to now is whether we go ahead and offer for it, Yes, or No? And we can test for ethical difference by looking for the question to which two opposite answers are given. (It is possible to exaggerate the importance of this binary moment, of course, just as it is possible to exaggerate the moment of decision in moral behavior as a whole. I offer it only as a formal test to distinguish real from imaginary ethical differences.)

Sven submits a truthful tax return, Kostas an untruthful one. The answers they have given to the same question are opposed like negative and positive values of the one integer. But does that mean they *disagree* about something? If Sven is simply acting morally and Kostas immorally, what are they disagreeing *about*? Only whether to be moral or immoral. On what the moral course really is, they may be entirely agreed. The binary difference seems to mean no more than the presence or absence of active moral responsibility. But *lack* of responsibility is not a *kind* of responsibility. What is not there doesn't count. (Remember the logical parable of the three cats on the mat: the ginger cat, the tabby cat, and the imaginary cat?) We should certainly not think that whenever someone acts immorally he or she must have an alternative set of moral beliefs to account for it. Sin lacks the dignity of a point of view. Only if Kostas has a different way of understanding his situation can we trace his difference with Sven back to a *disagreement*. He may, perhaps, believe that government documents do not require strict veracity; he may believe that tax laws are an unjust imposition; he may believe that his duty to his family is higher than his duty as a citizen. It doesn't matter whether he is right; the point is, there must be *something he believes*, justified or unjustified, if he is to have a disagreement with Sven. A disagreement has more propositional content than a difference of judgment; it is a clash of reasonings, which arises from a difference in describing the way the world lies.

"Ethical disagreement," then, does not mean the same as "sin." Indeed, if we think of sin as sheer willful disobedience, there can be no overlap at all between sin and disagreement; the very fact that someone has reasons for a contrary judgment means she or he is not willfully disobedient. But this voluntarist definition of sin is too narrow. There are culpable faults of thought, too, misunderstandings for which we are to blame. Some moral disagreements—perhaps most of them—are a matter for some blame in some quarter. Yet there is such a thing, as moral theology has long known, as "invincible ignorance."

3. Ethical disagreement may be talked about, then, when two conditions are met: *(a)* opposite practical judgments about what to do, deriving from *(b)* differing descriptive judgments about the way the world lies. But descriptive differences are also of various kinds. There are differing judgments of fact; there are differing judgments of circumstances; there are differing estimations of consequences. A special kind of disagreement arises when there are differing views, or interpretations, of some fundamental truth about the world, a "doctrinal" difference in the theological sense. And these are the disagreements which raise the most painful questions about our unity in the faith of Christ. One church may think that the colonial period of Africa's history was a disgrace to the European churches, another may think it was an honorable phase of Christian mission. Such a difference, however large its practical implications, may be tolerated with charity and good will. But if one church affirms that God created the material world, another that it was made by Satan, that will produce something worse than a major difference of practical judgment; it will constitute a disagreement that can hardly be sustained within Christianity.

And this raises the question of what is meant when it is said that a moral disagreement, such as that over homosexuality, is too small, too unimportant, for the churches to divide over. In the face of potential schism in the Anglican Communion, it invites immediate sympathy to ask, in bewilderment, how such a destructive outcome could derive from such a trivial cause.[4]

There is more than one way in which the concepts "small" and "large" may be applied in this context. In the casuistic moral-theological tradition it used to be said that moral offences might be discounted when they concerned "small" as opposed to "grave matter." If one unwittingly pocketed a large sum of money not one's own, one was obliged to make every effort to restore it; if one unwittingly pocketed a penny, one could cheerfully congratulate oneself on one's good luck. If one *deliberately* stole a penny, of course, an act of contrition was required, for theft is theft; yet even so, returning the penny might not necessarily be the highest priority among one's duties. "Scrupulosity," preoccupation with small matters, was thus recognized as a vice in itself.

Some points of moral disagreement among the churches may be settled by an appeal to "small matter." Suppose that in a Roman Catholic parish in Northern Ireland a well-known republican gangster regularly receives communion from an obviously complicit parish priest—what an irritant to the Protestant neighbors! What an embarrassment to the bishop! Yet the Catholic bishops have made their position quite clear. It is a single case, and an irregular one. So it may be "small matter" in the context of ecumenical relations, and everyone would be wise not to make a *cause célèbre* of it. But this illustration does nothing to illuminate our kind of problem. Nobody argues that the fuss over the New Hampshire consecration was overdone because, after all, it was only *one* gay bishop! The whole point was, a precedent was set, and was intended to be set.

4. For this reaction, see Christopher Lewis's contribution to *Gays and the Future of Anglicanism*, entitled "On Unimportance."

Much more potentially fruitful is the paradigm of "heavy" and "light laws" propounded by the rabbis to arrange the laws of the Pentateuch in some kind of moral ranking-order. In the New Testament we find Jesus himself taking up the rabbinic distinction between "heavy" and "light" commands of the law: the tithing of mint and dill and cumin is less important than justice, mercy, and faith; the supreme command is love of God and neighbor. Before we embrace this model with too much enthusiasm, however, we have to answer a difficult question about how it is to be applied. Once we have said that the law of love is architectonic and that ritual is secondary, how much more does the New Testament tell us about differences of gravity? Do our assumptions about the ranking-order of moral principles correspond to anything in the Scriptures, or are they imported from the common intuitions of our own time? Christians in any period of history, whatever their disagreements, seem to agree with one another on morality more than they agree with Christians of other ages on morality and more than they agree with one another on doctrine. Doctrinal preoccupations tend to be diachronic, linking past communities with present, while moral preoccupations are synchronic, characteristic of their day. The moral profile of Christians today is pretty recognizable across most varieties of church and churchmanship. They believe in international aid and fair trade; they believe in care for AIDS victims; they do not believe in racial discrimination; they believe in families; they tend to think the more abstract forms of capitalist financing morally perilous; they regard making money out of sex as debased, and so on. They have their major disagreements, it goes without saying, and perhaps these appear more ominous against the striking uniformity of their background. But this very uniformity marks contemporary Christians off from Victorian Christians, from early-modern or medieval Christians, and from the Christians of the New Testament era. If we ask why there should be such historical differences, the answer is simple: the priorities we hold are the result of shared judgments about the demands of the age in which we live and act. That is as true for us in our time as it was for the New Testament writers in theirs.

If this observation seems to support a strong historical relativism in regard to ethics, let us correct the impression by stressing its limits. It has to do with the issues we *prioritize*. It does not mean that the church in each age conducts its moral thinking in isolation from the traditions it has received, learning nothing from them and acknowledging no authority. It does not mean that there are no moral lessons to be learned from the New Testament. It does not mean that the only lessons to be learned from the New Testament are highly general moral categories ("justice, mercy, faith"), and that all its more detailed discussions may be set aside. The New Testament can and should exercise authority over our moral thought at both general and specific levels. Yet there remains a work of moral judgment that is properly relative to agents and situations, and this is what shapes the priorities that prevail in given periods. That is why it is more difficult for us to sympathize with the moral attitudes of earlier Christian generations than it is to share their doctrinal convictions; for with our contemporaries we share a common world with its urgent questions and moral challenges. The logic of human historicity is that living in a given age means having a distinct set of practical questions to answer, neither wholly unlike those that faced other generations nor mere repetitions of them. It is to be neither superior to nor independent of the past; but it is to be answerable for our own space and time and for its peculiar possibilities of vice and virtue.

Where does this leave the proposal about the light and the heavy? In the awkward position of a *petitio principi*. In warning us not to make light matters into communion-breaking disagreements, it trades on common priorities that we all assume, and offers the good, if undramatic, advice that we ought not to let ourselves be deflected from priorities we agree on. But what when we disagree? If disagreements did not arise, there would be no reflective way for Christians to respond to changing demands. They would just go on stressing what they had always agreed to be most important thing, and would take no notice of how new challenges were shaping up. So when some Christians see a more ominous threat in a new development than others do, the advice to concentrate on the most important things is no advice at all.

The problem with the proposal to solve this disagreement by dismissing the matter as "light," not "heavy," is that it has latched on to the rabbinic rather than the Christian version of the hierarchy of values. I do not say this to disparage the achievement of the rabbis. Their discovery of the difference between the light and the heavy was a great discovery, and without it Jesus's development of the theme would have been inconceivable. Nevertheless, Jesus and the early Christians did develop it, and they did carry forward the proposition of some rabbis that the highest law was not merely the weightiest of the laws, but in some sense *enveloped and contained* all the others. That is to say: the hierarchy of moral principles was not merely a matter of preferring A to B. The law of God had an organic logic, in which the varied and diverse subject-matter of the laws was brought under the hermeneutic control of a unifying and regulative demand, the law of love.

What follows from this is that the moral weight of any area of moral concern—let us say, the scope of any one of the commandments—will be relative to the way in which its demand interacts with the others and concentrates the regulative command of love upon a particular constellation of historical events and circumstances. The specific moral commands do not present sequestered and self-contained demands. They are different matrices for *one* demand, distributing the way it encounters us within the complex order of the created world. The essential task we face in relation to our own differences of moral judgment is to map those differences carefully, to establish their true dimensions. We face a task of moral description, in which we shall need to call upon all the categories of moral judgment offered us, in the Ten Commands and elsewhere, for a variety of relations and interactions in the service of love.

So we see how inadequate it is to exclaim, "But the issue is not such a very great matter, after all!" There are, indeed, smaller and larger differences; but—and the point is crucial—their size is not determined by the *matter* of the difference as such, but by the *relation* in which it stands to wider agreements and disagreements. The point at issue—whether homosexuality, capitalism, colonial slavery, or something else—is never the whole of what is at stake. Nobody has to make a decision about that and that alone. It would be nice to purify the question to the point when it was about one thing and one thing only; but if we had done that, it would already be nine tenths solved. The question is always, *what does it mean, in this constellation of circumstances,* to approve or disapprove of this or that line of conduct? What relations are present to us in and through it? How do the various refractions of the demand of love within the moral law come together to form an understanding of where we stand? So what looks "small" at first glance can become the subject of the day, the focus of everyone's attention, the test of where each and every person is morally situated, the divide between old friendships and new ones. From outside the historical context it may be hard indeed to comprehend why; but it is part and parcel of historical understanding that we should recognize how one issue acts as a conduit for others. The struggle in the fourth century can appear to be about an iota, but it seemed to those engaged in it to be a struggle over false gods. If we cannot see how that was so, it does not mean that it was not so. It simply means we have not entered into the intellectual dynamics of the time and seen how the largest of alternatives was shaping up for the church. Large alternatives always present themselves in petty choices.

And it is no different with our own age. Understanding the times we live in can be especially difficult. Our initial familiarity with them may be a positive hindrance; it is hard to gain perspective. We must first of all, therefore, take *seriously* the fact that homosexuality has become a dividing issue among us. There is no point in expressing scornful wonder. It is part of the shape of the history we have been given to live through—no more rational and no more irrational than any other history. We must cope with the history we have been thrown into, and reach such understanding of it as we can. To do this, we must ask what great issues this apparently "little" issue mediates, how what is fought over can have become the question of strange gods. But if we press forward resolutely along that path, we may begin to untangle the knot of associations, identify the strange gods, flush them out of their cultural hiding places and leave the question of homosexuality disenchanted of them, ready to be seen precisely for what it is and not as the bearer of some wider cultural decision. That cheerful rationalist Joseph Butler thought that "every thing is what it is, and not another thing."[5]

5. Butler, *Sermons*, preface §33

It would be truer to say that everything is something other than what it is, everything is charged with borrowed significations, alien references to things contiguous. A patient work of interpretation is needed. To try to handle the question peremptorily is to deny what it is we face, which is the culturally shaping force of systems of reference. And to deny that is to refuse the ancient challenge, "Know thyself!"

We return to the question from which we began: what room is there for a "pluralism" in the church's moral beliefs and practices, i.e., the acceptance of tolerable but ethically significant difference? Such an acceptance will not be possible, we must assume, when moral difference reflects significant doctrinal disagreement, bringing the common Christian faith into question. With this negative in place, can we now identify a positive possibility for moral pluralism?

As a definitional baseline, we may say that to recommend moral pluralism is to find not just moral difference but moral *disagreement* respectable. Until the final perfection of the church there will always be moral difference in that there will always be sin as well as righteousness. But what there need not always be is disagreement about whether a given practice counts as sin or righteousness. And pluralism aims to find such disagreement *respectable*, not merely to license it. In a civil political order some moral disagreements are licensed without being commended. When the state permits people to sex-select their children or plunge themselves hopelessly into debt by addictive gambling, it does not necessarily approve of these actions. (Whether we approve of the state's permitting them is a separate question.) We may accept people's freedom to follow such courses, and yet disapprove wholeheartedly. We may think that gambling-addiction should lie beyond the reach of the criminal law, and yet not hesitate to suggest to any addict with whom we have a pastoral relation that his addiction is bad for him and for all connected with him. But to advocate pluralism, we must paradoxically maintain a kind of *approval* of moral judgments of which we disapprove. On the one hand, it is not merely a question of recognizing that in different situations different judgments will be appropriate; for in that case there is no disagreement. To advocate moral pluralism is to say that something which should in principle not be done, should continue to be done all the same. And to advocate it plausibly is harder than may at first appear.

Let us take a paradigm case. Western liberals are inclined to view arranged marriage with disfavor. That young adults should be wholly responsible for finding and choosing their own marriage partners is, they are likely to think, undoubtedly better. There is always a risk of immature judgment, of course; yet the fact that the individuals take responsibility for their own decision at this critical juncture in their lives is morally fitting to their personal dignity, and offers a better prospect that a couple will be committed to each other over the long term. What space does this leave for Western liberals to speak in favor of the more ancient system? They can admit that it fits other expectations within societies that traditionally practice it—e.g., in respect of education, breadth of social contact, the role of affine-groups in providing cultural and economic opportunities, and so on. They can admit that when operated conscientiously it may serve the best interests of young couples *as they actually find themselves situated* in those societies. They can see that reform could not be achieved on this one point without renegotiating a whole range of other social conditions, so that a sudden breach in the tradition could be very difficult to handle; considerate and consultative ways of operating the system, on the other hand, might produce a slow and healthy evolution towards freedom. The Western liberal can grant all this without doubting that the modern Western policy is superior. On these terms Western liberals can be genuine moral pluralists in respect of the question.

This example draws our attention to a necessary condition for any appeal to pluralism. It can be made only on behalf of practices embedded in cultural contexts, contexts in which they serve to secure recognizable social goods. Pluralism, in effect, can only be made sense of in relation to cultural totalities, modes of social existence taken in their entirety. There is a range of different possible patterns for negotiating the challenges of human social existence as a whole. We by no means have to maintain our neutrality in respect of the various features of these; yet we may still recognize that the troubling features play a structural role within their systems. But this has an implication of major importance: the appeal to cultural pluralism can never support experimentation or innovation. It demands deference for established traditional differences, those related to broad patterns of social organization.

Imagine a Western visitor in a society where arranged marriage prevails asking a young woman why she permits her parents to choose a husband for her. If she is articulate, she may rehearse the virtues of the practice in relation to the society she belongs to: "I only know dull uneducated village boys, but my father has contacts with educated families in the city," and so on. If she is reflective, she may also concede the virtues of a system of free choice. And yet, "it is the way it is done here." Pluralism means accepting the validity of this last move, acknowledging a certain authority to embedded practice. But no innovation can be defended in that way; and it is curiously absent-minded of us if we don't find it odd when the defense appropriate to established practices is offered on behalf of innovations or experiments whose likely long-term effects are quite unknown.

Societies may, of course, sometimes be asked to engage in experimental change. But this requires reasons, and the reasons must be strong enough to bear the burden of proof. If the arguments offered are insufficient, the case for innovation is not made, and there is no question of the innovation's commanding respect. If, on the other hand, the burden of proof is met, its success consists precisely in undermining respect for a faltering practice. The most that can then be offered defenders of the *status quo* is the respect and forgiveness due to those who are wrong in good faith. But that is not pluralism either. Which is why I say that pluralism is difficult to argue for successfully. A plea for variety of moral practice very easily turns into an undermining of existing practice. Apart from culturally embedded practices, moral plurality quickly becomes self-contradictory, an assertion of p and $\sim p$ at the same time—or perhaps a delaying tactic while one clears one's throat and gets ready to swallow![6]

To assert the right of plural moral judgment requires a careful account of the systemic social differences that make that right intelligible. So explanation of difference is the essence of a policy of mutual forbearance. It risks adding insult to injury to demand forbearance while at the same time refusing ex-

6. And Professor Adams does not in fact succeed in carrying through her pluralist intentions with any consistency. She concludes her advocacy of live-and-let-live with a rousing call for everyone "to own up to the spiritual violence we have done to gay and lesbian, bisexual and transgendered persons" ("Faithfulness in Crisis," 78). The Church of Nigeria will manage things its own way, to be sure; but the rest of us are to apologize loudly for the Church of Nigeria!

planations. The sharp response to the innovations of Western Anglican churches from the churches of the ex-colonial territories owed much to the fact that the innovating churches had no program of mutual explanation in view. And here, perhaps, the churches of the South and East made a mistake. They attributed the North American uncommunicativeness to racism. It is, on the whole, more likely that the North American churches merely acted, in default of a thorough deliberative process of their own, under the force of strong cultural pressure, the reasons for which they never explained even to themselves, since an ill-conceived doctrine of pluralism persuaded them that thinking was an unnecessary labor. They may have suffered something worse than a bout of racism, if such a thing can be imagined; they may have suffered an implosion of their powers of practical reason, the result of long habits of irresponsibility. And since theology is nothing if not a discipline of common reasoning about God and our life together, unless they recover it, their days of being churches of any kind are numbered.

4 SCRIPTURE *and* OBEDIENCE

*O that my ways may be steadfast in keeping your
statutes!*

(Ps 119:5)

THE AUTHORS OF the *Windsor Report* thought it was unnecessary and inexact to speak of the authority of Holy Scripture;
to speak of the authority of God said everything that needed
to be said. And there is an element of truth in this, in that
the only authority these books can possibly command is the
authority of their role in God's self-announcement; apart from
that, they are records of a past culture that may interest us or
not, as we choose. Yet we cannot leave it at that. For God's
authority authorizes; and it is through authorized persons and
activities that we see the effective exercise of God's authority in the world. There is nothing wrong in speaking of the
authority of bishops, of councils, of preachers or of the community of the faithful; and at the other end of the spectrum,
there is nothing wrong in speaking of the authority of Jesus of

Nazareth. Neither is it inexact, then, to speak of the authority of apostles and prophets, called out by God to write with clarity and sufficiency of the events surrounding Jesus of Nazareth, their context in the history of Israel, and their universal meaning for mankind. These writings are God's chosen means, together with the sacramental acts of the church, of making his self-announcement known to all ages. Scripture is not the first moment of God's self-announcement; that is the historical deeds themselves by which he raised up Israel and Jesus. But neither is it a moment *after* God's self-announcement, a retrospective commentary that could be peeled away, leaving the core intact. Scripture is, we may say, God's administration of his self-announcement, the record he has authorized to it and the seal he has set on it to confirm that it is true.

If we need to say more about the Scriptures than that they are authorized, perhaps we may follow John Webster in speaking of their "sanctification" for their work.[1] That means simply that God has set them apart. As he has set apart a particular race and a particular member of that race for the salvation of the world, so he has set apart particular writers to bear a definite and decisive testimony to what he has done. It was, of course, a *human* testimony they had to bear, a work performed in human ways by human servants. In a thousand ways, the texts that lie between the covers of our Bibles show that they are the product of painstaking and creative human labor and reception. But we must be careful what we make of that word "human." If we glide from speaking of their humanity into implying some kind of inadequacy in them, as though their being human were a shameful secret we have laid bare, a deficiency we are now in a position to patch up, then it is we, not they, that

1. Webster, *Holy Scripture,* 17–39.

must stand charged with ignorance and superstition. The humanity of the Scriptures does not entitle us to patronize them. Just as we speak of the sinlessness of the human being Jesus of Nazareth, and some Christians speak of the immaculate human conception of the Virgin Mary, so we may speak quite appropriately of a perfection in Holy Scripture. Its perfection is sui generis, a fitness for its own assigned task. The perfection of the Psalms does not consist in their being the most perfectly metrical verses or containing the most perfect poetic imagery. The perfection of the letters of Paul does not consist in their being the highest examples of epistolary elegance. Neither does the perfection of the historical books consist in their being the most unambiguous records or the most discerning evaluation of sources. The only perfection that counts is this: that God *truly attests himself and his deeds* through this poetry, these letters, this history. The faith required of the reader of Holy Scripture is obedience to the testimony that God bears within them, and that is one and the same as the faith that leads to salvation.

In more ways than one the Christian world now finds itself living "after" the fundamentalist controversy, downstream of those white-water rapids that imperiled theological navigation for a century. There is a widespread sense, for one thing, that the historical exploration of the biblical texts has played itself out, that most of what can be done intelligently on those lines has been done, and that further work is subject to the law of diminishing returns. For another thing, the question of the authority of the biblical texts has been refocused from their historical veridicality to their moral serviceability. This makes a deal of a difference. Those who first raised problems about the Bible's historical veridicality thought they could be confident of its authority in everything that really mattered—i.e., faith and morals, two things that might, to a thoroughgoing liberal, melt into one. To the liberalism that grew out of the skeptical project of historical criticism, the moral authority of the Bible, or at least of the New Testament, was simply self-evident. Moral and religious goodness, it appeared, was either unaffected by the vagaries of history or was in a progressive compact with it. So far have liberal convictions undergone a sea change. Doubts about Scripture's authority today are focused on its competence to guide us through those highly contested moral discernments which have become so common a feature of the late modern world.

But in order to get a view of what authority means in this context, we need a clearer view of what it means to make moral discernments. Certain phantasmic conceptions, which liberals and conservatives often used to hold in common, and which hang around today's discussions like ghosts at the feast, had better be exorcised. Moral truths were conceived of as something like self-evident speculative truths, which, once properly grasped, could hardly be doubted. Christ was to be obeyed because, and to the extent that, his moral teaching self-evidently presented us with those truths to which the moral consciousness bore independent witness. Kant said as much in a famous assertion in the *Groundwork for the Metaphysics of Morals.* That meant that practical moral crises could be viewed only as temptations to the weak in faith, not as real dilemmas to which the answer could be in any doubt. They were challenges to our resolution, to be countered by a more unflinching reassertion of the principles we were taught from the beginning. (Think of the appalling assumptions that generate the melodrama of Scott's *Heart of Midlothian!*) Casuistry, which attempted to resolve dilemmas by making fine distinctions, was dismissed scornfully as a mean abuse of the intellect, designed to produce subtle denials of the obvious. Needless to say, the Bible's wholesale rejection of homosexual conduct was seen, by liberals as well as by conservatives, as entirely of a piece with its moral superiority over pagan cultural values.

But ethics has now fallen out of the realm of the self-evident into the realm of the contested, to which, in truth, it always belonged. And this has made moral consistency look less like a confident conviction of truths evident as the day, more like a faith in truths not seen. It restores to practical reason the atmosphere of insecurity and risk that is native to it. The prayer of the psalmist, "Give me life according to your word!" (Ps 119:107) is the prayer of the faithful reader of Scripture who is ready to take the risk of living by it. This reader does not know everything there is to know about Scripture or about the challenges of life; he does not have the answer to every question; but he is willing to rely on this teaching, to receive it on its own terms, questioning and being questioned by it, in the expectation that God will open up his way before him as he reads, recites, and constantly revisits those testimonies to God's purposes.

If we are inclined to say, as I am, that this is the *authentic* way of understanding obedient practical reason, more suited to the real meaning of discipleship, we should not do so glibly, underestimating the danger. That danger arises in relation to two conjoined intellectual tasks, for neither of which there can be secure rules, two "discernments" that simply have to be made, and may possibly be made wrongly with serious consequences. There is the interpretative task of discerning *what the text means*, on the one hand; and there is the conscientious task of discerning *ourselves and our position as agents in relation to the text*, on the other. The first discernment is *of* the text; the second discernment is *out of* the text. In the first discernment, the text is before us; we read about David, about Peter, about

Jesus, and have to decide what it is that is said about them there. In the second discernment the text is behind us; we do not read about ourselves in the same way that we read about David, Peter and Jesus. Yet it sheds light forward upon us. It provides us with the categories and analogies we need for questioning ourselves and understanding ourselves. The Scripture tells us not to bear false witness against our neighbor. Whether *this* particular ambiguous statement we have it in mind to make will be false, or merely discreet, is something that the Scripture will not tell us; we must judge that for ourselves with the aid of the Holy Spirit. Yet everything the Scripture does tell us about truth and falsehood will contribute to making that judgment possible. The authority of Scripture is proved, then, precisely as it does, in fact, shed light on the decisions we are faced with, forcing us to reevaluate our situation and correct our assumptions about what we are going to do.

Neither of these two discernments is without risk; yet the second is the more highly dangerous. The most mysterious question anyone has to face is not, *what does Scripture mean?* but, *what does the situation I am facing mean?* If we have even begun to appreciate the nature of this question, and how a false judgment of ourselves can lead us to destruction, we shall be on our guard against any hermeneutic proposal to *reverse* the sequence of discernments, starting with our own situation and turning back to Scripture to look for something there to fit it. That presupposes that we already know the answer to the one question we dare not presuppose an answer to. Nevertheless such proposals are common enough in theological discussion, sometimes with a liberal, sometimes with a conservative, slant. It hardly matters which, since the two come closest to each other precisely at the point where they are both furthest from the truth. If the conservative thinks that *all* the scriptural witness to moral behavior can and must be honored somehow, and the liberal that only *some* of it, or only *most* of it, must be honored, what difference does that make if each thinks that conclusion has been reached from some self-evident intuition about what the times require, so that the appeal to the Scripture merely confirms what has already been decided? This is not to take Scripture seriously as an authority. And it is not to take living in the present seriously as a risky business.

For our present purposes, and since much of our discussion so far has been concerned with the current dilemmas of liberal Christianity, let us take up a liberal version of this hermeneutic proposal. We shall have opportunity enough to identify the specifically conservative form of the temptation when we discuss the need for hermeneutic "distance." Help is at hand from a cautiously worded statement of Roman Catholic provenance, representing the proposal at its most modest, and therefore, perhaps, its most seductive. "Here and there," wrote Heinz Schürmann, "among the particular New Testament values and precepts . . . there are time-bound judgments of value and fact, and they show that the Holy Spirit has deepened moral sensitivity through the course of the Church's history and the history of mankind."[2] Bracketing out the mention of time-bound judgments of *fact*, which is irrelevant to our purpose, the important claim here is that some New Testament "judgments of value," being "time-bound," show us how moral sensitivity has "deepened" since they were made. These are, of course, only supposed to be occasional. Sufficient distinctions have been made before this point in the exposition to render most of the New

2. Schürmann, "How Normative," 43. We are told that Schürmann's conception of the relation of Scripture to moral doctrine was "adopted in general terms" by the International Theological Commission in 1974.

Testament amenable to our ethical reasoning without recourse to the "here and there." These occasional "time-bound judgments," then, are an intractable residue, a clinker in the furnace that refuses to burn up. When the author proceeds to urge that a "moral-theological hermeneutics" is in place to handle this recalcitrant material, we know that the word "hermeneutics" cannot bear its customary sense. It does not promise, as might be expected, an *interpretation* of these judgments; it promises only a refusal of them. What is demanded is a clear, though modest, right of repudiation in respect of some "judgments of value," not on the ground that the situation has changed, which could cause no one any difficulty, but simply on the ground that we have made some moral progress since the days when the Holy Spirit spoke through the apostles, and can understand their judgments as immature. It asserts the superior right of our preunderstanding.

It is decisive, of course, that this claim is made in respect of *New Testament* moral judgments. That something will have to be said of the "time-bound character" of some judgments in the *Old* Testament will surprise no one who has learned from the Epistle to the Hebrews to see the pre-Christian vision of the human goal as "fragmentary" and "diverse," looking for an "earthly" rest where the ultimate purpose of God was nothing less than a heavenly sabbath (Heb 1:1, 4:7). To take just one example from that book: the way we think of Joshua's wars of conquest will be affected by our looking for a "heavenly" rest. The conquest narratives will not be taken to afford, directly or indirectly, a moral norm for war making, and that not because of changed situations or perceptions, but simply because their salvation-historical position has been, as it were, overwhelmed by the advent of Christ. But this judgment is based on a Christian reading of history, in which Christ himself fulfils and transforms what has gone before. That is the framework in which the "then" of Joshua is differentiated from the "now" of the Christian epoch. To take the same way with the teachings of the New Testament, on the other hand, would be self-subverting. And to avoid this fall into incoherence, the liberal hermeneutic proposal faces, it would seem to me, a simple alternative. Either it posits some *further* climax of salvation-history over and beyond Christ, some "age of the Spirit" such as Montanus or Joachim conceived of, or a Hegelian dialectical history with an Absolute Future, something, at any rate, that will allow a "deepened moral sensitivity" to which the revelation of the incarnation looks immature and outgrown. Or else it makes a distinction between the normative position of Jesus himself and the subnormative position of the apostolic authors, refusing to claim on their behalf the kind of finality it claims for him. The difficulties into which each of these courses leads are too well known to be pursued in detail at this point.

Since we summoned a Roman Catholic theologian for a modest statement of a hermeneutic proposal that Anglican liberals would be likely to make with less reserve, let us look in the same direction to find a suitable corrective, equally modestly expressed. Jean-Yves Lacoste has written: "The image of the hermeneutic 'circle' is less illuminating than it seems. We can learn only to the extent that we can let the unanticipated put our expectations and our prejudices in question. Authentic discovery punches a hole in the circle, since only pseudo-questions carry their own answers ready and waiting in their bosoms. Pre-understanding without honest admission of non-understanding will hardly invite more than the most meagre discoveries."[3] Lacoste does not challenge the necessity

3. Lacoste, "More Haste, Less Speed," 272.

of hermeneutic preunderstandings. He insists simply that there can be no discovery that has a circular form; preunderstanding cannot have both first and last word. "Yet it is necessary," he continues, "for questions to be asked, and that means there must be a field of dialogue where the speech that answers my questions can become my very own speech."[4] The essential difference between two hermeneutic approaches emerges precisely at this point: the one sees Scripture's readers as armed with "deepened moral sensitivity," new moral confidence that has accrued to the elevated age in which they live and from which the text cannot deflect them, the other sees them as approaching armed with moral *questions* to which they seek answers that may become their "very own." What is at stake in resistance to the liberal hermeneutic paradigm becomes clear: the cause is the cause of *open questions*—questions that need opening and holding open because they are of such importance existentially to those who have to ask them. But to hold a question open with real existential commitment, and not merely to bedazzle the conversation with interrogatives darting round like bats in daylight, one must purposefully look to the source from which an answer is sought, an answer not already contained in the question, which is therefore capable of reforming and refining the question. And that is precisely what is meant by the authority of Scripture in Christian ethics.

Indeed, it is what is meant by the authority of Scripture as such. For authority is what evokes belief and obedience, and questions of belief and obedience are all, at root, moral questions—not in the superficial sense of being related to the details of our behavior, but as concerned with the way we dispose of ourselves in our living. What hermeneutic theory says about

4. Ibid.

preunderstandings applies, of course, to speculative and empirical questions too: the experimental scientist cannot ask questions of the readings he obtains without some preunderstanding of what those readings may indicate; yet he cannot discover anything unless those readings can redetermine his preunderstanding. But we leap into a whole new world of seriousness when the questions are the ultimate practical questions, questions about how we are to live the one life given us; and we leap into a whole new world of seriousness when we dare to ask these questions of God's chosen witnesses, the writers of the documents of the Old and New Testaments.

The liberal hermeneutic paradigm, fashioned by the controversy over historical biblical criticism, failed precisely because it thought it could count on there being a concrete moral truth immediately and categorically known to all, a peremptory and unchallengeable moral certainty. In this it failed to allow for danger. Action is always exposed to danger: we may turn out to have acted on false assumptions about the facts, to have misunderstood the situation in which we acted, to have formed an inadequate conception of our task, to have failed to envisage the good to be pursued, etc., etc. Nothing can guarantee us against such failures; nothing except perpetual vigilance can protect us from them. In failing to allow for danger, the liberal hermeneutic failed to pose the questions that engage us supremely in our self-disposal: questions of intelligibility and purpose in the life we live, questions of our responsibility for ourselves. Always pressing forward in pursuit of some speculative truth, it dared to take the answers to all these questions as read; in doing so, it bypassed deliberative reason and short-circuited the role of the intellect in the living of life.

The questions we pose to Scripture look for answers to help us live as those reborn from death and destruction, exercising our powers of thought and decision anew. We may not look for answers that will excuse us that task. Consider, for example, the question and answer of the psalmist: "How shall a young man keep his way pure? By guarding it in keeping with your word" (Ps 119:9). It is hardly surprising that a long-established line of historical criticism found this profound poem, the most existentially urgent document in the whole Old Testament, to be legalistic, formalistic and altogether uninteresting. That was because the critics never grappled with practical reason as the poet grappled with it. To the poet, presented here as a young man poised on the threshold of life with everything still to be determined, the question mattered. He had need of a word; he had a way to find, and was unsure of it; he wanted it to be not merely *safe* but *pure*—"uncompromised," as we might say, and worthy of a human being's one and only opportunity to live. But why a *word*? Because the only way we have of engaging with our living is by *thinking* about it, and thought requires that we discern a shape, a form, in how we live. An approach to practical reason must be existential, for it is our selves that are at stake in the answers we reach; it must be "poetic," for the task is not mere repetition, but creation in action; but it cannot be improvisatory, since it is a response to a context, and that context may at any point deceive us or trip us up.

   To a word of God we turn, then: a word that gives the world its original meaning and intelligibility, and gives our engagement with the world its meaning too. If we fail to envisage the practical question practically, and think of it as merely theoretical, then we shall feel ourselves imposed upon by the claim to authority and shall resist it by outright protest or by calculated dissimulation. Theoretical discussions always look askance at authority, for we can dally over them forever without putting ourselves or other people to the slightest inconvenience. If nobody needs to know whether Jesus was born in Bethlehem of Judea, a text that claims the authority to settle the matter strikes us as intrusive, hemming us in by forbidding speculation that he was born in Waco, Texas. But what if we do need to know? What if it is part of a message about how we may be saved? Then its claim to authority is the very opposite of intrusive; it is a welcome handhold that we may grasp in our struggle for deliverance. And when we come to St. Paul's observation that God has given an idolatrous culture over to homosexuality, or to Jesus's saying that a man who divorces his wife and marries another commits adultery, it is a radical judgment upon human culture and history, a judgment that presupposes the confrontation of God and world. It operates not simply to demand our assent or dissent; it operates to elicit moral decision from us about the kind of life we are to live in faithfulness to its judgment. Its role is to authorize us to live well, not to take authority away from us. So any judgment we make on the authority of that text is, at the same time, a judgment on ourselves, a moment of self-transcendence that it has brought us to achieve.

It sometimes happens, when gays and non-gays meet to explore questions of sexuality, that proceedings will be brought to an embarrassed halt by an impassioned avowal on someone's part of being personally affected: "It is me they are all talking about!" The correct response to such a declaration must be for everyone, of every approach and every point of view, to leap to his or her feet and chime in: "And me!" "And me!" Certainly we had better not approach the famous biblical texts on homosexuality as though we were not personally affected! What business could we possibly have with them if our only interest were to frame a theory of sexuality, or perhaps a history of sexuality, for scientists or philosophers to discuss? We had better come to them knowing that we need the help of God's word if we are to find our way through this idol-ridden sphere, and that our own sexuality and idolatry—nothing less!—are under scrutiny in those texts. The dangerous possibility of moral skepticism had better be always present to our minds, and we had better know the terror of waking up one day to find that the living of our lives has become worthless, in our own sight and in God's. We had better stumble across homosexuality, our own or other people's, as a genuinely unknown quantity; we had better ask about it as those who need to be told, rather than reckon we already know all there is to know. If its opportunities and threats press in on us with bewildering complexity, leaving us at a loss as we search around for a way of sorting out the multiple layers of our experience, then the authority of Scripture may begin to mean something serious to us.

Better an honest bewilderment than a perfect theory. Then, with our preunderstanding up in the air, we shall understand well enough that St. Paul's observations about the relation of homosexual practice to an idolatrous culture are only one moment in the story. Yet we shall be very unwilling to leave that moment out, since we shall be only too conscious of our own predicament with the idolatry of our culture. The danger lies, we shall know, precisely in oversimplification. But oversimplification consists of ruling inconvenient angles out, and we can hardly avoid oversimplification by failing to think about the subtle undercurrents and connections that bind a given sexual dilemma to a given cultural complex. If we cannot approach this text as a clue to a problem weighing sorely upon us (whether as homosexuals ourselves, or as those who share a social space with homosexuals, two categories that include most people in the West), we shall certainly experience it as a pointless imposition. Then we shall rebound in panic, assert the right of our preunderstanding, and briskly close down every question. Protective of a freedom that will, in the end, be no more than purely notional, we shall put ourselves on guard against any insight in any text that might actually teach us something helpful. If only we understood what freedom really meant, and how difficult freedom is to accomplish, we would surely ask that text to give us rivers of living water!

5 HERMENEUTIC DISTANCE

Therefore we must pay greater attention to what we have heard, so that we do not drift away from it.

(Hebrews 2:1)

A DISCIPLINE OF biblical "hermeneutics," i.e., of interpretation, has no point unless we are resolved to be obedient. That will serve as a summary of the argument of the fourth of these "sermons"—and if it seems to leave a number of loose ends hanging, let them hang a bit longer while we press on to the other side of the matter; for without seeing both sides, we cannot get the question of scriptural authority properly in view. The other side is this: obedience is a duty that needs the discipline of hermeneutic reflection if it is to be carried through. We cannot "obey" in a vacuum of understanding.

To get a purchase on the point, let us begin from the case that seems to belie it: what we sometimes call "implicit" obedience. That epithet suggests that there is no room to stop to think. The command is barked out, and the troops leap to it, as in the old sergeant major's quip, "When I say 'jump,' you jump, and ask how high on the way up!" Is this not the right model, after all? Must we not obey God blind, acknowledging that the ways of providence are beyond our grasp? The story of Abraham's sacrifice of Isaac would hardly make sense if there were nothing laudable in simply doing what God commands, questions aside.

Yet even "implicit" obedience demands a measure of understanding. There is an old (and overfamiliar) joke about a man who sought guidance by opening the Bible at random; and coming at first attempt on the statement that Judas went and hanged himself, arrived on the second at "Go, and do thou likewise!" It is not a very funny joke; but a joke it is, not a tragedy. What makes it a joke? Jokes are about fools, and the hero of this joke is certainly a ripe fool who did not understand something very elementary about commanding and being commanded. Commands are events that occur within a relationship. They are given *by* somebody *to* somebody at a particular juncture. The order barked out at the new recruits by the sergeant major needs a parade ground for its context. There must be an understood relation between barker and barked-at. Otherwise what is barked can have no reference, and if it has no reference, it cannot be obeyed. Imagine walking quietly down the street and hearing a voice mysteriously borne through the air: "Present arms!" What are you to do? You will probably suppose you have overheard something not intended for your ears, from a nearby military barracks or a film set. Possibly, though, you think it was the voice of an angel sent to warn or command you—but then you will have to give your mind seriously to interpretation. The one thing you cannot do is simply present arms, like recruits on a parade ground. You don't have arms, only an umbrella. They can obey "implicitly," you can't. And they can only obey by virtue of what is understood within their situation: that they are recruits in training, that they are standing on a parade ground, that the loud-voiced man with the red face shouting at them is their sergeant major, and so on. Implicit obedience needs a frame of reference. Even Abraham had to reckon that this was YHWH speaking to him, the same YHWH whose promise had led him out of Mesopotamia to the land his descendants were to occupy, who could bring his purposes to bear in the teeth of seeming contradiction. The point is emphasized by the writer to the Hebrews: "He considered that God was able to raise men even from the dead" (11:19). That "considering" did not *detract* from his implicit obedience. It made it possible.

I knew someone who had a curious experience in the course of her early education when, seated at the back of a classroom next to an unsoundproofed partition, she ended up learning the next-door class's lesson instead of her own. If a child is to obey when the teacher says "get out your poetry books!" she must be able to tell whether it is *her* class that is being spoken to and *her* teacher who is speaking. To obey we need a context, and we need to relate ourself correctly to the context. The fool in the joke does not know how to relate himself to the commands he reads in the Bible. The problem lies not in the commands, but in a failure of practical reason in himself. We may be tempted to call him "literal-minded," but that doesn't quite get to the bottom of the problem. The biblical texts he landed on make perfectly good literal sense when read on their own terms; nothing would be gained by trying to read them figuratively or allegorically. But he is unable to read them on their own terms at all. Preoccupied with finding a reference to himself, he diverts their literal sense from its proper context into his, and so arrives at a conclusion that they could never, literally or otherwise, have intended.

Commands are acts, and acts are performed at certain times and in certain circumstances for certain definite purposes. Divine commands are acts of God. They exert a claim upon their own historical context primarily, on those to whom they are directly addressed. But because any act has a certain intelligibility in its context, and the context of God's acts is his constant will to bless and redeem the world, God's commands may always have implications for other times and circumstances. The Decalogue was not of interest *only* to a barbarous people gathered at the foot of a mountain in Arabia long ago. We, too, in our time and setting, have ways of honoring our father and our mother and of not coveting our neighbor's goods. But in order to judge the bearing of these commands on other times and circumstances, we must observe their place in their historical context first. If we say, "That applies to us, too!" we are *already* engaged in moral reasoning.

Some of the commands in the Bible are so very "bare," so free of wider implications, so wholly defined by their historical situation, that they could never be obeyed more than once, even analogously: "Go into the village opposite you," Jesus told his disciples, "and immediately you will find an ass tied, and a colt with her; untie them and bring them to me" (Matt 21:2). It might be an edifying liturgical innovation if on Palm Sunday a village congregation would walk across the fields to greet its neighbors and be met there with a suitably domesticated beast of burden for the minister to be escorted back on, all waving palms and singing "All Glory, Laud, and Honor"! Not even on the widest construction, however, could this be obedience to the command that Jesus gave his disciples. That command cannot be obeyed now. On the other hand, there are commands whose content can always make some claim upon obedience, however different the circumstances. Consider the passage in the Sermon on the Mount (Matt 5:21–48) where Jesus says, "You have heard that it was said . . . but I say to you. . . . Be reconciled to your brother . . . if your right hand causes you to sin, cut it off. . . . Do not swear. . . . Do not resist one who is evil. . . . Love your enemies." These are not at all like "untie the colt." They claim to direct our action in certain kinds of situation that arise recurrently.

But these again divide into two types: moral rules and public laws. The moral rules in the Sermon on the Mount are concerned with dispositional attitudes—conciliatoriness, self-discipline, restraint, forgiveness, and so on. They are radically and surprisingly expressed, without much interest in whether we will find them easy to obey or not. They have nothing much to say to such dilemmas of practical casuistry as, "What if my brother refuses to be reconciled unless I join him in a solemn oath of undying hatred to our enemy?" Such questions are left, as it were, for later. As a result, these moral rules are capable of directing our conduct in a wide variety of circumstances and producing a very varied style of conformity. By contrast, public laws are designed to be straightforward and easy to keep with a measure of uniformity in execution. We have an outstanding example of a legal code in Deuteronomy 14–23. Shaped, very evidently, out of preexisting legal traditions, it aims to maintain a practical continuity with these while achieving certain dominant reforming aims. It chooses its topics apparently randomly, in the light of questions that have come up and legal rulings that are to hand. It has a lot to say about detailed dilemmas, comparatively little (though not nothing) about underlying attitudes. Moral rules and public laws look different, and they do different jobs. In obvious ways, moral rules are more "portable," more easily applied to changing situations. We still have brothers to be reconciled to, even if there is no temple to leave our gift in (cf. Matt 5:23–24). We would have considerable difficulty in obeying the Deuteronomic law of slavery, however sympathetic we might be to its intentions.

These two types of generic instruction, as they appear in the Bible, share a common feature. They are framed by a narrative context. The metaphor of "framing" could be misleading, though, for a picture frame is designed to display the picture, and may be taken off and changed, but this framework is integral. Narrative is a constituent element in these texts' moral claim upon us. The legal code of Deuteronomy 14–23 is preceded by twelve chapters of mixed narrative and exhortation, explaining how this law code originated in the birth of the nation and the ministry of Moses, and why a code originating in Israel's nomadic past should have authority over an settled agricultural society governed by a monarchy and civic institutions. This setting is continually relevant for understanding the commands as they arise. When told that we must leave the gleanings of the grape harvest for the stranger passing by (Deut 24:19–21), we are reminded that God heard our cry when we were strangers in the land of Egypt (Deut 24:22). The Sermon on the Mount, similarly, is situated in St. Matthew's Gospel as a prelude to Jesus's ministry and as a climax to the account of his birth and commissioning. This, equally, is not irrelevant to those who come to this text for guidance. When we are told to resist not evil, we are prepared to hear how Jesus refused to call on legions of angels to resist arrest in Gethsemane (Matt 26:53–54). The difference in the content of the two texts corresponds to the difference in the narrative that supports them: on the one hand, a narrative about the founding of a holy nation; on the other, a narrative about the fulfillment of history and the redemption of the world. Neither is "timeless," if by that we mean detached from any historical context. But there is a sense in which we can call the Sermon on the Mount "timeless," while Deuteronomy is not. Here is the point at which the particular history of a nation with which God dealt is taken up into God's all-embracing act of world redemption; here is the event in which we are all in every age involved, and here are the commands that belong to that all-embracing event. At the center of the biblical message is an announcement of what God has done in history—"when the time had fully come, God sent forth his Son" (Gal 4:4)—and in that announcement all the authority of the biblical texts finds its source. Biblical commands speak with authority to us because that deed of God in history speaks with authority to us. Let us sum it up like this: it is not *the commands the Bible contains* that we obey; it is *the purposes of God that those commands reveal*, taken in their context. The purposes of God are the ultimate reason why anything at all is good or evil to do. The Bible is authoritative for ethics because it speaks of those purposes and demonstrates them through God's acts in history.

We began from commands because they are a limiting case, raising the question of "implicit" obedience most sharply. There are, of course, other forms of moral instruction in the Scriptures. An ancient and uncouth tradition of hermeneutics looked exclusively to commands as a source for ethics. A fifth-century work called *Speculum 'Quis ignorat?'* wrongly attributed to St. Augustine, begins: "Who does not know that within Holy Scripture there are propositions to be understood and believed, and commands and prohibitions to be observed and acted upon?" and proceeds rather tediously to attempt a list of all the commands in Scripture, so that we may have a compendious code of instruction from which nothing is omitted. It is a model of how not to approach the question, for the effect, of course, is to omit what must on no account be omitted from any view of the Bible's moral instruction: stories, hymns of praise, prophecy, wisdom, parables, lists of virtues, and so on. These all teach us to direct our ways pleasingly to God. We can learn of the wrong of adultery from David and Bathsheba, and not only from the seventh command of the Decalogue. But of all these other styles of moral communication, the same must be said as was said about commands: they lay claim upon our action by virtue of what God has done for us and with us.

Is that to say that everything in the Bible is ethics, and that there is no specifically moral teaching, distinct from history or doctrine? No. There is moral teaching as distinct from doctrine in the same sense that there is practical reason as distinct from theoretical reason. The narrative of how Abraham took his men and chased after the four kings to recover Lot is, viewed in isolation, simply a factual proposition with no term beyond itself. But it does not stand in isolation. It is integrated into the Pentateuch, and the Pentateuch is integrated into Scripture. Our reading of Scripture, viewed as a whole, always tends towards a practical term, how we are to live before the living God of Abraham. There are texts that focus especially upon this practical cutting edge; yet everything in Scripture has a bearing towards it and nothing is simply irrelevant to it. Yet it is not wrong to treat those texts where narrative and doctrine and liturgy crystallize into direct moral instruction as having a special interpretative weight. For these afford a paradigm of how faith works in action, and so serve to protect our moral reflection from falling into a kind of speculative hermeneutical fancy. They are a check on what we are doing with the Bible. If we cannot make our interpretation accommodate the passages where the biblical authors give direct practical guidance, something must have gone wrong. That is why such texts as the condemnations of homosexuality should continue to demand our careful attention, even though they should never be treated alone and in isolation. They are a test of our capacity to achieve a faithful overall reading of the Scriptures. If we can make nothing of them, we should go back to the beginning and start again.

All this takes us a considerable distance from "implicit" obedience, a response that requires no thought or consideration but only immediate conformity. There are occasions on which nothing but implicit obedience will do. But recognizing those occasions depends on a general understanding that we have to think through patiently and reflectively. And when the church is at sea, for one reason or another, over how to read the message of the Gospels, only patient attention to reading, interpretation and obedient thought will bring it to harbor. A shrill call for implicit obedience never substitutes for careful exploration of what it is that must be obeyed.

Is all this just another way of intellectualizing the demand of God? Does it subvert the call for obedience, which ought to be a matter of immediate devotion? To the first of these questions we should answer, Yes—in a way; to the second we may answer, No. Yes, in that our obedience *must be thoughtful obedience.* This "must" is, in the end, not so much an obligation as a simple necessity. Moral instruction is directed to what we "do," and nobody "does" without thinking. If obedience is what is required, thought is what is required—thought about how we may frame our action obediently to the demand. But thoughtful obedience does not exclude immediate encounter with the commanding God. Moments of fear and trembling may befall us; and these are not an *alternative* to the "rational worship" of Romans 12:1–2, by which our minds are renewed to "appreciate distinctions." It is really just another way of saying that the obedience to Scripture that is required of us is the obedience *of faith.*

And in that obedience of faith there has to be a "hermeneutic distance." That term refers to the gap between the reader and the text, the gap that understanding has to bridge. This "distance" is often misunderstood. It is not *historical* distance—that particular turn in hermeneutic theory led, in my view, into a blind alley. There is no reason why I should find the gap wider when reading Plato than when reading Lévinas. Of course, texts that come from unfamiliar cultural backgrounds present special tasks; but if we are ready to take up those tasks and familiarize ourselves with their backgrounds, they need not be any more alien to us in the end. Possibly they will be less so. We may suppose all too carelessly that just because we are contemporary with Lévinas, we shall understand his meaning and objectives without much effort. The distance we have to insist on, rather, is that which secures the objective standing of a text, and especially of a text that claims to speak to us in the name of God. The distance between the text and ourselves can never be, and should never be supposed to be, swallowed up by our understanding. Whatever I may have concluded from my reading of the Scriptures, my conclusion must be open to fresh scrutiny on fresh reading—and will in fact always be, whether I know it or not, because the Scriptures will be its judge. If, after reading the Bible faithfully, I am confident enough to make a ringing declaration of what I have understood, and if my confidence is wholly justified as far as it goes, that still does not mean that my declaration was simply identical to what was contained in the Bible. I may declare that the eternal Word of God, consubstantial and coeternal with the Father, was incarnate of the Virgin Mary; I may be perfectly entitled to think my statement "biblical," as well as "catholic" and "orthodox," and whatever other epithet may underline its authenticity as an expression of Christian belief; and yet it remains the case that those words are not in the Bible, and their authority is always a matter of demonstration and argument in the light of other words that are in the Bible. The authority of Scripture cannot be made over in full plenitude to my words, or to any other words.

There is, of course, a proper authority attaching to a faithful formulation. Creeds, declarations of church councils, Reformation articles and confessions, even the propositions of major theologians have exercised wide authority in the church, and deservedly. Are there moral formulae that have equivalent standing to these doctrinal formulae? Probably. But the drafters of these formulae were not appointed eyewitnesses of the incarnation, as Peter and James and John were eyewitnesses of the incarnation, and so the question whether they have adequately caught the Scriptures' implication at this or that point will always be worth discussing, even if the result of the discussion is the same every time. A seriously meant inquiry into what the Bible means and how it may apply to us can never be out of place in the church. We must not, then, in the supposed defense of a "biblical" ethic, try to close down moral discussions prescriptively, announcing that we already know what the Bible teaches and forbidding further examination. It is the characteristic "conservative" temptation to erect a moment in scriptural interpretation into an unrevisable norm that will substitute, conveniently and less ambiguously, for Scripture itself. The word "authority" means, quite simply, that we have to keep looking back to *this* source if we are to stay on the right track. Anything else is unbelief—a refusal to open ourselves to the question, What is God saying to us through his word?

The three temptations of Jesus, temptations, as St. Luke recounts them, of body, soul, and spirit, culminate on the pinnacle of the temple where the devil invites Jesus to demonstrate his belief in Scripture as God's word. Jesus replies, "You shall not tempt the Lord your God." (Luke 4:12). The fulfillment of the word is sure; but it is not for us—not even for Jesus—to impose on God the manner and time of its fulfillment. At the point of greatest confidence between God and man, where God has shown to man his mind and his purpose, the Son of Man stands back, refuses to seize the initiative and waits upon the unfolding of the Father's purposes that have already begun to unfold. The interpretation of Scripture is a matter in which we wait upon God—not, of course, as though we had understood *nothing* of his mind, but simply because we have not understood *everything*. The text and my reading of the text are two things, not one, and the first is the judge of the second. I can always read further, study harder, think deeper. To precipitate myself from the pinnacle of the text, and demand that angel wings shall bear my interpretation up, is to cut short the task of waiting and attending; it is to tempt the Lord my God.

Why should we find this so difficult to accept? We are anxious for the church. We are anxious for ourselves. We are anxious about the consequences of admitting any indeterminacy in our understanding of the text, which might give a hostage to fortune. Once we acknowledge hermeneutic distance, we fear, "anything goes." A host of false prophets will take advantage of our respectful distance. They will rush forward to wrest Scripture from its plain sense, pervert it into authorizing what cannot be authorized. And, of course, this fear is, in the short run, likely to prove well grounded. The public discourse of theology is, indeed, one where anything has the habit of going. False prophets are, and always will be, quick to rush forward. So we must simply expect to hear abominations and absurdities put forward with implausible but brazen claims to be consistent with, or authorized by, Scripture. To this annoyance we are called, as Christ warned and as generations of the faithful have since proved. The question is, what sacrifice of faith we would make if, to avoid this annoyance for ourselves and to spare the church its turmoils, we were to close down on the reading and interpretation of Holy Scripture, if we were to declare that there was nothing to discuss any more. To our fears, all too well grounded in the short term, we must reply with the question: is the Spirit of the living God an adequate match for human perversity? Is Jesus's promise about the gates of hell meant seriously enough to be relied on? Are we prepared to encounter false interpretations with the weapons of true interpretation, the weapons that are "not worldly, but have divine power to destroy strongholds . . . [taking] every thought captive to obey Christ" (2 Cor 10:4–5)? Precisely those weapons—hand-to-hand, thought-to-thought, unpicking the web of error strand by strand—cannot be used without discourse, without argument and debate, without proper distance on, and attention to, the text in itself, without the waiting and searching that every true work of interpretation demands.

Granted that this is what we are called to, we may ask: Do we, does the gospel, then, have no *formal and institutional* defense against indefinite prevarication and distortion? Indeed we do, and it does. There is within the church the *ministry of the word,* which has the duty of ruling false interpretations out and ruling true interpretations in. That is what our priests and bishops are charged with, and they do it not by suppressing or forbidding the discussion of the biblical witness, but by waiting on the mind of the church where it is genuinely seeking to understand, and by confirming the mind of the church where there are well-established lines of understanding. In a situation of controversy, this ministry will exercise a proper caution and refuse to allow the church to be swept off its feet by sudden enthusiasms, or shamed out of its traditional judgments by the power of new fashions. It will create and hold open the space for properly disciplined and biblically founded common inquiry.

And may it also from time to time pronounce, as Richard Hooker hoped it might, a "judicial and definitive sentence, whereunto neither part that contendeth may under any pretence or colour refuse to stand"?[1] The difficulty is, as Hooker himself was forced to recognize, that if the mind of the church is in fact unsettled and uncertain, declaring that a pronouncement is definitive will not settle it, but will only heighten the tension. In James Joyce's story "Grace," the ideal of a judgment that settles everything is subjected to some teasing, as an enthusiastic Irish layman, aiming to save the soul of a dissolute colleague, gathers with some friends around his bed and renarrates, suitably reinforced by some "special whisky," the history of the ratification of the infallibility dogma at the First Vatican Council:

> "In the sacred college, you know, of cardinals and archbishops and bishops there were two men who held out against it while the others were all for it . . .
>
> "Ha!" said Mr. M'Coy.
>
> "And they were a German cardinal by the name of Dolling . . . or Dowling . . . or –"
>
> "Dowling was no German, and that's a sure five," said Mr. Power, laughing.
>
> "Well, this great German cardinal, whatever his name was, was one; and the other was John MacHale."
>
> "What?" cried Mr. Kernan. "Is it John of Tuam?"

---

1. *Of the Laws of Ecclesiastical Polity,* preface 6.1.

"There they were at it, all the cardinals and bishops and archbishops from all the ends of the earth and these two fighting dog and devil until at last the Pope himself stood up and declared infallibility a dogma of the Church *ex cathedra*. On the very moment John MacHale, who had been arguing and arguing against it, stood up and shouted out with the voice of a lion; "*Credo!*"

"*I believe!*" said Mr. Fogarty.

"*Credo!*" said Mr. Cunningham. "That showed the faith he had. He submitted the moment the Pope spoke."

"And what about Dowling?" asked Mr. M'Coy.

"The German cardinal wouldn't submit. He left the Church."

Mr. Cunningham's words had built up the vast image of the Church in the minds of his hearers.[2]

But precisely that "vast image" of church authority is the problem. The bishops cannot and must not substitute their own pronouncements for a hard-sought unity of the Spirit. Yet that does not mean that the bishops have nothing to contribute. What they may and can do—in support of the search for unity, not in suppression of it—is to secure the *tradition* of interpreting God's word as a critical point of reference, and so defend the identity of the community as grounded in faithfulness to the word of God. In this way they may restrain the tendency to anarchy and strife that naturally attends on excitement and uncertainty; they may give structure and order to the processes of faithful inquiry, by keeping before the church's eyes

2. Joyce, "Grace," 130–31.

a clear sense of what comes first and what comes after, what is legitimately in doubt and what cannot be in doubt. And in this context—not to suppress dissent or preclude discussion, but to give the discussion the direction it needs in the service of the gospel—they may perhaps declare that some aspect of a question that was once open is now closed, or that some other aspect of a question cannot be opened until more fundamental questions have been dealt with. In these conditions, their gift of the Spirit will be shown, by facilitating real convergence, to have served the search for unity in God's will.

The Anglican bishops at Lambeth 1998 sought to exercise this gift—and though, perhaps, they did not exercise it perfectly, they spoke with a degree of coherence that was remarkable considering the reports of procedural mayhem that surrounded the occasion. In "rejecting homosexual practice as incompatible with Scripture," they clearly did not suppose they had achieved a simple closure of all the moral questions; they had simply provided a reference point in Scripture to which all answers to these questions would be responsible. They sought to establish some practical conditions for an orderly exploration. Chief among these, they "could not advise" the blessing of same-sex unions or the ordination of those involved in them. An open exploration could hardly go forward if new facts were deliberately being created on the ground by unilateral action. There was, of course, no leonine roar of *Credo!* from the opposition. That was hardly to be looked for, or even desired. What could have been looked for and desired was some patience and restraint. Those who thought it too much to show *that* degree of deference to the authority of the church's ministry refused something far greater than poor Dr. Döllinger ever did. But the last word has still to be spoken in response, and the effect of the Lambeth bishops' service still to be seen.

Meanwhile here we are with five chapters behind us discussing the questions of the church's order, the influences to which it has been subject, and the authority that it must confess. It is quite enough. In the two that remain, we shall turn our eyes back, and forward, to the content of the interrupted exploration, and to some questions that are certainly at issue in it.

6
CREATION, REDEMPTION, *and* NATURE

Creation waits with eager longing for the revealing of the children of God.

(Rom 8:19)

WHEN THE GOVERNING committee of the Church of Sweden proposed to its General Synod the sacramental celebration of same-sex marriage, it wrote: "Here the distinction between what belongs to creation and what belongs to salvation loses its significance."[1] Innovative as the sacramental proposal was, it is the doctrinal proposal that is likely to shake the foundations. The creation of the world by God and its redemption in Jesus Christ are the poles in relation to which Christians have consistently narrated the moral history of the world. There are moments in the narration, of course, that do not lie at either pole but in between them—e.g., the sacraments themselves, which have no place either in the Garden of Eden or in the

1. Church Board of the Church of Sweden, *Life Together*.

New Jerusalem. But these still depend on the *distinction* of creation and redemption; they are sustained by the dynamic tension between them. If the distinction between creation and redemption has no significance, then a sacrament has no significance either. The narrative of creation and redemption has accompanied and disciplined Christian attempts to think about the moral dilemmas thrown up by every age: slavery, war, technology, wealth and markets, etc., etc. In each dilemma, they have asked, what gifts of the Creator are to be rejoiced in here? What evils are to be repented of and lamented? What transformations are yet to be hoped for? As these strands in each dilemma have been separated and clarified, so resolution has seemed possible. But now, it is suggested, the same-sex question is better thought about without this narration. In contemplating a same-sex union we need not ask whether we are rejoicing in the bounty of creation, lamenting the distortion of human affections, or looking forward to the lineaments of the new creation. What could such a proposal amount to—in relation to this or to any other question?

When people ask with greater or lesser bewilderment why *this* issue should have proved so divisive in the churches of our time, one answer lies close to hand: it is anxiety about doctrinal revisionism. The origins of this anxiety lie more than a century back, in the growth of critical academic theology, that speculative anthill from which so many questions have marched forth to nibble at the Christianity of the Scriptures and the creeds. But the focus of anxiety now is not now upon university departments, where reconstructing Christianity from the ground up is out of fashion, but upon diocesan offices and synods. Yet if this is the true meaning of the crisis over homosexuality, it remains to be seen *whose* meaning it is. Is doctrinal revisionism a frontier reached by gay Christians in pursuit of their moral challenge to the church? Or is the gay movement a frontier reached by a liberal church leadership in its pursuit of a doctrinal-revisionist agenda? It was because the answer to this question did not seem at all obvious, that the authors of the "St. Andrew's Day Statement" ten years ago framed their contribution in the form of a doctrinal confession, and asked gay Christians to say how far they could go along with it. Nobody can speak for gay Christians about doctrine except gay Christians, and until an intellectual gay voice is as widely heard in the Christian community as it has long been outside it, there is little point in anyone asserting what gays do or do not believe in. There have been straws in the wind, however, suggesting that not all gays are enamored of the liberal bear-hug.

The dialectic of creation and redemption is not merely one episode in the struggle between orthodoxy and revision. It is its central and decisive battleground. It gives their shape to the creeds that differentiate Christianity from deism. What is it, then, that tempts Christians to loosen their hold on it? What is the underlying doubt that causes them, with greater or lesser embarrassment, to shuffle uncertainly towards doctrinal revision at this decisive point? The answer is, as I take it, a simple moral mistake, centrally characteristic of liberal Christianity. The mistake is called "historicism," and it consists in confusing the good with the future. It induces a profound loss of nerve over any claim to discern the good hand of God within the order of a good creation.

I want to explore this answer more deeply with the help of a recent essay by Professor R. M. Adams, a Christian philosopher with a well-earned reputation for having breathed new life into moral philosophy by recovering the central importance of the notion of the good.[2] Adams's short contribution to the pro-gay cause is an essay in three parts, of which the first sets out a critical challenge to the objection that homosexuality is "unnatural." He makes a deft job, as one would expect, of marshalling some of the more common objections to the use of "nature" as a normative category: it depends on an Aristotelian conception of species; laws of nature are merely statistical; a species is simply a population of similar genetic traits; the use of "natural" and "unnatural" to express moral discrimination is untheoretical, supplying no reason for favoring or disfavoring anything. Natural teleology is of interest today, Adams holds, only to some Roman Catholics. (That it was the view of Hooker, Taylor, Butler and all the classical Anglican divines, this generous Presbyterian omits to mention, sparing our blushes!) What "most of us" think, Adams holds, granting too much too quickly, I would judge, to the views of Richard Dawkins, is that functional behavior is measured by the successful gene propagation of individual organisms. At any rate, in discriminating between good and evil behavior, as we must, we should not confuse genuine moral intuitions with subjective likes and dislikes. Adams shudders at the thought of eating grasshoppers, though he knows some people like them.

So far the common objections to the objection. Pausing at this point, we may observe that "so far" is not actually *very* far. One might, I think, concede more or less everything Adams says in this section of his essay, and still go on saying that homosexuality was "unnatural." One would have to allow, of course, that the term was derived from a now-outdated Aristotelian notion—one would be mistaken, but one would have to allow it!—yet that need not rule out a post-Aristotelian correlation

2. Adams, "Human Nature." Adams's major contribution to the philosophy of the good is *Finite and Infinite Goods*.

of kinds and goods. One would have to allow that expressing a moral intuition in this way was untheoretical, needing
a deeper level of justifying description; but for most people
most of the time it is enough to be reasonably sure that such
a deeper description could in principle be given. But of which
moral intuition may that *not* be the case? Express the view that
it would be "unnatural" for a human infant to be brought up by
chimpanzees. Call it "unnatural" for deaf parents to want their
child to be as deaf as they are. Observe that it is an "unnatural"
diet that destroys the human body by clogging up the valves of
the heart with trans-fatty acids or coating the lungs with tar.
Contrast a Caesarean operation with "natural childbirth." All
these uses of "natural" and "unnatural" are subject to the same
line of criticism as calling homosexuality unnatural—and that
does not make all, or any, of these moral intuitions wrong; it
merely means that they require further explication and justification. Adams's argument is addressed simply to the efficiency
and clarity of one element of our moral vocabulary; and from
such an argument as that one can never expect to reach a substantive conclusion that different sexual orientations are of no
more moral importance than differences of taste over eating
grasshoppers.

So we could stand stubbornly by the substance of the
objection that homosexuality is unnatural, while conceding
more or less all these objections to the objection. But I think
it would be injudicious to concede anything like as much as
this. In the first place, consider the bogey of Aristotelianism.
One so deeply versed in seventeenth-century moral thought
as Professor Adams can hardly be unaware that the wide cur-
rency given to the category of "nature" in that period actually
owed less to Aristotle than it did to Stoic influences mediated
through Cicero. As the philosophers of the early Enlightenment

used it, "nature" can be seen to do a fairly precise job, and to do it tolerably well. That job was to focus attention on the dual constitution of the human being as body and soul, at once a free, self-directing, spiritual entity and at the same time a material organism. The virtue of "living according to nature" was precisely that of harmonizing the demands of these two aspects of one's being, achieving a rational self-direction that respected the structural limits and possibilities of the bodily condition. "Natural" and "unnatural" are terms that come into play when questions arise about how we shall conduct ourselves as embodied souls and ensouled bodies.

At the cost of a slight detour from Professor Adams's argument, we should note that there are strong Christian grounds for interest in such a line of questioning. It is commonly said—though the generalization has nothing to recommend it other than the charm of naiveté—that Christianity traditionally despised and ignored the body. The opposite is the truth. Belief in the incarnation made any such attitude impossible. Even in the eighteenth century, when the temptation for enlightened souls to take wing was, perhaps, at its height, Christians would sing:

> Soul! Make no offence of this,
> That the Light of spirits' bliss,
> True likeness of God's radiance,
> Takes disguise of servile stance![3]

Christianity has, in fact, harped upon the body. It has harped upon the conditions of the body's mortal existence, and it has harped upon the body's share in the hope of the kingdom of God. "No one hates his own body," says St. Paul, "but nourishes and cherishes it" (Eph 5:29). And if Christianity

---

3. From Salomo Franck's libretto for Bach's Cantata BWV 186, *Ärgre dich, o Seele, nicht*; translation mine.

has earned little credit for its harping, that is because its late modern critics have their own ideas of what should be said about the body, which often begins and ends with the body's erotic powers. Talk of the body's sickness or death is all too easily dismissed as talking the body down. *Gute Nacht, o Wesen!* Christians sing to their dying bodies with all due respect and seriousness.[4] But it is not a song the late modern eroticist wants to hum along to!

To "cherish" the body is to care for very much about the body besides its erotic powers. It is to care for its internal organs and their functions, for the extraordinary capacities of its hands and feet, for its processes of growth. It is to take care of its weight, its rhythms of sleeping and waking, its powers of hearing and seeing. Even if we make a sharp distinction between the *created* and the *fallen* body, so bracketing out illness and death, we can hardly attend to the body and cherish it if we fail to notice its temporality, its exposure to physical risk, or its processes of aging. Jean-Yves Lacoste has reminded us recently that the phenomenon of fatigue cannot be assimilated to illness and suffering.[5] Yet sickness and death should not, in fact, be excluded from our view, for Christians have historically seen mortality not as an accident befalling human bodies, but as a created possibility of bodily life that never need have become an actuality. But above all these things, we have to cherish the body's role in interpersonal communications, its essential sociality. It is through the face that one human being is known to another, and all types of relation are built up through the body's strategies of nearness and distance: its attraction and repulsion,

4. Bach again. These words are from the seventeenth-century hymn "Jesu, meine Freude," by Johann Franck, used as the basis of the motet of that name, BWV 227.

5. "Petite phénoménologie de la fatigue," in *Presence et Parousie*.

its power to dominate and threaten, and its power to charm and endear. And this entails the learning of disciplines that surround the body's bearing of itself. We can none of us endure everybody else's bodies intruding constantly on our own; society is enabled by sustaining spaces around bodies, by holding the body back as well as bringing it forward, by turning the eyes away from it as well as fixing our gaze upon it. Gesture, clothing, styles and patterns of movement, all contribute to form the software by which the body loads its repertoire of social arts and achievements.

The *erotic* body, in fact, stands out as the exceptional moment in the repertoire. Here the body conveys a hint of eternity that beckons and calls us from beyond it; here it reaches out to point beyond itself. It was surely an irrevocable insight on Plato's part (whatever reservations we may have about the rest of his theory of love) to see in eros an *implicitly philosophical* reaction to the human body. It is possible, of course, to use the word "erotic," as a great many of our contemporaries do, simply as a synonym for sexual desire. But that is to miss almost everything of interest that has been thought about the erotic. Eros is precisely *not* sexual impulse; it is an aspect of the spiritual life of mankind, though inevitably engendering bodily experiences to accompany it since we are psychosomatic beings whose every moment is a mediation of the spiritual through the bodily. Reflecting on the body, it responds with yearning for its lurking hint of beauty and truth. It responds to something beckoning through it from beyond it. Precisely that moment of reflection is the temptation, as Plato, again, understood. The familiar body, the body that we live in, object of wonder though it is, is too essentially present to us, too intimate, too enclosing—let us say, too *heavy* to beckon us beyond itself. But the body of the spiritual imagination is light and elusive. If we fail to carry the act of reflection through to its conclusion, if we fail to inquire what the erotic body is a medium *for,* then we end up investing our perfectly ordinary experiences of sexual attraction with an ontological weight that is, in fact, a borrowed transference, and in our confusion we fail to understand either ourselves or our bodies. We cannot and should not take that moment of rapture in the presence of the beautiful body quite at its face value—though we cannot and should not ignore it, either. We must interrogate it for its meaning. So Plato taught, and much Christian philosophy after him; for Christianity mostly (though not universally) found this aspect of Plato's thought suggestive and helpful. His warning has been echoed in most Christian thought about the erotic; it was certainly echoed by Rowan Williams, in his characteristically indirect way, in the much-celebrated but little-understood essay on "The Body's Grace." An unwelcome warning, perhaps, to an ethical intuitionism that puts its trust in the immediacy of feeling; and since Plato, by and large, is more spoken of than read, Christianity has had to shoulder the blame for the reserve—though it never was a reserve *at the body,* but a reserve *at the erotic image* of the body. Ever since St. Paul, it has been the *phronēma sarkos,* "the mind caught on the flesh," not the flesh itself, that has caused alarm.

The "unnatural," then, is a falling short, or perhaps an overreaching, of the transcendence of the soul over the body. Still, Christianity has not been content to leave philosophical programs for transcendence where it found them; and that is because it has had a more complex and more critical view of transcendence than most philosophy has had. There is bad transcendence as well as good. And there is a transcendence *of* the terms of creation as well as a transcendence *within* the terms of creation. Getting a distance on the body is not an end in itself, and may even be a temptation. The key to achieving the *right* distance is to locate the powers of the soul precisely where every created power of human nature must stand, under the judgment of God and awaiting his transforming redemption. The language of "nature" and its concerns for the body-soul relation must be framed within a fully theological account of creation and redemption.

What we have achieved by our digression into the concept of the "natural" is to identify a range of features in human existence that ought to excite our wonder and admiration, and can clearly ground some moral discernments. These then point the way to the understanding that a doctrine of creation can supply. Adams, for his part, having cut short his treatment of the natural with the common objections, finds himself at a loss, when in the second part of his essay he addresses creation, to know what moral discernments this category could possibly disclose. What worries him especially is the difficulty of speaking of a world at the same time created and fallen. If we distinguish a "natural" created world from an "actual" fallen world, he complains, it "breaks the epistemological teeth" of the concept of the natural and unnatural. Is war natural, or merely actual? And how would we know the difference? We can only pretend to do this, he fears, on the basis of "presuppositions" about the purposes or commands of God, which look as though they are smuggled in to make sense of a creation that, on its own, is unable to tell the difference between good and evil. But this is altogether too skeptical. There are some value distinctions we may make quite clearly simply by reflecting upon the way the world works.

Consider, for example, how we know the difference between the health of a natural organism and its sickness—let us say, between the flushed cheek caused by a high temperature and the ruddy glow in the cheek promoted by a vigorous walk.

We could, of course, say that nature knows of no such distinction; that it is only our own preferences that make us call the one flushed cheek "health" and the other "sickness." But the preferences are obviously not arbitrary; they have to do with the predictable outcomes of high fevers on the one hand and of good circulation on the other, with the subjective experiences we have of the one and the other, and with our innate resistance to the prospect of dying. This is all "nature," too. Nature is, to be sure, highly dialectical. She assigns death to all living organisms, and then instills in the higher and more organized ones a passionate opposition to the fate she has appointed. Yet, though there may be various ways of making sense of this, saying that nature knows no distinctions is not one of them. At the very least, nature knows that life is better than death! We may be guided by the book of Genesis and the Gospels to understand life and death theologically as the imprint of our creation and our fall—but we do not need the book of Genesis and the gospels to tell us that there *is* an order of value in which life is preferable to death. We only need—just once in our life—to be dangerously ill, or to find ourselves at the bedside of someone else in that condition, and to wonder at the remarkable conviction with which we hold on to the good of life.

To take the step from a philosophy of nature to a theology of creation is not to abandon one set of interests in favor of another. The revealed purposes of God in creation will direct our attention back to *the world*, i.e., the totality of what there God has made, and teach us how to see the good he has given us within it. Any purposes God has in making the world are to be discerned in the world; they are not set apart from it somewhere else. Any discernment of how the world works will, pari passu, be a discernment of the purposes of God. No "presupposition" is required for this discernment other than that it is a *morally intelligible* world, a world in which there is good and evil to be distinguished, a world fit for humans to act in. All we need to assume is something that Adams, at any rate, is always quick to grant, namely, that the goods of this world are ontologically more basic than the evils.

What theology as well as philosophy must seek in the world are simply *the conditions of intelligibility of human life*, which is at once bodily, and therefore mortal, and yet "with eternity in its heart," transcending its bodily state and aspiring to all the goods there are—not only bodily satisfactions but moral recognitions, intellectual comprehensions, and even fellowship with God. To pose the question of homosexuality in *these* categories is precisely to ask about its intelligibility. Can there be any sense in an affection that appears to defy the logic of human bodily sexuality? Or is it not defiance after all, but a new disclosure of the good? These are questions that have to be raised (as, indeed, they are constantly raised by homosexuals), if we are to treat sexuality with the seriousness that the task of living a human life invests it with.

But Adams makes a different and unnerving move. A wedge is driven between creation, which is all about "beginnings," and goods, which are located in "the future." There are, it appears, purposes of God in creation. Loosely following the Western tradition, Adams conceives of three purposes that might be discerned in sexuality: a procreative purpose, a unitive purpose, and a cooperative purpose. But when we think of how these are to be fulfilled, our imagination is not tied to the way the world actually functions. Each of them, he argues, can be realized just as effectively in independence of the others, and that has the advantage of giving space for sexual partnership between what he calls "physical and genital" homosexuals. (The apparent conviction that homosexuality and heterosexuality are "physical," indeed "genital," conditions is one of the more baffling features of the argument at this point!) For procreation, it is enough that the heterosexuals get on with their usual business, or if they are unwilling or insufficient, the IVF industry can be stepped up. For the unitary good, homosexual partnerships are as good as heterosexual. For cooperation of the sexes, what is needed is equal job opportunities and women in the boardroom. All of which construes God's purposes in a purely voluntarist and arbitrary sense, detaching them from the philosophical task of understanding the goods of human existence as we find it. When the tradition spoke of three God-willed goods of sexuality, (offspring, faith, and sacrament, in Augustine's formulation), it did so precisely to point out the convergence of the three in one and the same natural institution. The point of the analysis was to account for the form of marriage as all human cultures knew it, not to reinvent the world. Once we separate God's purposes in creation from the inherent goods of creaturely existence, there is little reason to hold on to the view that God meant anything at all by making the world.

Creation narratives focus our attention on beginnings, he tells us, and though beginnings pretend to provide fixed norms, they cannot do so. Sexuality and sociality have changed, and change is only evaluated in the light of eschatology. How, then, are we to situate ourselves at the end of history, to evaluate it? Through "the goods God offers us to love." That is puzzling, indeed. The whole normative content of creation has been transferred to eschatology, moved out of the world we inhabit into a world yet to be revealed, *and then assumed to be immediately accessible to moral judgment!* Actually, the conflation of the good with the future is a confusion. Goods, as such, are not in the future tense; we do not predict them. Neither are they in the past tense; we do not narrate them. Goods are in the present tense, offered to us as the objects of our action, here and now. But we are historical beings; we live by narrative and hope; we grasp the present tense as set "between" past and future. That is to say, the present in which we live and act always has its two horizons, reaching back and reaching forward. We focus our attention on the good presented to us by approaching it through narrative and projecting it through hope. Christians have their own reasons for doing this: they have encountered a God who has made himself known as Beginning and End, Alpha and Omega, whose beginnings are a faithful token of his endings. They therefore speak not only of a good to be loved in action here and now, but of a good to be looked for in the future. But philosophy is not free simply to borrow the notion of a future good from Christian faith and substitute it for the present good. Philosophy knows nothing of the future.

It is, of course, right that philosophers should speak as believing Christians. It is right that they should do their philosophizing in a conscious openness to theology. By doing both these things, R. M. Adams has earned our appreciation. But it is not good that they should confuse understanding the world as it presents itself with random elements of eschatological proclamation. The result of that will be a deformation both of theology and philosophy. Theology needs the philosopher's reflection on the moral sense of the world, in order to think seriously about the fulfillment of creation. For without the love of what is, the "new creation" is an empty symbol—or is it a clanging cymbal? New creation is creation renewed, a restoration and enhancement, not an abolition. Not everything that can be thought of as future can be thought of as the kingdom of God. A brave new world of cyborgs is not a kingdom of God. God has announced his kingdom in a Second Adam, and "Adam" means "Human."

One thing at risk in Adams's approach, as in a thousand less articulate and less measured approaches along the same path, is the disappearance of scientific knowledge from the criteria of moral responsibility. We are invited to set the observation of nature aside, to cast ourselves on novelty. It is, indeed, striking how scientific curiosity—inadequate, one-sided and inconclusive as much of it may have been—has come to be banished from the discussion of homosexuality. Adams has done us the service of displaying the intellectual underpinnings of this development: a concept of value that has parted company with a concept of reality, a division between the good and the real. But moral responsibility to the real is precisely what the dialectic of creation and redemption in Christian theology safeguarded. Intellectually the outcome is curious and a little depressing: not only the approximations of medicine and psychology, but even the cultural-philosophical legacies of a Foucault—hardly a defender of the traditional view of created goods, but resolutely interested in the complicated constructions of human culture—disappear over the edge of an increasingly moralistic public discussion of the gay phenomenon.

It would be ungrateful to leave our critique at that point. For Professor Adams has a final turn to make, which may, after all, really prove helpful. From the notion of the good as future he steps back, in a kind of gracious retreat, into speaking of the good as "vocation." A vocation is not a future; it is a future horizon to which we respond in the present, and it corresponds to a past horizon expressed in the idea of an agent or a situation that has summoned us. "God *has* called me," we say, "that I *may* do, or be, this special thing." Now, vocation cannot provide a comprehensible idea of the good on its own. To appreciate its contribution, we have to tie it back into the goods of creation, from which Adams has apparently sought to cut it loose. A "vocation" is a *special* calling to a *distinct* good, different from that to which others are called. It is a distinct path of human action, offered to this person or that, but not to all. It is not a vocation to love one's neighbor; it is not a vocation to refrain from stealing; these are commands that apply to all. But it may be a vocation to serve the community by writing novels or driving buses. And it is an obvious question to raise in the face of any strikingly distinct line of conduct, whether it can be understood as a special vocation. The answer will depend on how and to what extent it can be a true way of realizing goods that are for all humankind. We may sensibly talk of the vocation of a Goya or a Bosch to depict the horrific and the disturbing in their art; we may not sensibly talk of a vocation of a Hitler or an Attila to realize the horrific and the disturbing in their military endeavors. Why this distinction? Because artistic representation can benefit us simply by expanding our imaginations; warfare can only serve us as it is kept within the constraints of justice and directed to the end of peace. The distinction turns upon what it is to be human. A vocation, which necessarily departs from the general rule, needs to be recognizable as a *human* form of service to the human community. How this observation may help open up the question of homosexuality is something to which we must turn in the seventh and last of our "sermons on the subject of the day."

7 GOOD NEWS *for the* GAY CHRISTIAN?

> *He will feed his flock like a shepherd, he will gather the*
> *lambs in his arms, he will carry them in his bosom, and*
> *gently lead those that are with young.*
>
> (Isa 40:11)

IN A THOUGHTFUL response to the *St Andrew's Day State-ment* of 1996, Rowan Williams asked how the authors might address "the good news" to a certain type of homosexual Christian for whom he had a special concern.[1] Speaking in the first person, this Christian (to whom we shall assign the masculine pronoun) declares: (i) that he desires to live in obe-dience to Christ; (ii) that he is unable to see himself reflected in the description of homosexuals in Romans 1, since he is not "rejecting something I know in the depths of my being";[2]

---

1. For the text of the "St. Andrew's Day Statement," see Bradshaw, *Way Forward?* 5–11; for Rowan Williams's response, see Williams, "Knowing Myself," 12–19.

2. Williams "Knowing Myself," 17.

(iii) that he conducts a life of moral struggle like other Christians; and (iv) that it is "hard to hear good news" from a church that insists his condition is spiritually compromised.[3] This question frames very neatly the challenge the church faces. We may wonder whether the Archbishop's ideal homosexual Christian is idealized. We may wonder whether he is typical. But doubts of this kind are no reason to refuse the challenge. If there are homosexual Christians who see themselves in this way, then, precisely because they intend to take the disciplines of the Christian life with perfect seriousness, we may and must listen and speak to them with perfect seriousness about the good news in Jesus Christ. However, there is another question that ought to be raised alongside the first, and addressed to anyone who sees him- or herself in this portrait of the homosexual Christian. To raise this second question is not to evade the first; rather, it is to search out the shape that an answer to the first must take. This second question, too, is put by Rowan Williams: "How does the homosexually inclined person show Christ to the world?"[4] For if the gay Christian is to be addressed as a believer and a disciple, a recipient of the good news, he has also to be addressed as a potential evangelist. But we must take this second question a little further. The good news meant for the human race is meant for the church, too. What good news does the gay Christian have to bring to the church?

There is an elementary point about Christian ethics that I have sought to emphasize ever since the opening pages of my *Resurrection and Moral Order* published twenty years ago: there is no Christian ethics that is not "evangelical," i.e., good

3. Ibid.
4. Ibid., 18.

news.[5] There can be no change of voice, no shift of mood, between God's word of forgiveness and his word of demand, no obedience-without-gift, no gift-without-obedience. The gift and the obedience are in fact one and the same. They are the righteousness of Jesus Christ, encompassing and transforming our own lives, past, present, and future. To preach the good news, then, is precisely what we do in expounding Christian ethics, if we expound Christian ethics faithfully. Preaching the good news is the only form of address of which the Christian church as such is capable, whether speaking to Christians or to non-Christians. When we use any other form of argument— quoting opinion-poll statistics, for example, or reporting the result of scientific experiments, or suggesting some practical compromise—the relevance of what we say depends on how well it is formed to serve the evangelical message. If the church speaks not as witness to God's saving work but as a pundit or a broker of some deal, it speaks out of character.

Yet to preach the gospel, whether to Christians or non-Christians, is not a simple matter of offering reassurance and comfort. The gospel, too, has its "hard words." The righteousness of Jesus Christ is not comfort without demand, any more than it is demand without comfort. It is never less than that *demanding comfort* by which God makes more of us than we thought it possible to become. And from this there seems to follow an important implication: the gospel must be preached to the gay Christian on precisely the same terms that it is preached to any other person. "The 'hard words' theology is given to speak," as Jean-Yves Lacoste has written, "are still words of salvation, meant for mankind *as* mankind, not as Jew or Greek."[6] This

5. O'Donovan, *Resurrection and Moral Order*, 11–30.
6. Lacoste, "More Haste, Less Speed in Theology," 275.

should not be unwelcome to a gay Christian. What, after all, would it mean if we set gays aside from the bulk of humankind, offering them some special reassurance not meant for the children of Adam and Eve?

This was the point that the authors of the *St Andrews Day Statement* made when they wrote: "We must be on guard . . . against constructing any other ground for our identities than the redeemed humanity given us in [Christ]." These words met with a somewhat unsympathetic response. Either they seemed too obvious to be necessary, or they seemed too arbitrarily restrictive. From either point of view, it could be thought that the authors had some obscure polemical intent in writing them. What they had in view, in fact, was simply to assert the theological ground of human solidarity in creation, fall, and redemption, embracing gay and non-gay alike. If anyone thinks *that* point too obvious to mention, notice the range of inhuman views freely attributed by liberal polemicists to their opponents, as well as the range of "posthuman" views freely advocated by postliberals![7] Homosexuality is not the determining factor in any human being's existence; therefore it cannot be the determining factor in the way we treat a human being, and should not be the determining factor in the way a human being treats him- or herself. Gays are children of Adam and Eve, brothers and sisters of Christ. There is no other foundation laid than that. "He will feed his flock like a shepherd"; from which it follows, *simpliciter* and without adjustment, that he will feed gays like a shepherd, too.

Yet, it can be replied, there are other, less fundamental senses to the concept of "identity." Can we not speak of a "homosexual identity" in this less fundamental way, as we might

7. Cf. Waters, *From Human to Posthuman.*

speak, without denying anything in human solidarity, of a racial identity or of a class identity? And may we not ask how the good news may be addressed specifically to it? Since Gregory the Great's *Pastoral Rule*, bishops and other preachers have been preoccupied with how to address the gospel to sections of the flock with special needs—a gospel for the rich, a gospel for the poor, a gospel for the powerful, a gospel for the powerless, etc., etc.—which, as Gregory claims, "solicitously oppose suitable medicines to the various diseases of the several hearers."[8] I have to confess a reservation about this. I am not sure that it can be disentangled from Gregory's idea of the preacher as a *rector,* or "ruler," who safeguards and services a certain kind of Christianized social order built on role differences. Gregory's preacher strives to make role differences comfortable for everyone, chiefly by preventing them being overstated—excellent managerial sense, no doubt, but not the primary business of a Christian evangelist. The gospel is addressed to human beings irrespective of their condition, and there is no prima facie place to dismember it into a series of gospels for discrete social sectors. Why would there be a gospel for the homosexual any more than a gospel for the teacher of literature, for the civil magistrate, or for the successful merchant (to name just three categories that the early church viewed with the same narrowing of the eyes that a homosexual may encounter today)? It is for the church to address the good news, we may say; it is for the recipient—homosexual, pedagogue, politician or captain of industry—to hear it and to say *how* he or she hears it in and from this or that social position.

Yet there is more to be said than that. The gospel does have implications for the way we conduct ourselves in the world, and

8. Gregory the Great, *Pastoral Rule,* 3.36.

the way we conduct ourselves in the world is differentiated as the forms and circumstances that constitute the world are differentiated. There are special needs because there are special contexts within which the Christian life has to be lived out. Traditionally these have been discussed in Christian theology under the heading of "vocation." The preaching of the gospel can and must address distinct vocations, even though it must address them only in the second place, after it has spoken to us all as human beings, not in the first place. "He will gather the lambs in his arms, and gently lead those that are with young" (Isa 40:11). Let us imagine a gay person who has "heard" the message of the gospel but is yet unaware of any bearing it may have for his homosexual sensibility. Must there not be some *following up* of the good news, something to relate what has been heard to this aspect of his self-understanding? It is helpful to keep the analogy with teachers, magistrates, and financiers in our mind. Suppose a Christian teacher who has found in the gospel no implications for how literature is to be read and taught; or a Christian politician who has found no special questions raised by the gospel about policies for military defense; or a financier to whom it has not yet occurred that large sums of money should not be handled in the way a butcher handles carcasses. A pastoral question arises. In the light of the gospel, neither literature nor government nor money are mere neutral technicalities. They are dangerous powers in human life, foci upon which idolatry, envy, and hatred easily concentrate. Those who deal with them need to know what it is they handle. The teacher, politician, and banker who have not yet woken up to the battle raging in heavenly places around the stuff of their daily lives, have still to face the challenge of the gospel. Is it any different with the powers of sexual sensibility?

Of course, this pastoral train of thought does not entitle us to demand that the gay Christian (or the teacher, politician, and banker) should repent without further ado. Theirs is a position of moral peril but also a position of moral opportunity. In preaching the gospel to a specific vocation, we must aim to assist in *discernment*. Discernment means tracing the lines of the spiritual battle to be fought; it means awareness of the peculiar temptations of the situation; but it also means identifying the possibilities of service in a specific vocation. The Christian facing the perils and possibilities of a special position must be equipped, as a first step, with the moral wisdom of those who have taken that path before, the rules that have been distilled from their experience. A soldier needs to learn about "just war," a financier about "just price," and so on. Again, can it be any different in the realm of sexual sensibility? Discernment is not acquired in a vacuum; it is learned by listening to the tradition of the Christian community reflecting upon Scripture. In this exercise, of course, we cannot rule out the possibility that we may reach a "revisionist" conclusion. No element formed by tradition can claim absolute allegiance. But the right to revise traditions is not everybody's right; it has to be won by learning their moral truths as deeply as they can be learned. Those who have difficult vocations to explore need the tradition to help the exploration. The tradition may not have the final word, but it is certain they will never find the final word if they have failed to profit from the words the tradition offers. And if it should really be the case that they are summoned to witness on some terra incognita of "new" experience, it will be all the more important that their new discernments should have been reached on the basis of a deep appropriation of old ones, searching for and exploiting the analogies they offer. No one who has not learned to be traditional can dare to innovate.

If this gay Christian, then, directed to traditional rules of sexual conduct as bearers of help, complains that the good news is difficult to hear because his position is treated as compromised from the outset, he has misunderstood something. There is only one position compromised *from the outset*, and that is the position that is "revisionist" from the outset, determined by the assumption that the church's past reflections on the gospel have nothing helpful to offer. Certainly no one who sets out from *that* starting point will end up in catholic communion, for catholic communion presupposes a catholic mind. But the believer whom Rowan Williams introduces does not set out from there. He pleads that his purpose in life is "not just fulfillment . . ." but to become "transparent to Jesus, a sign of the kingdom."[9] He accepts, in other words, the *St Andrew's Day Statement's* point that discipleship cannot be without a price in self-denial but asks whether that price may not be paid, pari passu with the married, in the "daily discipline of a shared life." And then he asks how that daily discipline can fit in with its two exclusive categories of "marriage" and "singleness."

Two points about the Statement's appeal to these categories bear repeating.[10] First, the claim that these categories are mutually exclusive and comprehensive, covering the whole field of possibilities between them, is advanced on the authority of tradition, not of Scripture. Second, the Statement does not itself assert that "all who understand themselves as homosexual are called to do without such a relationship" (i.e., "exclusive, intimate and permanent," such as characterizes marriage), but says, "Some readers will draw this inference, others may not." A

9. Williams, "Knowing Myself," 18.

10. Cf. O'Donovan, "Reading the St Andrew's Day Statement." Also available online at http://www.fulcrum-anglican.org.uk/page .cfm?ID=63.

development of the tradition is therefore not ruled out, though serious conditions for recognizing such a development are stipulated. Further than that the *St Andrew's Day Statement* did not intend to go. Of course, no secret was made of the fact that the authors of the *Statement* approached the discussion with the assumption that the right category for the relationships of gay people was singleness, not marriage, and that this implied doing without an exclusive, intimate, and permanent relationship. But it was never the intention of the *Statement* merely to declare what its authors supposed to be the case. Its intention was to pose open questions to gay Christians that might elicit what *they* supposed to be the case. It was an invitation to dialogue within the basic terms set by Christian faith. The authors knew full well that other answers might be given to these questions than the answers they themselves would give, and they wanted to discuss those other answers too. They spoke to gay Christians as those who wanted to know, not as those who already knew. It had better be admitted straight away that the question-posing approach of the "St. Andrew's Day Statement" proved a communicative failure. It did not elicit the reflective answers to its questions to gay Christians that it hoped to elicit. Commentators, friendly as well as hostile, refused to take its questioning at face value, filled in the assertions they thought the authors intended to be read between the lines, and cheered or jeered accordingly. The strategy for opening dialogue fell victim, in fact, to the prevailing hermeneutic of suspicion. Yet I still find it difficult to conceive any other strategy that could ever lead to a process of mutual exploration.

Liberal Christianity has no need to ask such questions, because it reckons it knows what gay Christians need, which is, "stable relationships." Stable conjugality is the point at which liberalism has made its own peace with the tradition. Or, to put it more unkindly, it is its characteristic form of prudishness. There is, of course, a lot to be said in favor of stable relationships; but before settling on this as the decisive point, I would like to hear the question discussed by gays rather than by liberals. Is this in fact the key to *their* experience? Or is there something important in the roaming character of some gay relations? There is room here for a seriously interesting discussion among gay people which will be instructive to us all. What the gay experience really is, is a question of huge importance both to gays and non-gays. By no means everyone who speaks from that experience believes that marriage is the right model for conceiving their relationships. Some have seen it as the "bourgeoisization" of gay experience; and there are major advocates for the pattern of friendship. Such a debate among gays, if conducted frankly and in public, will provide the essential core reflection, helping the rest of us feel our way towards an understanding of the dynamic of the experience and a sense of how the good news may bear most importantly on it. If gays are to pursue this debate well, they will need to engage in analogical thinking, which is central to moral reasoning. They will need to ask themselves about likenesses of experience and about unlikenesses, about ways in which known patterns illuminate unknown, about the extending of paradigms to encompass new types.

Rowan Williams's hypothetical gay Christian, then, framed and posed precisely the question that we need his help to answer. And at this point, the author intervened, apparently in his own person, to sharpen the question: If you do not accept that homosexual desire is itself a mark of disorder, can you confidently say that the presence of this desire must always be a sign that sexual expression is ruled out?[11] This way of putting the question actually turns it on its head: instead of starting from given social forms, marriage and singleness, and using these as a baseline from which to reach out analogically to interpret an elusive and mysterious experience, it starts from an experience, and reaches out to posit a corresponding social form. Wrapped up in this is a certain psychological positivism, an unbiddability characteristic of romantic, pre-Wittgensteinian psychology. Within, we have a self-interpreting mental state, "desire"; outside, we devise an action to "express" it, i.e., lead the mental state uncompromised from the inner expanses of the mind to the public world. Inner certainties demand untrammeled expression. But that approach can only invite a skeptical reply. What is this inner certainty certain *of*? How can we know what the desire is *for*? The language of "expression" is treacherous. It lets us suppose that our desires are perspicuous, when they are not. Sexual desire in particular is notoriously difficult to interpret; the biblical story of Ammon and Tamar (cf. 1 Sam 13) is just one of many ancient warnings of how obscure its tendency may be. It is characteristically surrounded by fantasy, and fantasies are never literal indicators of what the desire is really all about, but are symbolic revealer-concealers of an otherwise inarticulate sense of need. But the point holds also for many other kinds of desire—let us say, the desire for a quiet retirement to a cottage in the countryside, or the desire to own a fast racecar. We cannot take any of them at their face value. "It wasn't what I really wanted!" is the familiar complaint of a disappointed literalism. To all desire its appropriate self-questioning: what wider, broader good does this desire serve? How does it spring out of our strengths, and

11. Williams "Knowing Myself," 18.

how does it spring out of our weaknesses? Where in relation
to this desire does real fulfillment lie? It is in *interpreting* our
desires that we need the wisdom of tradition, which teaches
us to beware of the illusory character of immediate emotional
data, helping us to sort through our desires and clarify them.
The true term of any desire, whether heavily laden or merely
banal, is teasingly different from the mental imagination that
first aroused it. And gays have no infallible introspective certainties in relation to their desires that would put them outside
the common human lot of self-questioning. "I became a great
question to myself!" said Augustine.[12] And it was the question
of *himself* that the gospel helped him address fruitfully.

None of which is to accept, what textbooks and pundits
wearisomely repeat, that a homosexual is someone *essentially*
characterized by an inevitable homoerotic desire. That would
be to close down the exploration of the gay experience with a
vengeance! Neither is it to accept the equation, too attractive
to some liberals as to some conservatives, of desire (or sexual
desire) and sin. It is perfectly possible to think of desires as no
matter for blame, and yet be persuaded that their literal enact-
ment cannot be their true fulfillment. Think of the desires we
conceive in relation to our enemies when we are angry, or of
the desires we conceive in relation to money and possessions!
Desire is, however, one aspect of what Christian doctrine used
to speak of as "concupiscence," a brokenness of the world reflected in a confusion of desire that our human society itself
instills in us. A recovery of the length, breadth, and depth of
the doctrine of original sin would rid us of a lot of misunderstanding at this point. The gay Christian who complains that
the good news is difficult to hear because his position is treated

12. Augustine *Confessions* 4.4.9.

as compromised from the outset could learn that it is not his position but the position of the human race that is compromised from the outset. The emotional resources with which anyone faces the world are a measure of the solidarity of human experience from which we have learned what it is to love other human beings in different relations; and in learning we are all, though in different ways, hindered. If the distinctiveness of gay experience reflects original sin in some way, it is because it also reflects the fractured quality of society and its loveless disorder, a disorder for which we all share common responsibility and all pay the common price, the fruit of our uneven social formation.

This train of thought offers us an insight into one aspect of the challenge presented by the gay experience, its novelty. The world has never seen a phenomenon like the contemporary gay consciousness. There have been various patterns of homosexuality in various cultures, but none with the constellation of features and persistent self-assertion that this one presents. And we need hardly be surprised at this turn in history if we reflect on the extraordinary discontinuities that exist between late modern society, taken as a whole, and traditional societies. To understand contemporary homosexuality without achieving some understanding of late modernity as a civilizational phenomenon is out of the question. But then, how can we understand late modernity without understanding contemporary homosexuality? Can we pretend to take a reading of the spiritual condition of our ultratechnological age without reading deeply the distinctive and novel forms of emotional experience that it has generated? It does not matter whether we suppose this society and its emotional forms will be short lived or long lived. The point is, they are of our day; they constitute a horizon of our mission. To live in our time, as in any other, is to have a unique set of practical questions to address.

If the first good news for the gay Christian, then, is that the "great question," the question of the self with all its pain and its hope, can be opened illuminatingly in the light of the righteousness of Jesus Christ, there is also a second good news. There is a neighbor with whom to explore the meaning of the contemporary homosexual situation, a neighbor who also needs, for the sake of his or her own integrity, to reach answers to questions which the gay Christian is especially placed to help search out. There is a neighbor for whom strict equality of regard and open candor—"irresponsibility," in the very best sense of that ambiguous word—makes it a primary obligation to put these questions and search for answers with a persistent patience not to be cut short by the concerns of purely managerial efficiency. The negotiation of soft and evasive compromises will not appeal to that neighbor, because the gay Christian's true self-understanding and well-founded self-acceptance in the grace of God is a matter to be safeguarded in their relationship as surely as the integrity of the questioning itself. One name for this open and candid neighborly relation is "friendship."

> But always to rigorous judgment and censure
> freely assenting, man seeks in his manhood
> not orders, not laws and peremptory dogmas,
> but counsel from one who is earnest in goodness
> and faithful in friendship, making man free.[13]

It is this open and candid relation that a liberal Christianity has refused by its managerial juridicalization of the gay Christian's claim, by its "laws and peremptory dogmas," designed to settle questions without exploring them, to adjust

13. Bonhoeffer, "The Friend," *Letters and Papers from Prison*, 390.

relations without justifying them, to reassure the uncomforted without comforting them, in short, to manage the situation. The juridical language of justice and rights offers the gay Christian a certain kind of recognition; the language of questioning friendship offers another quite different one. At the level of existential reality, the two are incompatible. The gay Christian today is therefore faced with a straightforward choice, a choice about the foundation on which he or she is to live. As always, the good news has a hard word in it: we can't have it both ways. The role of attorney's client, the perpetual petitioner before the court of pleas, is open and inviting, and there are plenty to welcome the gay into it—for the time being. But the catalogue of candidates for emancipation will be extended further, and the gay cause will lose the interest it once had—irrespective of whether it has won the concessions it fought for. The role of friend among friends, on the other hand, questioned and self-questioning, joined with those in pilgrim search for the new name that no man knows except the one to whom it is given, is an altogether different role, and perpetually available to those who seek it. The gay Christian thus faces in a particular way the choice that constitutes the human situation universally: whether to follow the route of self-justification or to cast oneself hopefully on the creative justification that God himself will work within a community of shared belief.

In this second choice nothing less is offered the gay believer than is offered to any and every believer: a role in attesting the work of God, in speaking to others of the redemption he has wrought. "How does the homosexually inclined person show Christ to the world?" Williams asks. Again, it is an obvious first step to ask why there would be a different answer for a homosexually inclined person than for any other person. At the deepest level there can be no difference. It is one and the same gospel witnessed to by gay and non-gay, a gospel of redemption from the enslavement of sin and of the purification of desire. Yet gifts are given differentially to members of the body of Christ; vocations are distributed variously to serve the common mission. Some are given in the form of special skills and abilities, some in the form of special opportunities, especially opportunities of special experience and suffering. From the place of special sensibility in which the homosexual Christian may find him- or herself, we may hear a testimony to the way the world confronts our mission in our time, to its fragmented identities, its disjunctions of feeling, its cruelties, its dislocations and the peculiar possibilities of redemption that God has put at its heart. The rest of us cannot do without this torchlight shone through the fog of the late modern world in which we, too, must grope our way.

What if the challenge gays present the church with is not emancipatory but hermeneutic? Suppose that at the heart of the problem there is the *magna quaestio,* the question about the gay experience, its sources and its character, that gays must answer for themselves: how this form of sensibility and feeling is shaped by its social context, how it can be clothed in an appropriate pattern of life for the service of God and discipleship of Christ? But suppose, too, that there is another question corresponding to it, which non-gay Christians need to answer: how and to what extent this form of sensibility and feeling has emerged in specific historical conditions, and how the conditions may require, as an aspect of the pastoral accommodation that changing historical conditions require, a form of public presence and acknowledgment not hitherto known? These two questions come together as a single question: how are we to understand together the particularity of the age in which we are given to attest God's works? And then the gospel has good news for us all: there is a friendship in which the most difficult questions about the self and the world in the era of time that is given to us can be explored and inquired into, a community in mission that can engage in the most difficult hermeneutic tasks. The good news preached by the church to the gay Christian coincides here with the good news preached by the gay Christian to the church. The content of that good news, perhaps, can be summed up simply by saying that the word "church" can achieve its proper content. The church is our neighborhood in the confession of Christ and obedience to his law, a neighborhood suffused with his love, a communion of mutual service and recognition.

The old-style liberalism that used to preside over the church's dilemmas in a confident spirit of practical compromise began from the assumption that everyone was divided from everyone else by recalcitrant disagreements. The Lord, the liberal prophets announced, had sent a perpetual famine of his word. We should stop asking questions of one another and hoping for answers, and eat the dry bread of commonsense compromises. Those who remember Pentecost may reasonably doubt that this was ever the wisest counsel for the church. But at the very least we cannot know whether and how much of a famine of the word there is in any disagreement until we submit it to the disciplines of patient common inquiry. No disagreement refuses to be analyzed, and its constituent elements sorted out according to size and shape. No disagreement does not lure us on with the hope, however distant, of a genuine resolution. Can we promise ourselves, then, that if the churches would only discuss homosexuality long and fully and widely enough, they would end up agreeing? Well, we are not entitled to rule out that possibility. But suppose it were not true; suppose that after careful exploration and a search for common ground, there was an agreement-resistant core at the center of the issue—a problem about how modernity is viewed, for example, or about the ontological status of self-consciousness; it might still be possible to set the residual disagreement in what the ecumenists like to call "a new context," and (who knows?) learn how to live with it. We have a parallel in the difference between indissolubilist and nonindissolubilist views of marriage, a traditional point of tension between Catholic and Protestant. That disagreement has not gone away; but if today it bulks less threateningly than it once did, that is because we are so much more clear about the extent of the agreed ground all around it—God's intentions for marriage, the pastoral desiderata in dealing with broken marriage, and the like. It no longer evokes threatening resonances. It is a problem reduced to its true shape and size.

There are no guarantees. There never are in the Christian life. But that is not a reason not to try. And seriously trying means being seriously patient. Anyone who thinks that resolutions can be reached in one leap without long mutual exploration, probing, challenge, and clarification has not yet understood the nature of the riddle that the ironic fairy of history has posed for us in our time.

BIBLIOGRAPHY

13th Lambeth Conference (1998). Resolution 1.10. "Human Sexuality." No pages. Online: http://www.lambethconference.org/resolutions/1998/1998-1-10.cfm. By permission, the Secretary General of the Anglican Consultative Council 2006.

Adams, Marilyn McCord. "Faithfulness in Crisis." In *Gays and the Future of Anglicanism*, edited by Andrew Linzey and Richard Kirker, 70–80. Winchester: O Books, 2005.

Adams, Robert Merrihew. *Finite and Infinite Goods: A Framework for Ethics*. New York: Oxford University Press, 1999.

———. "Human Nature, Christian Vocation and the Sexes." In *The Bible, the Church and Homosexuality*, edited by Nicholas Coulton, 100–113. London: Darton, Longman & Todd, 2005.

Anglican Communion News Service. "Anglican Communion Primates Meeting Communiqué." No pages. Online: http://www.anglicancommunion.org/acns/news.cfm/2005/2/24/ACNS3948

Bonhoeffer, Dietrich. "The Friend." In *Letters and Papers from Prison*. Enlarged edition. Edited by Eberhard Bethge. Translated by Reginald H. Fuller. New York: Macmillan, 1972.

Bradshaw, Timothy, editor. *The Way Forward? Christian Voices on Homosexuality and the Church*. 2d edition. London: SCM, 2003.

Breidenthal, Thomas E. "Disagreement as Communion." In *Gays and the Future of Anglicanism*, edited by Andrew Linzey and Richard Kirker, 188–98. Winchester: O Books, 2005.

Butler, Joseph. *Sermons: Sermons I, II, III, Upon Human Nature, or Man Considered as a Moral Agent*. Edinburgh: T. & T. Clark, 1888.

Church Board of the Church of Sweden. *Life Together.* 2005. Online: www.cofe.anglican.org/info/ccu/new/response.html.

Forsyth, P. T. *The Principle of Authority in Relation to Certainty, Sanctity, and Society: An Essay in the Philosophy of Experimental Religion.* London: Independent, 1913.

Frost, Robert. *Collected Poems of Robert Frost.* London: Jonathan Cape, 1943.

Gregory the Great. *Pastoral Rule.* In *Nicene and Post-Nicene Fathers: Second Series,* vol. 12: *Leo the Great, Gregory the Great.* 1890–1900. Reprint, Grand Rapids: Eerdmans, 1978–1979.

Joyce, James. "Grace." In *Dubliners,* 117–34. New York: Viking, 1967.

Hooker, Richard. *Of the Laws of Ecclesiastical Polity.* 4 vols. Edited by Georges Edelen et al. Cambridge: Harvard University Press, 1977–1982.

Kierkegaard, Søren. *On Authority and Revelation: The Book on Adler, or A Cycle of Ethico-Religious Essays.* Translated by Walter Lowrie. Princeton: Princeton University Press, 1955.

Lacoste, Jean-Yves. "Du phénomène de la valeur au discours de la norme." In *Le Monde et l'Absence d'oeuvre,* 109–27. Paris: Presses Universitaires de France, 2000.

———. "More Haste, Less Speed in Theology." *International Journal of Systematic Theology* 9 (2007) 263–82.

———. "Petite phénoménologie de la fatigue," in *Presence et Parousie,* 309–22. Geneva: Ad Solem, 2006.

Lambeth Commission on Communion. *The Windsor Report* 2004. London: Anglican Communion Office, 2004.

Lewis, Christopher. "On Unimportance." In *Gays and the Future of Anglicanism,* edited by Andrew Linzey and Richard Kirker, 149–58. Winchester: O Books, 2005.

Linzey, Andrew, and Richard Kirker, editors. *Gays and the Future of Anglicanism: Responses to the Windsor Report.* Winchester: O Books, 2005.

Newman, John Henry. "The Parting of Friends." In *Sermons, Bearing on Subjects of the Day.* London: Rivington & Parker, 1843.

O'Donovan, Oliver. "Reading the St. Andrew's Day Statement." In *Anglican Life and Witness: A Reader for the Lambeth Conference of Anglican Bishops 1998,* edited by Chris Sugden and Vinay Kumar Samuel, 38–51. London: SPCK, 1997.

———. *Resurrection and Moral Order: An Outline for Evangelical Ethics.* 2nd edition. Grand Rapids: Eerdmans, 1994.

Proudhon, Pierre-Joseph. *What Is Property?* Edited and Translated by Donald R. Kelley and Bonnie G. Smith. Cambridge Texts in the History of Political Thought. Cambridge: Cambridge University Press, 1994.

Rashdall, Hastings. *Conscience and Christ: Six Lectures on Christian Ethics*. London: Longmans, 1915.

Ratzinger, Joseph. "The Church's Teaching: Authority, Faith, Morals." In *Principles of Christian Morality* by Heinz Schürmann, Joseph Cardinal Ratzinger, and Hans Urs von Balthasar, 47–76. Translated by Graham Harrison. San Francisco: Ignatius, 1986.

Schürmann, Heinz. "How Normative Are the Values and Precepts of the New Testament?" In *Principles of Christian Morality*, by Heinz Schürmann, Joseph Cardinal Ratzinger, and Hans Urs von Balthazar, 9–44. Translated by Graham Harrison. San Francisco: Ignatius, 1986.

"St. Andrew's Day Statement." In *The Way Forward? Christian Voices on Homosexuality and the Church*, edited by Timothy Bradshaw, 5–11. 2d edition. London: SCM, 2003.

Vasey, Michael. *Strangers and Friends: A New Exploration of Homosexuality and the Bible*. London: Hodder & Stoughton, 1995.

Waters, Brent. *From Human to Posthuman: Christian Theology and Technology in a Postmodern World*. Burlington, VT: Ashgate 2006.

Webster, John. *Holy Scripture: A Dogmatic Sketch*. Current Issues in Theology 1. Cambridge: Cambridge University Press, 2003.

Williams, Rowan. *The Body's Grace: 10th Michael Harding Memorial Address*. London: Lesbian & Gay Christian Movement, 2002.

———. "The Challenge and Hope of Being an Anglican Today: A Reflection for the Bishops, Clergy, and Faithful of the Anglican Communion." Address, Convention of the Episcopal Church USA, June 27, 2006. Accessed March 14, 2008. Online: http://www.archbishopofcanterbury.org/640.

———. "Knowing Myself in Christ." In *The Way Forward? Christian Voices on Homosexuality and the Church*, edited by Timothy Bradshaw, 12–19. 2d edition. London: SCM, 2003.